Exploring the Power of Nonviolence

Syracuse Studies on Peace and Conflict Resolution
Robert A. Rubinstein, *Series Editor*

Other titles from Syracuse Studies
on Peace and Conflict Resolution

Back Channel Negotiation: Secrecy in the Middle East Peace Process
ANTHONY WANIS-ST. JOHN

A Band of Noble Women: Racial Politics in the Women's Peace Movement
MELINDA PLASTAS

41 Shots . . . and Counting: What Amadou Diallo's Story
Teaches Us about Policing, Race, and Justice
BETH ROY

Globalization, Social Movements, and Peacebuilding
JACKIE SMITH AND ERNESTO VERDEJA, EDS.

Human Rights and Conflict Resolution in Context:
Colombia, Sierra Leone, and Northern Ireland
EILEEN F. BABBITT AND ELLEN L. LUTZ

Not Just a Soccer Game: Colonialism
and Conflict among Palestinians in Israel
MAGID SHIHADE

A Place We Call Home: Gender, Race, and Justice in Syracuse
K. ANIMASHAUN DUCRE

Re-Centering Culture and Knowledge in Conflict Resolution Practice
MARY ADAMS TRUJILLO, S. Y. BOWLAND, LINDA JAMES MYERS,
PHILLIP M. RICHARDS, AND BETH ROY, EDS.

Western Sahara: War, Nationalism, and Conflict Irresolution
STEPHEN ZUNES AND JACOB MUNDY

Exploring the Power of
Nonviolence

Peace, Politics, and Practice

Edited by
Randall Amster and Elavie Ndura

With a Foreword by Michael N. Nagler

Syracuse University Press

∞ The paper used in this publication meets the minimum requirements
of the American National Standard for Information Sciences—Permanence
of Paper for Printed Library Materials, ANSI Z39.48-1992.

For a listing of books published and distributed by Syracuse University Press,
visit our website at www.SyracuseUniversityPress.syr.edu.

ISBN: 978-0-8156-3340-2 (cloth)   978-0-8156-3344-0 (paper)   978-0-8156-5253-3 (e-book)

Library of Congress Cataloging-in-Publication Data

Exploring the power of nonviolence : peace, politics, and practice / edited by Randall Amster
and Elavie Ndura ; with a Foreword by Michael N. Nagler. — First Edition.
    pages cm. — (Syracuse studies on peace and conflict resolution)
    Includes bibliographical references and index.
    ISBN 978-0-8156-3344-0 (cloth : alk. paper) — ISBN 978-0-8156-5253-3 (e-book)
    1. Nonviolence. 2. Nonviolence—History. 3. Nonviolence—Study and teaching.
    I. Amster, Randall, author, editor of compilation.   II. Ndura-Ouédraogo, Elavie.
                        HM1281.E87 2013
        303.6'1—dc23   2013035808

Manufactured in the United States of America

Contents

Foreword
Michael N. Nagler • *ix*

Preface
Randall Amster • *xiii*

Acknowledgments
Randall Amster and Elavie Ndura • *xvii*

Introduction
*Love-Force and Total Revolution: Twenty-First-Century
Challenges to Global Nonviolence*
Matt Meyer and Elavie Ndura • *1*

PART ONE: **Histories and Theories of Nonviolence**

1. Varieties of Nonviolence and Cultural Change
World History Lessons for Our Global Present and Future
Antony Adolf • *21*

2. Historicizing Nonviolent Protest
The Role of the French Revolution
Micah Alpaugh • *41*

3. "I Was and Am"
*Historical Counternarrative
as Nonviolent Resistance in the United States*
Jenice L. View • *57*

4. Traditional Indigenous North Americans, Nature, and Peace
Pat Lauderdale • 78

PART TWO: Nonviolent Movements

5. Nonviolent Civil Insurrections and Pro-Democracy Struggles
Stephen Zunes • 99

6. Apathy, Aggression, Assertion, and Action
Managing Image for Nonviolent Success
Tom H. Hastings • 117

7. Our Actions Are Louder than Words
Gender, Power, and a Nonviolent Movement toward Peace
Supriya Baily • 135

8. From the Headwaters to the Grassroots
Cooperative Resource Management as a Paradigm of Nonviolence
Randall Amster • 150

PART THREE: Nonviolence Pedagogy

9. Direct Education
Learning the Power of Nonviolent Action
George Lakey • 171

10. Teaching Peace in Higher Education
The Role of Creativity
Laura L. Finley • 189

11. Fostering a Culture of Nonviolence through Multicultural Education
Elavie Ndura • 206

PART FOUR: **Ethics and Practices of Nonviolence**

12. Bowen Theory and Peacemaking
Human Evolution through Nonviolent Conflict Resolution
Wayne F. Regina • 223

13. Forgiveness, Reconciliation, and Conflict Transformation
Tülin Levitas • 240

14. Toward a Moral Psychology of Nonviolence
The Gandhian Paradigm
Nancy E. Snow • 253

Conclusion
*Cultivating Transformative Wisdom and the Power of Peace
to Create Futures of Nonviolence*
Elavie Ndura and Randall Amster • 268

References • 275

Contributors • 311

Index • 315

Foreword

Michael N. Nagler

It was nearly a century ago that Mohandas Gandhi wrote in *Young India*, "It may be long before the law of love will be recognized in international affairs. The machineries of Governments stand between and hide the hearts of one people from those of another." Unfortunately, these words remain equally true today.

When the editors of this compelling volume were, I imagine, faced with a way to bring order to a highly diverse set of minds without inhibiting their diversity, they did so by posing a question along the lines of this quote, a question that captures an essential tension in the development of nonviolence around the world and its implicit challenge to traditional ways of thinking. They ask, "Is there a natural nexus between love and revolution, a meeting point where the two enrich one another and spur on greater possibilities for lasting, positive change? Indeed, that nexus may be what we refer to as 'nonviolence' in its broadest sense: a philosophy grounded in universal love, and a set of practices with revolutionary potential."

Facts on the ground would seem to indicate that such a philosophy and practice are in fact emerging. It is a little-known detail that more than half of the Earth's population now lives within a regime that has experienced—well within living memory—a signal nonviolent movement or uprising that has changed its history for the better. But beyond the sheer size of the development of what Orville Schell has dubbed "the other superpower: civil society and common people on the march," I would further point to at least three qualitative developments that are, if anything, even more significant in their potentials.

Since the cross-fertilization between India's freedom struggle and the American civil rights movement, many civil-society movements—including nonviolence-based insurrections—have become more conscious of each other around the world and have begun (perhaps for the first time in history) to create institutions for systematic learning, such as the Centre for Applied Nonviolent Action and Strategies (CANVAS) that disseminates "best practices" that were originally gleaned from the successful Serbian *Otpor!* (resistance) movement that brought down then-Yugoslav President Slobodan Milošević in 2000. The importance of this learning—and the parallel manner in which indigenous societies are finding ways to be more integrated with one another and the rest of the world without surrendering their character—cannot be overemphasized. In this regard, books like the one you before you are no mere academic exercises, but can play a key role in precipitating change by encapsulating such mutual learning.

Peacekeeping itself has developed a few new institutions, such as Unarmed Civilian Peacekeeping and the Nonviolent Peaceforce, both outgrowths of Gandhi's Shanti Sena (Peace Army). The spread of concrete nonviolent interventions, especially in war-torn and conflict-ridden environments, helps to connect theory with practice and promotes a spirit of direct engagement with both people and place. The authors in this volume likewise strive to make these crucial interconnections and encourage hands-on nonviolence.

Last but not least, there has been a remarkable development in science. On every level from quantum theory (in whose vision the world becomes a deep unity in which consciousness, not matter, and events, not things, become the primary constituents of reality) through neuroscience to the social and behavioral sciences, the values and processes of unity, cooperation, and empathy have been discovered as fundamental principles of nature. Perhaps one day there will be a fascinating study of how this remarkable shift came about. Suffice it to say here that "science" and "history"—which for so long have been carelessly thought to demonstrate the impossibility of nonviolence, and to demonstrate the "natural" place of killing in the order of nature (notions carelessly projected onto human nature)—are now revealing inspiring possibilities for the ultimate realization of the "beloved community." This nascent "science of nonviolence" is greatly enhanced by the contributions of scholars and activists such as those collected in this edition.

We are well past the popularized "innate aggression" theorists of the 1970s, and more responsible scientists today speak openly of "altruism," which, however, could still be thought to be based on "rational-actor," cost-benefit calculation. Going further, behaviorists such as Frans de Waal, and social theorists such as Jeremy Rifkin and Frances Moore Lappé, speak confidently of "empathy" as the reason for pro-social behavior. Moreover, thanks to a remarkable discovery made as recently as 1988 in Parma, Italy, we can point to a neural basis for empathy in the primate-human brain: the famous "mirror neurons," or as neuroscientist V.S. Ramachandran calls them, "Gandhi neurons," that fire in response to another's actions, emotions, and perceived intentions. One begins to feel that we have only begun to understand the human capacity for identification with the other—for genuine compassion and empathy—that is a key to nonviolent transformation.

In this sense, we should also talk about love. While love must play, I agree, a central role in any movement that can even pretend to save us, it is famously true that the word "love" covers a multitude of meanings, some of which can be vacuous at best, and dangerously misleading at worst. So what is the love in which revolution must be grounded? No one sophisticated enough to be reading this book will believe that it is the mushy sentiment of the mass media (or believe almost anything else in the mass media, for that matter). No, this is the love of which Gandhi stated, "It's not nonviolence until you love your enemies." It is the love of which the modern and very nonviolent saint Swami Ramdas spoke when he was once asked, "Is hate the opposite of love," and replied, "No. Love has no opposite."

In short, we are not talking simply about an emotion; although positive emotions can help, they are only representations of something deeper than our conscious awareness. We are talking about a force. The contributions to this volume, in their several ways, bear witness to that realization, namely that we seek a force that is grounded in practices that not only seek to free us from overt violence in the outer world, but more broadly work to bring healing energy to human relationships and thus create lasting change. The essence of that "love" has to be unlocked within us and expressed into the world around us. We are finally waking up to this challenge, as these essays show.

In my view, this is the final answer to the central question posed in this important volume on whether love can be joined with revolution: love *is* the revolution. By linking this essential insight with the scholarly and pragmatic nonviolent interventions explored here, we bring ourselves one step closer to the realization of Dr. Martin Luther King Jr.'s "beloved community." I encourage you to read these words with an eye toward finding "revolutionary love" in your own thoughts and actions.

—Berkeley, California, October 2010

Preface

Randall Amster

The new millennium finds humanity situated at a critical crossroads. While there are many hopeful signs of cross-cultural engagement and democratic dialogue, it is equally the case that the challenges of warfare and injustice continue to plague nations and communities around the globe. Against this backdrop, there exists a powerful mechanism for exploring fundamental issues and transforming crises into opportunities: the philosophy and practice of nonviolence. Sometimes mischaracterized as a form of passivity or inaction, nonviolence actually has been and remains a proactive force for positive change in a wide range of contexts, from education and ethics to peacekeeping and politics. The expert authors brought together in this volume collectively deploy the essential teachings of nonviolence across the spectrum of contemporary issues, yielding a potent mechanism for overcoming challenges and creating positive alternatives in this time of "people power" movements appearing around the world.

In particular, the contributors to this volume address a range of key queries, including: How can we encourage systemic thinking and a critical exploration of the concept and application of nonviolence? What lessons can be drawn from the practice of nonviolence that can inform our engagement with the pressing issues that we face today? How does nonviolence function as a method, an end goal, or both? How can pedagogy promoting nonviolence be practiced at all educational levels? What political, social, and economic structures best assist human communities in practicing and attaining nonviolence? What strategies can activists share about the ways in which they have utilized nonviolence in the quest for peace and justice? Where is nonviolence being practiced today, and how is it connected to issues of power and ethics? In seeking to address these and similar questions, the authors in this work take the teachings and practices of nonviolence, and pass them through the prisms of both current events and academic inquiry.

One of the dominant renderings of nonviolence comes through its association with charismatic leaders such as Mohandas Gandhi and Dr. Martin Luther King Jr. Unquestionably, both of these iconic figures (along with other luminaries from history) have done much to advance the narrative and utilization of nonviolence as a tool for social and spiritual transformation alike. Yet in so doing, the pursuit of nonviolence has arguably been constrained as much as it has been enabled by the significant historical shadows of King and Gandhi. Interestingly, neither saw nonviolence as a tool merely for the evolved and enlightened among us, but rather as a pathway to a world in which the virtues of equality and opportunity would be available to all without regard to station or privilege. In this sense, nonviolence can be seen as inherently radical in its full dimensions, and moreover as something to be disseminated widely rather than being merely the province of history's giants. It is in this spirit of engaged application that the notion of nonviolence advanced here slips its untenable bonds and appears as a primary motivation for scholars and practitioners across an amazingly broad range of perspectives.

Nonviolence can be a powerful tool for individuals, communities, and nations alike to utilize in confronting and transforming the myriad issues that define our time. In tracing the scope of this potential power, what we aim to convey here is a sense of nonviolence as a living theory, a pragmatic guide, and an end in itself. This "living nonviolence" is strong-willed, adaptive, compassionate, and contentious. It delegitimizes forces of repression and prefigures a just future. It strives to break the cycle of violence through patience, empathy, and the refusal to participate. It is idealistically utopian, calling upon our better instincts, and eminently practical, guiding our choices in the world as we find it. Nonviolence is equally concerned with the measure of our values (ethics), the utility of our actions (efficacy), and the power of our creativity (aesthetics). It is, in short, a way of life as much as it is a political ethos or spiritual edict. This lived nature of nonviolence becomes evident in the unique and evolutionary ways it is applied by the authors here as a foundational component of their work.

The resultant collection comes at a crucial juncture in history. People worldwide are actively looking for coherent strategies to manage social and ecological issues in new ways that do not replicate the same forces that helped to create the crises in the first instance. Given the skilled contributors and the breadth of topics covered here, we believe that this collected edition will be of use to scholars, practitioners, educators, and policymakers across a gamut of fields and disciplines. In touching upon and drawing from areas including peace studies, political science, philosophy, history, psychology, religion, ethics, and education, this work moves the discussion of nonviolence beyond any disciplinary or ideological confines by applying its teachings and values to a wide array of social, political, and ecological concerns. In the end, we have sought to demonstrate that a contemporary and forward-looking conception of nonviolence—one that advances our aims beyond merely seeking to attain the absence of violence—can serve as a powerful tool for imagining and constructing a more just and peaceful world.

We invite you to share in this work.

Acknowledgments

Randall Amster and Elavie Ndura

This book was inspired by the theme and proceedings of the Peace and Justice Studies Association's (PJSA) annual conference, held in October 2009 on the campus of Marquette University. We would like to acknowledge the contributions made to the study of peace, conflict, and nonviolence by the Board and Members of the PJSA, a number of whom are included in this volume. The dynamic nature of these annual gatherings continues to inspire our work, and we are extremely appreciative of the foresight exhibited by the PJSA in selecting timely and relevant conference themes that serve to advance the field.

Further, we are grateful beyond mere words for the contributions from all of the authors in this volume. By taking up the challenge of integrating nonviolence with their own areas of expertise, and doing so with great enthusiasm and maximum professionalism, they have demonstrated the best qualities of academia and have embodied the virtues of peaceful concourse all at once. These expert colleagues in the field deserve special recognition for contributing to a very effective peer-review process of the chapters included in this volume, thus ultimately enhancing the quality and distinction of the work. Thanks are likewise due to the skilled editors at Syracuse University Press, who have worked diligently to help bring this volume to fruition.

We also express our deepest gratitude to Queen Shahuri for willingly and expediently sharing her extraordinary intellect and talents to assist us with the formatting of the works cited in this volume. Our respective universities have provided us with the intellectual support and scholarly resources that make projects such as this possible in the first place. And our families continue to provide the motivation for our work, as well as the wellspring of love and gratitude from which our desire to embrace nonviolence flows.

Finally, we want to express our sincere admiration for all of the modern-day satyagrahis struggling in kindness and compassion for a better world for ourselves and our children. This book is for you.

—September 2012

Exploring the Power of Nonviolence

Introduction

Love-Force and Total Revolution: Twenty-First-Century Challenges to Global Nonviolence

Matt Meyer and Elavie Ndura

At the risk of seeming ridiculous, let me say that the true revolutionary is guided by great feelings of love. It is impossible to think of a genuine revolutionary lacking this quality. . . . One must have a large dose of humanity, a large dose of a sense of justice and truth in order to avoid dogmatic extremes, cold scholasticism, or an isolation from the masses. We must strive every day so that this love of living humanity is transformed into actual deeds, into acts that serve as examples, as a moving force.
> —Ernesto "Che" Guevara, "From Algiers"

The only dream worth having is to dream that you will live while you're alive and die only when you're dead: To love. To be loved. To never forget your own insignificance. To never get used to the unspeakable violence and the vulgar disparity of life around you. To seek joy in the saddest places. To pursue beauty to its lair. To never simplify what is complicated or complicate what is simple. To respect strength, never power. Above all, to watch. To try and understand. To never look away. And never, never, to forget.
> —Arundhati Roy, *The Algebra of Infinite Justice*

At the 2010 War Resisters International (WRI) conference held in Ahmadabad, India, Gandhian activist and scholar Narayan Desai (2010) explained the common transliteration of the word *satyagraha*. Developed by Mohandas Gandhi as a young solicitor based in Durban, South Africa, satyagraha has most commonly been described as meaning "truth force." Gandhi relied upon truth as one of his more powerful weapons, speaking truth to power and sometimes equating the force of truth with nonviolent resistance, itself, as when he titled his autobiography, *The Story of My Experiments with Truth* (1929). Everyone, Gandhi observed and believed, has a bit of truth in their story and perspective. Our job as revolutionaries working to transform society to a more just place hinges on understanding the truths of one's adversaries, and creating new truths that will liberate both the oppressed (in particular) and the oppressor, who could be freed from enforcing immoral decisions and committing inhumane acts. In an era in which "truth commissions" have become almost faddish—utilized to de-escalate violence, but not necessarily to remove structural inequities—it is easy to see how Gandhi's concept of truth could get lost.

Desai (2010), however, was concerned about more than simply the corruption of satyagraha's most popular meaning. He argued that the phrase "truth force" adequately describes only one-third of satyagraha's full meaning. Gandhi's concept of satyagraha in both theory and strategic practice, Desai explained, also includes the power of "soul force" and "love force." It is this final definition, Desai suggested, which was most lacking in the work of modern-day progressive organizations, including nonviolence movements. A history of poetry, prose, and sonnets could attest to the abiding and historical power of love. Using love as a powerful force for social resistance, and for structural and revolutionary change, however, provides a distinct set of challenges for the nonviolent tactician.

In apparent contrast to the power of love to build an effective movement lies social change activists' striking need for confrontational struggle. At a time when the richest 500 individuals on the planet possess wealth equivalent to hundreds of the poorest nation-states (United Nations Development Program 2007), and when democracy to most people means little more than pulling a lever once every few years to choose between electoral candidates who represent nearly identical privileged interest groups, the need for radical change is a "self-evident truth" (to paraphrase a centuries-old North American revolutionary movement). The socialist and communist experiments of the last century, given barely enough time to develop out of infancy, and even less room to develop alternatives to the dominant political and economic paradigms of their time, have been officially declared dead; the academy's dearth of popular discourse on those experiments gives credence to that postmodern declaration, whatever the realities on the ground might suggest. Anarchism remains largely untested in a large-scale context, while its opposite, liberalism—though championing the concepts of "hope" and "change" through the election of an unquestionably intellectual adherent, an American president of African descent criticized mightily by the reactionary forces of the U.S. mainstream—illustrates the hard work and persistence needed to achieve even the most minimal of non-structural changes.

For many, philosophical nonviolence seems hardly a revolutionary choice, with practitioners appearing to be more concerned with reconciliation than with justice, remaining vigilant whenever the "wretched of the earth" take up arms in self-defense, but forgiving the masters of destiny when compromises with capital "must" be made. And though the leadership of women demands to be heard in grassroots and high level spaces all around the globe, the anti-patriarchal critiques offered by feminism in all its varied forms have been surgically removed from many of these forums (Van Wormer 2008). It seems, indeed, that revolutionary thinking and action are in need of revitalization today.

Is there a natural nexus between love and revolution, a meeting point where the two not only logically co-exist, but enrich one another and spur on greater possibilities for lasting, positive change? Has the absence of love as a force for the acquisition of "power with," as opposed to "power over," hindered the development of successful revolutions worldwide? And is there an untested ideology of "revolutionary nonviolence," a set of tactical and strategic principles that fall short of religious dogma, but which provide guidelines reaching far beyond the dichotomized thinking of those who view armed guerrilla liberation movements as antithetical to the pacifist pure-of-heart? (Dellinger 1970). Can revolutionary nonviolence, if properly defined and developed, tap an uncharted "love force" that can lead us to greater, united, on-the-ground victories for people's movements everywhere?

We answer these queries decidedly in the affirmative. Furthermore, we believe there are clues suggesting that this answer is correct, and where to look to prove it. From the mid-1980s to the present, stories of struggle—mainly from the Global South—illuminate the active potential of these standards. Throughout Africa, radicals of all tendencies have looked beyond the confines of their ideological bases to engage in civil resistance, which demands that the status quo be shifted in the direction of justice (Meyer and Ndura-Ouédraogo 2009). Though far from defining their struggles as explicitly nonviolent, national and Pan-African leaders have thought deeply regarding the effectiveness of both pacifist political workers and military warriors (Sutherland and Meyer 2000). In Latin America, the ballot box once used to rubber stamp Western-funded puppet regimes (when dictatorships turned sour) has now become a tool of mass sentiment, bringing progressives and radicals to state power in unprecedented numbers (Barrionuevo 2010). In Asia, movements against corporate enclosures and neo-colonial invasions are growing more regular, while simultaneously taking a greater variety of forms (Padel 2010). At the opening plenary of the aforementioned WRI conference, Indian social critic Arundhati Roy suggested that these new campaigns amount to a "biodiversity of resistance" in a world with little breathing space for knowing how to fight (Roy 2010). These efforts—revolutionary nonviolence in practice—might well amplify their effectiveness if a collective love-force were to be tapped.

It is certainly not a coincidence that the research and practice developed by Narayan Desai attempts to blend all three aspects of Gandhian satyagraha into a comprehensive program for people's power. Desai's own precedent for building the Institute for Total Revolution, housed in the same province in which Gandhi built his first ashram, was the work of his colleague and mentor, Jayaprakash Narayan. For Narayan, living in India after independence, nonviolent methods were a given, though the cult-of-personality process of turning Gandhi into an unreachable saint figure had already begun. The communist revolution led by Mao Zedong in neighboring China was of special interest, as Narayan, a committed anti-capitalist, worked to merge socialist and pacifist ideals. The basic principles—fundamental redistribution of wealth and the extension of human rights for all—existed in both systems. The basic method, the building of a mass movement, was also a feature of both, though Narayan believed that the military factor was often used to unsuccessfully attempt short-cuts around mass organizing.

"There is no remedy," argued Narayan (2002, 65), "but a vigorous social movement, a peaceful struggle against the evil. Likewise, the implementation of land reforms, homestead tenancy legislation, removal of corruption in the administration, etc. All this requires a mass awakening and a mass struggle. The youth, including the students, must naturally be in the vanguard." Jayaprakash Narayan's use of the phrase "total revolution," which Narayan Desai has adopted, was developed during Narayan's work in his native Bihar, an eastern province where he based many of his campaigns against Indira Gandhi and the conservatives whom he felt were misleading the country. "The question [of power] is even larger [than working against one powerful leader]," Narayan (2002, 65) wrote. "It is how to bring about a systemic change in society; i.e.[,] how to bring about what I have called a total revolution: revolution in every sphere and aspect of society." Narayan explained:

> The question becomes harder to answer when it is added that the total revolution has to be peacefully brought about without impairing the democratic structure of society and affecting the democratic way of life of the people. Put in this way, even the most legalistic and constitutionalist democrat would agree that all this could never be accomplished if the functioning of democracy were restricted to elections, legislation, planning and administrative execution. There must also be people's direct action. This action would almost certainly comprise, among other forms, civil disobedience, peaceful resistance, non-cooperation—in short, satyagraha in its widest sense. One of the unstated implications of such a satyagraha would be self-change: that is to say, those wanting to change must also change themselves before launching any kind of action. (Narayan 2002, 66)

The India of the 1970s may have only been a mild precursor to the industrial incursions of today, but Narayan and Desai understood then the need to connect the personal and the political, science and utopia, and love and revolution. Desai posited that society has been racing to keep up with the rapid technological explosions of our time by making social revolution. With more revolutions taking place over the last several decades than have taken place over the last several centuries, Desai suggests that it is the destructive force of new weapons that gives revolutionary nonviolence its strategic edge. "Science and technology have converted the world into a small nest," he wrote in *Towards a Nonviolent Revolution* (1972, 3). If it is inevitable, and an historical necessity, that rapid changes take place, it is the responsibility of disciplined nonviolent cadre to cope with the crises that arise when societies are restructured. It is not the role of the pacifist to be neutral in the face of violence, but to actively engage in building a peace army, ready and willing to take the same casualties that a traditional army would have to endure. Desai's concept of Shanti Sena (Indian peace brigades), sought to bring together a group of radicals based on love of all people, struggling together in constructive programs to make life at the local levels an engaging and dynamic joy (Desai 1972).

When contemporary writer and activist Samarendra Das (2010) of India's Orissa region, working with the local Kondh people to protect their sustainable and self-sufficient communities, speaks of "making resistance fertile," it is in the tradition of the Shanti Sena. Discussing the challenge to practitioners and researchers more generally, Desai has reiterated that "actual power lies at the heart of the people, in the spirit of the soul . . . but that power doesn't crystallize; it doesn't become effective until a people feel themselves, and feel their own power" (2010). Desai believes that Brazilian educator Paulo Freire holds the key to the first step towards feeling one's own power: conscientization—the ability to properly and forcefully name one's own reality and world (Freire 2000; Freire and Maceo 1987). The next step, organization, requires changes in values, attitudes, relationships, institutions, and the structures that we produce. Finally, once organization is achieved, we must go beyond reason to faith; we must have faith in ourselves, in our comrades, for the cause, about the means that we will employ, and in the irrefutable fact that we will overcome. If we use "an overflowing love force," Desai (2010) predicts, "we will have dialogue not debate, and we will not only win, we will win over."

The most significant and widespread applications of Gandhian nonviolence utilized in revolutionary situations have occurred across the continent of Africa (Meyer and Ndura-Ouédraogo 2009; Sutherland and

Meyer 2000). These began, of course, with Gandhi's own development of satyagraha in the streets of Durban, South Africa. Despite divisive limitations common to the population groupings of that era, there can be little doubt that Gandhi played a substantial and positive role in the development of at least the Indian community. It seems clear, as well, that there was substantial political cross-fertilization of the struggles of Indians and Africans in turn-of-the-century South Africa. Gandhi and his Phoenix Settlement maintained social and political contact with an African industrial school, the Ohlange Institute and its leader, John Dube, who was to become the first president-general of the African National Congress (ANC) (Nauriya 2006). The ANC's predecessor, the South Africa Native National Congress—which came together in reaction to the formation of the British and Afrikaner-led Union of South Africa—was a far greater show of inter-ethnic "unity" than the Union ever could be.

The organization's founding constitution (not that of the Republic) called explicitly for "passive" and peaceful action. A related group, the African Women's Passive Resistance, initiated in the Orange Free State in 1913, more directly relied upon direct action and civil disobedience to dramatically show their outrage at the segregation and injustices of white supremacy in the heart of southern Africa (Nauriya 2006). In later years, non-cooperation took on extensively greater importance, from the efforts of ANC President Albert Luthuli (Luthuli 1963), to the massive boycotts, fasts, and alternative structures of the United Democratic Front of the 1980s, which followed the ANC call to make the apartheid regime "ungovernable" (Sutherland and Meyer 2000). Research by contemporary Indian scholars suggests that Gandhi's own ideas about strategy, non-racialism, and politics evolved and expanded with his extended experience in Africa (Nauriya 2006); it is easy to chart that this reciprocal relationship between his African and Indian experiences also continued after Gandhi's death and India's independence.

African and Pan-African leaders outside of the South African context used their own terminology and put their own cultural and strategic spin on satyagraha methodology. Trinidadian historian and journalist C. L. R. James was one of the most influential and thoughtful of these, recognizing even in the context of his traditional Marxist background that there was something uniquely powerful about the Gandhian approach (Presbey 2009). When Kwame Nkrumah led the people of Ghana to independence in 1957 using what he termed "positive action," it was widely recognized that an Africanized version of satyagraha had been developed, including the popular heralding of Nkrumah as "Africa's Gandhi" (Sutherland and Meyer 2000). James suggested that what was needed in the African arena was a quality more correctly called "organized spontaneity"—i.e., a capacity among masses of people to act suddenly, without training, when a confluence of forces was taking place. Leaders like Gandhi and Nkrumah, James believed, understood how to "read" historical moments that presented opportunities for mass nonviolent action (Grimshaw 1992). But while James, Nkrumah, and other Pan-African independence leaders agreed that militant non-military methods, such as those used by Gandhi in India, evidenced a "tactical inventiveness," they did not all agree that principled or philosophical commitments to nonviolent social change were needed for nonviolence to "work" in ending colonialism and winning state power.

Though Tanganyika and Zanzibar gained their political freedom without bloodshed, their founding father, Julius Nyerere was always clear that he saw nonviolence as no more than an effective tactic. Yet Nyerere maintained decades-long respectful dialogue with key Pan-African pacifists such as Bill Sutherland, and well understood that "flag independence" was little more than a crumb without the complete decolonization of the continent's economies, a transformation that would surely require tremendous, organized, and mass civil resistance (Sutherland and Meyer 2000). Zambia's Kenneth Kaunda is probably the only modern statesman in the world with significant political background on and philosophical commitment to Gandhianism (Kaunda 1980). But even intractable armed struggles like the people's war fought in Mozambique suggest a greater reliance on non-military civil non-cooperation than is often assumed or understood (Meyer, forthcoming).

It should also be clear, in any case, that the latest generation of peaceful campaigners in parts of war-torn Africa have an often-sophisticated analysis of the dialectical nature of violence and nonviolence. In the contemporary context, survivors of some of the world's worst atrocities have become proponents of some of pacifism's most indigenous and ingenious ideas. The Rwandan group MEMOS, for example, works as an explicitly and philosophically nonviolent organization, training youth to learn from and use the past in building for peaceful resolution of conflicts in the present. Critiquing the popular "commemorative" version of reconciliation without historical memory, MEMOS struggles to link those who focus exclusively on genocide and crimes against humanity with those who work against "the crimes of war" (Murangwa and Higiro 2008). Forming, in practice, a more holistic program of positive action, MEMOS joins others (individuals and organizations) in Rwandan civil society who are committed to relying on African norms (Sebarenzi 2009). The community-based, "truth-telling" Gacaca courts are the most well-known of these culturally rooted resistance and reconciliation tactics, which also include INGANDO peace camps or retreats, Ubudelte initiatives, which foster locally-based economic solidarity, and the use of Abunzi: respected neighborhood leaders who serve as mediators and are formally trained in Rwandan developed programs of conflict resolution (Ndangiza 2008). Burundi's *abashingantahe* constitutes a similar community-based mechanism for resolving conflict nonviolently.

In the final days of the racist apartheid regime in South Africa, the ill-informed insistence that "nonviolence wouldn't work" following the 1960 Sharpeville Massacre shifted, in some peace studies circles, to a caricatured postulate that South Africa was the latest great success story for the power of nonviolence. In fact, the Mozambican and South African struggles have more commonalities than differences, not least of which being the basic philosophical commitment to the need for a military component in the freedom struggle. Leaders of both nations, however, also harbored serious concerns regarding the long-term effects of armed tactics, and understood the strategic possibilities inherent in civil insurrection, non-cooperation, and civic resistance. South African Nobel laureate and Truth and Reconciliation Commission (TRC) Chair Archbishop Tutu (1994) has most popularly brought to wide international attention the term *ubuntu*, an African Bantu concept suggesting that every human is only fully human in the context of their relationship with other humans. Similar concepts, such as the Botswanan idea of *bogosi*, promote values close to the concepts of principled nonviolence and peacemaking (Molomo 2009). Though study still needs to take place regarding the long-term justice-based effects of South Africa's TRC (Chapman and Van der Merwe 2008), one link between these contemporary cross-continental initiatives is that, at the risk of seeming ridiculous, ambitious experiments in new modes of struggle are being explored and utilized.

The cross-pollination of radical movements has not taken place only between Africa and Asia; the struggles of Latin American have undergone similar transformations. While it is common knowledge that South Africa's Truth and Reconciliation Commission drew extensively from lessons learned in the Chilean forum of a similar nature, recent research has also detailed the African roots of Che Guevara's own words regarding the revolutionary power of love (Guevara 2001; and see the epigraph above). Love-force has always been a central part of the work and scholarship of leading Chilean nonviolent activist Roberta Bacic, who served as a key staff person for the precursor to Chile's Truth Commission as well as for War Resisters International. In reviewing the work of African and Latin American peacebuilding efforts, Bacic (2002) notes that reconciliation can often be a meaningless or even insulting concept if justice is not served. In an interview with a grieving compatriot about the loss of a loved one, Bacic (2002, 20) decried that "truth without justice is not truth; it only means the acknowledgement of what has happened." The struggle for truth with justice—for historical memory perhaps without violent recriminations, but certainly not without consequences—is an urgent task for adherents of revolutionary nonviolence. If guided by love—for the individuals surrounding someone, as well as for "the people" in general—this struggle may help us rebuild the Left in a more powerful form.

"Rebuilding the Left," especially in light of the post-9/11 world, has been a particular preoccupation of another Chilean activist-intellectual, Marta Harnecker. Far from an advocate of nonviolence or Gandhianism, Harnecker has been well positioned—thanks to her Marxist background and her leadership of Cuba's research institute Memoria Popular Latinoamericana—to review and support the Bolivarian revolutions from a unique perspective. Her observations align with the postulates put forth by Bacic, Desai, and our African comrades. First, indigenous and mass movements must be taken more seriously than they have been in the past by leftist political parties. Second, the idea that power was only or primarily located in the apparatus of the state must be thoroughly dismissed (Harnecker 2007). Finally, in developing clearer definitions of revolution and reform suitable for a new generation of struggle, Harnecker (2007, 131) asserts that "neither the use of violence, on the one hand, nor the use of institutions and the promotion of reform, on the other, can be used as the criteria for drawing a line of demarcation." Instead of drawing lines between pacifists and guerrillas, she spotlights the more essential dichotomy: between those seeking total, structural transformation of societies plagued by injustice and inequality, and those solely seeking minor changes in order to make the existing society a bit less unjust.

The lessons coming out of modern-day Venezuela echo a strategic orientation that looks to the grassroots for ways of strengthening international peace movements. The logic of collectives, communes, farms, and workplaces, which have multiplied by the tens of thousands under the presidency of Hugo Chavez, helps demonstrate the needs that, when not met, underlie all contemporary warfare. One community leader, Maria Vincenta Davila of the Mixteque Communal Council, expressed both shock and understanding when she realized that war was "convenient" to her neighbors to the north. Despite decades and centuries of colonization, land theft, and unequal distribution of resources, Davila's convictions against the military industrial complex are based on her own notions of love for her brothers and sisters of North America, who should be more involved in acts of mutual solidarity and support (Martinez, Fox, and Farrell 2010). US-based solidarity activist and poet Margaret Randall (2002), whose experiences stem mainly from the previous generation of struggles in Central America and the Caribbean, also characterizes her life as "profoundly informed by love and adventure," focused as she is on searching for humanistic values and ways of combating systems of violence and greed. She is one of many who have sought to redefine "terror" in an era where war criminals get elected to high office, and activists—such as Puerto Rican independentistas Oscar Lopez Rivera and Carlos Alberto Torres—spend more than thirty years in US jails for the "thought crime" of seditious conspiracy (Morales 2010).

Mexico's Zapatistas, originating as an armed group committed to self-defense and defense of indigenous lands, showed their true colors when they initiated one of their many largely nonviolent campaigns with the release of the Zapatista Air Force: thousands of paper planes! Though still facing terrible repression at the hands of the Mexican government, the Zapatistas provided an inspiring example that has nevertheless failed to successfully mobilize significant amounts of transnational solidarity amongst revolutionaries across the ideological and tactical spectrum. Yet, most who have gotten closest to these peaceful warriors in the southernmost corners of North America agree that their notions of autonomy and dignity are vital signposts for the entire global movement (Weinberg 2000). Furthermore, when one "rides" with the Zapatistas, it has been said, it is in the spirit of resistance and in "the language of love" (Norrell 2009).

It is, indeed, time for progressives of the Global North, literally fluent in the romance languages of Europe, to learn a new language of solidarity as Mozambique's Samora Machel defined it—not as charity, but as mutual aid in pursuit of shared goals. It is time for solidarity of love to flow northwards, to those truly in need of aid: the underdeveloped peace and justice movements of the western world. There can be little question that the movements of the Global South, so prevalent at World Social Forums and other manifestations of alternatives to the current order, are the advanced practitioners of "total revolution," seeking paths to a nonviolent world through nonviolent methods and a non-dogmatic understanding of the connections between means and ends.

The power of nonviolence, in and of itself, is in little danger of atrophy. Western practitioners of nonviolence, on the other hand, may fall victim to their own marginalization, made irrelevant by an inability to see outside Eurocentric boxes. It is heartening, perhaps, to see streams of commentary on the Peace and Justice Studies Association (PJSA) listserv in response to a search for "the missing Mahatma," looking for a great soul such as Gandhi or Dr. Martin Luther King Jr. in the West Bank, Israel, and Palestine. But revolutionary nonviolent individuals and organizations have long been present throughout the Middle East, which is in no particular need of another leader-icon to show it the way to the Promised Land.

On March 21, 2010, one such individual—International Solidarity Movement co-founder Huwaida Arraf, a Palestinian-American and recipient of PJSA's annual Social Courage award—was beaten and arrested for standing in the way of Israeli police shooting at unarmed demonstrators (King 2010). Many more, in Palestine and elsewhere, have had much worse done to them over the course of many years of movement-building. And much critical thought has been given to the problem of social movements built around singular, charismatic, male leaders. But we forget.

Historical amnesia sometimes leads us to understand our solidarity and internationalism only in terms of what we can lend, and not what we must learn. Closer to home, however, this forgetting has also led us to soft-pedal critiques of sexism within our organizational midst and history (Sharoni 2010). If, as Johan Galtung (2010) has predicted, the US empire will fall in 2020 and a blossoming may occur out of the embers of the old regime, it seems doubtful that this could take place without a reassessment by progressive US peace and justice practitioners. It will be difficult to build that "beloved" community if we do not more directly and honestly confront the ethnocentrisms, racisms, sexisms, and heterosexisms of our individuals and institutions. Where, after all, would the love be in that?

Baby steps may yet take us in interesting directions. Environmental activists and antiwar activists seem to understand the need to find common ground, as do conscientious objectors and those working for resistance from within the military. Some staunch anti-racists have shifted from the finger-pointing of a previous era, substituting a gentler approach to the divisions that persist among progressive people. Signe Waller (2002), for example, in documenting the 1970s and 1980s struggles against the Klan in Greensboro, North Carolina, titled her memoir *Love and Revolution*. Even Colombian crossover pop star Shakira made it clear in her acceptance of an International Labor Organization medal for her work promoting social justice: "Gandhi used to say, 'Be the change you wish to see in the world,' and I've followed that maxim" (ANI 2010). There are limitless possibilities for a rich series of overlapping social change movements, if only we know the path to follow in building principled unity and struggle.

In our estimate, peace scholars and practitioners from the Global North would do well to take the lead from, and listen carefully to, our sisters and brothers in Asia and the Pacific, Africa, Latin America, and the Caribbean. We would do well to understand that we have less to teach others than we often presume. We would do well to keep clear distances from the false dichotomies developed in decades past: presumed rifts between socialists, communists, and anarchists, and divisions still fostered by passive pacifists and armchair advocates of armed struggle alike. Unity is a precious commodity amongst the sectors of the movement that have moved beyond infantilist sectarianism. We would do well to build coalitions that make our peace studies more multicultural, and our multicultural education more firmly emboldened by an understanding of the role the military plays in fostering racism, sexism, and class divisions (Ndura-Ouédraogo and Meyer 2009). We would do even better to work to make our nonviolence as revolutionary as possible and the revolutions of the world as nonviolent as possible.

It may well be in our own histories, deep in the forgotten pieces of past struggles, that signposts point the way towards developing our own indigenous forms of radical movement suited for the current era. The Left Forum, one of the largest multi-tendency progressive conferences held annually in the United States, featured a collage featuring Reverend King (alongside Minister Malcolm X) as one of its central images in 2010, captioned "The King of Love." It behooves all the people of the world who admire King's message to understand the ways in which he used reforms to foster an agenda of total revolution. We would do well to remember, far beyond King's dreams, his concrete suggestions for building social change. King (quoted in Carson and Shepard 2001) taught through words and actions that a true revolution requires the questioning of the fairness and justice of many of our past and present policies:

> A true revolution of values will soon look uneasily on the glaring contrast of poverty and wealth. With righteous indignation, it will look across the seas and see individual capitalists of the West investing huge sums of money in Asia, Africa and South America, only to take the

profits out with no concern for the social betterment of the countries, and say: "This is not just."

Dr. King challenged Western arrogance and the dominant paradigms of race, class, and militarism, and he posited that a true revolution of values would always seek to create a new world order where humankind and the common good command individual and collective loyalties.

His call for a worldwide fellowship that would lift neighborly concern beyond one's tribe, race, class and nation is in reality a call for an all-embracing and unconditional love for all people.

King defined love as the force that all of the great religions have seen as the supreme unifying principle of life. Contemporary scholar-activist Cornel West elaborated on that concept when he explained that to step in the name of love, with religious fervor and a dangerous honesty and freedom, means taking the risk of "stepping on nothing." Those who are committed, however, keep on going because "no empire can give . . . and no empire can take away" the things that sustain them. Furthermore, West posits that justice is nothing less than "what love looks like in public" (West 2008). We are called to heed these many and varied invitations to struggle for a new world in a new way. With revolutionary nonviolence, we may see a world only imaginable if we intentionally dedicate our hearts and minds to loving our fellow human beings. With a radical love-force, we may find ways to create sustainable revolutionary relationships, and pursue together the common good.

Part One

Histories and Theories of Nonviolence

As a set of practices and values that are frequently deployed for political transformation, the "nonviolence paradigm" has counted many successes over the course of its history. Mohandas Gandhi's resistance to British imperialism in India and Martin Luther King Jr.'s stewardship of the civil rights movement in America are generally invoked as archetypal examples of the theories and strategies of nonviolence. Beyond these iconic episodes, there are innumerable uses of nonviolence throughout history dating back at least to the early days of the Judeo-Christian tradition. More broadly, nonviolence as a way of life and a set of political practices has been deployed by societies from time immemorial, comprising in many ways the baseline of our humanity.

This history, however, has also created for some an impression of nonviolence as stale, antiquated, and unfit for use in a complex modern world that is dominated by the outward appearance of force as the prime mover of social and political realities. In this view, nonviolence comes to be seen at best as a noble, if futile endeavor, and at worst as a dangerously ineffective strategy that actually works against meaningful change. In both cases, nonviolence is often taken as a static, doctrinaire perspective that is practicable only for saintly souls or a privileged few among us. While these critiques ought to be taken seriously, they may be contrasted with the recognition that, by and large, the bulk of humankind lives closer to the tenets of nonviolence than might often appear from the state of the world and media constructions of societies everywhere.

In this light, nonviolence can be reinterpreted as a complex, evolving, and widely practiced set of theories with deep historical roots as well as strong resonances in the present. Yet, in order to keep it vital, the ways in which it has been utilized and continues to be theorized need to refreshed and reinvigorated. The chapters in this part of the book do precisely that, divining the essence of nonviolence from historical episodes where it has either been undervalued or even omitted altogether. Antony Adolf sets the tone for this analysis by reimagining nonviolence as a set of dynamic and multiple "nonviolences" that can serve to "offer a renewed transformative framework for engaging our pasts, presents, and futures alike." For Adolf, this historically informed paradigm is "predicated upon coordinated pluralities of nonviolence of proven effectiveness rather than a single generic and/or hegemonic one," thus breaking beyond the static or unitary boundaries sometimes ascribed to the theory. In the end, Adolf's work helps to frame the larger discussion of an "evolutionary nonviolence" by providing us with an emerging set of strategies "toward constructive change locally and globally for a world and species that direly needs it: ours."

Where Adolf takes a broad-based, holistic view of nonviolence, Micah Alpaugh wades deeply into an important historical episode (the French Revolution) and draws critical lessons from this exploration that still have great relevance in today's world. Alpaugh's work asks us to reconsider the past through a lens of nonviolence, which could serve as "a boon to the study of nonviolent protest elsewhere." Scholars and theorists in peace-related fields, in Alpaugh's view, "have largely focused on Gandhian and post-Gandhian traditions, in some respects underestimating trends already developing previously." The French revolutionary period in particular was "an important point of expansion in the history of nonviolent protest, contributing both the intellectual justification for such movements—popular sovereignty—and many of the tactics through which to conduct them." By rediscovering the essence of nonviolence contained within this history, Alpaugh asks us to move beyond "a doctrinal position" toward a more organic perspective that involves the "conscious attempt to adopt alternatives to violence, especially in situations . . . where its outbreak could easily occur."

Building upon these themes, Jenice View reflects upon a deep-seated history of American violence, particularly vis-à-vis people of color. Even measures taken ostensibly to benefit oppressed peoples have often replicated society's inherent "structural violence," and some reeducation programs from the recent past can be seen as attempts to "kill the [Indian, African, Mexican, Asian], and save the child," or "otherwise create a reverence for European culture, manual labor, and second-class citizenship." Despite such provocations, View discerns that people of color in America generally have "maintained a posture of nonviolent resistance," in the hope that the development of historical "counter-narratives of their labors and sacrifices to build the American Empire, would compel respect from rational members of the academic elite and lead to more equitable political and economic policies." While this hope yet remains unfulfilled in many respects, some gains have been made. In particular, "heritage curricula have been promoted for nearly 100 years as counter-narratives to the hegemonic academic texts that ignored the histories of people of color." Still, for View, a sense of "fierce cultural debate" pervades US classrooms and society at large, necessitating a set of strategies "to overcome racialization and internalized oppression, as well as to promote nonviolence and human rights in classrooms."

In this light, Pat Lauderdale's evocative and pragmatic analysis of native North American societies as living laboratories for the cultivation of nonviolence takes on enhanced significance. Beginning with the apparent reality that "the role of the modern state in most nations now is intimately related to the exacerbation of violence," Lauderdale counterposes an indigenous framework that devolves upon "an emphasis on decentralization via the deconsolidation of power by grassroots communities and government, the preventative processes related to violence within community, and an emphasis on equality before efficiency." As an historical proposition, native cultures "practiced many forms of nonviolent resistance against genocide and ethnic cleansing," and, perhaps even more to the point, cultivated an inherent "respect for diversity, community, and the care of nature [that] are central to civil law and peace." Without idealizing these lessons, Lauderdale concludes that "traditional North American Indians created complex, yet clear paths to peace [that] did not lead to simple social techniques or punitive moral standards for a nation, which empirically have led to more violence." Rather, the essence of nonviolence is contained in these histories and theories that have oftentimes been excluded from our social and political narratives.

1

Varieties of Nonviolence and Cultural Change

World History Lessons for Our Global Present and Future

Antony Adolf

Introduction: From Nonviolence to Nonviolences

When we look back upon the world history of nonviolence so as to improve current and prospective nonviolent ventures, what are we looking for? Are we seeking instances of the absence of violence alone, as the term may in its strict negating sense suggest, or are we looking for exacting kinds of presences, or—assuming such can be the case—for something in between? Given nonviolence's multiplicity of contextual meanings, let alone its various historical, present, and potential future applications, is it not more accurate to speak of nonviolences in the plural unless a very particular kind of nonviolence is intended? These are not fanciful philosophical questions or hair-splitting semantics, nor are they mere bookish musings that should be shelved. Rather, they constitute the ongoing, pragmatic examinations of pivotal forms of nonviolence that have had the greatest impact throughout history, and which retain merit today. What is the value of such bold enterprises, which are the subject of this very book? Without overstating the point, the aim is to ensure the survival and prosperity of humanity and all life on earth.

Constructively comparing and contrasting basic varieties of nonviolence as they were put forth within their diverse cultural contexts can

21

serve as a point of entry. We will focus on four distinct but interrelated categories here, as much for their contemporary as for their historical value. They are:

(1) *Spiritual Nonviolence*: derived from beliefs that incorporeal elements (e.g., deities, spirits, forces, etc.) have a perceptible influence on the corporeal and vice versa (Strain 2005, 42; Kool 1993, 95–6; Indian National Commission for Cooperation with UNESCO 1970, 176);

(2) *Physical Nonviolence*: derived from the actual or potential interaction between two corporeal elements (e.g., human bodies, materiel, organisms, etc.) (Mayton 2009, 226; Levy and Moulton 2007, 271; Parrish 2006, 41);

(3) *Structural Nonviolence*: derived from social (intra-group) and collective (inter-group) structures (e.g., economic, political, cultural, etc.) (Toussaint 2008, 5; MacQueen 1992, xii; Cerutti and Ragionieri 1990, 23); and

(4) *Intellectual Nonviolence*: derived from the human mind (e.g., science, philosophy, art, literature, etc.) (Chapple 2002, 20; 1993, 97).

However, comparison of these approaches would remain simply a point of entry, a step into but not a stride within, if we fail to find common denominators and guiding principles that can shape futures with both less violence and more peace. Finding key instances of these—or at least finding out how to find them—is the first of our two purposes here.

What becomes clear in pursuing this objective is that, except in special cases, nonviolence is generally aimed not at accepting situations as they are, but at transforming them into something "better," the nature of which is often highly disputed. Exploring this transformative quality of nearly all varieties of effective nonviolence is our second and ultimate purpose here. As both a cause and consequence of cultural change on local and global levels, the principles and practices that have made this distinct and unitive form of nonviolence—transformative nonviolence—the most effective, historically (Easwaran 1999, 196; Potorti 2003, 53), are examined to draw pragmatic lessons that can inform and reinvigorate nonviolent transformations now and in the future. The groundwork will be laid by encounters with exemplars of each of the four categories of nonviolence in sequence—spiritual, physical, structural, and intellectual—ultimately returning most explicitly to "transformative nonviolence" itself.

Spiritual Nonviolence: Incorporating the Incorporeal

Imagine that a group of leaders of Buddhists, Christians, Hindus, Muslims, and Jews decided to embark on a joint nonviolent venture, each insisting that their faith be considered. Would the venture be doomed from the start, or are there proven ways for diverse spiritualities and religions to work together nonviolently? Of the four categories of nonviolence presented, none is more elusive yet historically widespread, paradoxically, than the spiritual. Our encounter with spiritual nonviolence here will be based on what we hope will be a simple but pragmatic one: an incorporeal entity to which believers ascribe agency. Also to note is that spirituality as used here encompasses much more than the organized and institutionalized religions that are built around them, sometimes to their benefit, and often to their detriment. Gandhian *satyagraha* and the Christian law of love as expressed in Jesus's Sermon on the Mount are already well-known expressions of spiritual nonviolence, so our focus will be on key tenets of Daoism, and particularly on a specific Daoist practice dating back to the seventh century BCE in Ancient China that is linked to the notion of *wu-wei* (Slingerland 2003). Focusing on this one spiritual tradition can, both strategically and allegorically, inform the analysis of spiritual nonviolence and its utilization within other traditions.

The diverse texts, beliefs, and practices grouped under the moniker "Daoism" share two beliefs (Kohn 2000). The first is a belief in the *Dao*, an incorporeal agent that is omnipresent in our material world, and which shapes and is shaped by corporeal beings, binding them by being below, in, and above their surfaces. Dao is frequently translated as the "way" or the "path," but these English terms can be deceiving because they imply a static stiffness and self-subjugation that are anathema to the Dao of the *Dao De Ching*, the dynamism and empowerment of which is most important to advocates and scholars as a wellspring of spiritual nonviolence. The authorship of that foundational text is attributed to Lao-Tzu, who was an older contemporary of Confucius and Zhou Dynasty bookkeeper before becoming an itinerant sage. Over the course of close to three millennia since, his sometimes enigmatic teachings have been crystallized into a few potent ones. Most prominent are the so-called "Three Jewels of the Dao," which refer to compassion, moderation, and humility. Together, they form a nonviolent ethical praxis for approaching everyday life on a spiritual basis, and for guiding interactions with others in ways similar to those proposed by later philosophical and spiritual movements elsewhere. The deeper one goes into this spiritual reservoir, the more nonviolent values surface.

More so than most spiritualities, Daoism attunes its adherents to the repercussions of ecological violence, since it perceives all living beings, and even inanimate ones, as part of and a channel for *ch'i*, the life-force permeating the universe. This is the second belief all Daoists share. Under this view, reckless agricultural or industrial practices harm the ch'i of an area, of its living beings, and ultimately of the earth, itself. Political leaders, states, armies, economies, groups, individuals, and so on, are all part of ch'i, but each can paradoxically also harness ch'i regardless of existing stations and relations—a radical concept in its day, not unlike Buddhism's analogous impulse. Daoism's inherent antiauthoritarianism could lapse into chaos if it were not for ch'i as a binding force through those who, knowingly or not, can consciously manipulate and be manipulated by it. The Dao, then, becomes something of a vessel and a vehicle for those who are attuned to it, the spiritual nonviolence of which lies equally in belief, interpretations of occurrences based upon belief, and actions taken upon either, the three being inseparable. The task of those who study spiritual nonviolence is to explore and examine the connections between these concepts; the task of those who practice spiritual nonviolence is to make the most of them.

Even nonbelievers of any spirituality or deity gain by learning about the beliefs of others, because this knowledge helps in ascertaining what motivates, deters, and enhances the odds of nonviolent ventures succeeding. Ethical secularization of spirituality can also help create common ground, especially in inter-spiritual situations. With Daoism, ethical secularization becomes especially possible with respect to the *De* element of the *Dao De Ching*, a concept that combines inner strength and virtue, and which has been pragmatically reinterpreted throughout Daoism's history. De results from following the Dao, but the concept also parallels tenets found in all major world religions, including Christianity, Judaism, Islam, and many non-religious codes of conduct, several of which are discussed below. In effect, inner strength resembling De is often the source of nonviolent action, is always guided by virtues of a given denomination, and/or is considered a virtue in itself (Dasgupta 1984, 14). Inner strength is often taken for granted when writing and teaching about nonviolence, but never when practicing it. Therefore, an important distinction is to be made between active nonviolence—deliberately engaging De (or any nonviolent behavior a spirituality prescribes)—and passive nonviolence reflecting a predisposition to De (or to any nonviolent predilection a spirituality requires). The congruities between doing and being become much more evident with the central concept associated with De and Daoism's most explicit tie with spiritual nonviolence: *wu-wei*.

Technically defined as "non-action" or "non-interference," wu-wei in a more comprehensive sense means letting ourselves and the world be in such a way that the Dao may take its course. Thus, in the *Dao De Ching*, "the kingdom is made one's own only by freedom from action," and "when opposing weapons are crossed, he who deplores the situation conquers" (Ames and Hall 2004, 57). Here, negativities of nonviolence take on paradoxically positive attributes: what is not done is not done on purpose by a person or people, rather than there being a mere absence of violence as the state of conditions. Nonviolent practice attributed to the Dao, which can be harnessed through wu-wei, is in fact the source and destination of our agency; insofar as we stray from the Dao's nonviolence we deviate from that to which we owe our existence and which constitutes our very core. Being anything but nonviolent contravenes the spirituality of wu-wei and Daoism equally, not to mention other spiritualities. Wu-wei as spiritual nonviolence, then, should not be confused with Tolstoyan non-cooperation or Thoreau's civil disobedience, which are associated with—but are not inextricable from—spirituality, and can work even if the world were devoid of Dao. Whether or not wu-wei can also work in such circumstances may be a moot issue, given that adherents would need new spiritual and non-spiritual reasons to practice it.

In contrast, the social (within-group) and collective (between-group) implications of wu-wei (as opposed to the more individualistic nonviolences just mentioned) are so pervasive that it is impossible to fully understand wu-wei outside them (Adolf 2009, 2–14). With wu-wei, optimal Daoist governments are those that are least perceptible, that is, governments that do the most by doing the least. In this sense, Daoist politics are closer to modern laissez-faire and libertarian positions than interventionist socialist ones. In the influential words of the *Zuangzi*, an accretion of Daoist texts attributed to a fourth-century BCE official of that name: "The inaction of heaven is its purity; the inaction of earth is its peace. So the two inactions combine and all things are transformed and brought to birth . . . heaven and earth do nothing and there is nothing not done. Among men, who can get hold of this inaction?" (Watson 1968, 191).

It follows that not participating in or collaborating with violent governments are the best ways to resist them, and withdrawing from warlike cultures is the best way to change them. This is what we may call wu-wei's peculiar "active-passive" nonviolence, which could not exist without the spirituality in which it is based. The ideal Daoist society, then, is one in which individuals are free to follow the Dao as idiosyncratically revealed to them, regardless of class or clan, and with little or no government to inhibit the flow of ch'i. This was a revolutionary idea in its time, and may remain so today. With wu-wei, in contrast to later forms of nonviolence and especially recent ones, transformation through spiritual nonviolence occurs not by doing something, but by purposefully doing general and specific nonaction, since the underlying spiritual reality of the world is understood to act and not act on its own.

Daoism was so popular by the seventh century CE that T'ang Dynasty emperors gave it official sanction, and it has remained a strong and peaceful undercurrent in Chinese culture ever since, arguably matched only by Confucianism, Buddhism, and Communism (since the 20th century) in influence. Nevertheless, Daoism has been bastardized—as all spiritualities have at some point, sometimes extensively—into violent forms, paramountly during the so-called Yellow Scarves or Yellow Turban Rebellion in the second century CE, which was carried out in the name of a "Way of Supreme Peace" (Taiping Dao).

Spirituality without vigilance can and has led to violence, and so observers must always be on guard to not let such latent possibilities become potent actualities. Unfortunately, few religious and cross-religious nonviolent movements have achieved results as significant as those achieved by individual personalities. For example, compare Christianity with Tolstoy in thought and Martin Luther King Jr. in action; compare Hinduism with Gandhi, who also drew heavily on Christianity; and compare Buddhism with the Dalai Lama, including his expert use of non-Buddhist secular frames of reference. Of course, implicitly nonviolent inter-religious initiatives have been successful in achieving their otherwise specific aims even if they have not been explicitly nonviolent. A paramount exception may be found in the world's youngest religion, Baha'i, which draws upon other major religions for its concepts of spiritual nonviolence and seeks to overcome centuries of violence committed in the name of religion (Miller 1974). Although the faith's founder's high-level, late-life disarmament efforts came to naught, the doctrines he espoused and the faith's practitioners have proven the viability of spiritual and inter-spiritual nonviolence regardless of what one believes, and especially if one does.

Physical Nonviolence: Location, Location, and NVDA

To return for a moment to modern environmentalism, the roots of which can be traced to eighteenth- and nineteenth-century Romanticism: environmentalism is physical nonviolence incarnate, specifically as it relates to protecting living beings from harm in a particular location, but also when referring to protecting the earth as a whole. However, as Timothy Morton (2007) makes clear in *Ecology without Nature*, too often the environment is understood as something that needs to be "saved," and which lies somewhere "over there," when in actuality every place is an environment that warrants protection, if not preservation. In Morton's view, it is our naïve notions of "nature" that allow us to maintain this fictitious distance, putting humans in a perceived, imaginary, and privileged position above nature and interacting with it from the outside in; in actuality, it is our many environments, human-made or not, that permit us to exist as we do.

Along similar lines to this nuanced environmentalism, physical nonviolence refrains from causing physical harm to beings (usually humans) in a particular situation, as in, "They protested nonviolently in front of the Supreme Court for lifting the limits on corporate campaign contributions." This can also be thought of globally, as in "The organization seeks a world without violence, and takes pragmatic steps towards achieving it, beginning with the often hidden or overlooked violence in their members' communities." However, these two contexts—particular and global situations—give the impression that there is an in-between zone. There is not. That conflicts take place on street corners or whole continents does not change the complicity that comes with awareness of either. That I know gang violence, lone wolf attacks, rapes, and so on recur in my city or state puts me in the same position as knowing that war is ongoing in this or that region: I am (imaginarily) immune from them. In actuality, I am already involved in them by being aware of them and doing something or nothing about them (Adolf 2010a). There is no place "outside" of violence as long as violence exists, and pretending that there is prevents us from eliminating violence once and for all.

In effect, what we are exploring here is locative physical nonviolence without the absence of violence, that is, in the ever-presence (but not omnipresence) of violence. Only this formulation of physical nonviolence can adequately encompass the life/death line at which it begins, but does not end. Another fruitful ground for critical inquiry that can inform nonviolent undertakings today can be located through what Glenn Paige (2009) calls the "killing zone" (where people kill) and its correlate, "killing-free" zones (where people do not kill) in his foundational "nonkilling" paradigm for the political and social sciences. A paradigm, based upon Paige's work, for historical analysis of our presents and near-futures has also been put forth (Adolf and Sanmartin 2009). In brief, these analyses conclude that it is inaccurate and nonsensical to think or believe that killing preponderates nonkilling historically, since humanity and life on Earth would not exist as it does if this were the case, if at all. Soldiers do not kill their friends; they only seek to kill their foes, which suggests that nonkilling is a precondition of life and history that must built upon to be effective, in addition to comprising a foundational moral imperative. This is where an important theoretical break with serious practical repercussion occurs between concepts of nonkilling and nonviolence, notwithstanding equally significant continuities.

By definition, victims die when nonkilling ends, but life can survive nonlethal violence, whether it take the form of physical or emotional violence (Adolf and Sanmartin 2009; Adolf 2010b). The well-researched "cycle of violence" can only be vicarious when it comes to killing (Hazler 1996; Schmidt 1993). So it is not nonsensical, as it is with nonkilling, to think or believe that violence preponderates nonviolence historically, regardless of the fact that it is inaccurate quantitatively. Qualitatively— since awareness of violence makes us complicit, and therefore there is no place "outside" of violence—it is certain that violence preponderates nonviolence and will continue to do so until all violence everywhere has ceased. "So, what to do about it?" is the pragmatic question, and the answer is to begin by balancing our complicity in violence by awareness with a comparable complicity in nonviolence by awareness. This can be accomplished by acknowledging and building upon the circumstances that make violence less likely and nonviolence more likely, beginning with effective forms of nonviolence education as a sub-discipline of the established field of peace education. In 2009, Kenya became the first country to propose compulsory peace education in an effort to avoid repeating the violence that disrupted recent elections, and that has plagued the region, generally. To be effective, such programs cannot be merely inserted into existing curricula because doing so would sustain the delusion that nonviolence is somehow separate from everything else we do and are. Rather, a comprehensive peace curriculum should be grafted onto and fused with existing curricula in all disciplines, which is not an entirely new notion, given the way that "green" efforts have achieved widespread acceptance in fields from business to engineering.

The point this analysis has been building toward is that there are always two categories of location involved in violence and nonviolence:

the first is ever-present in the psycho-physical sense just described, and the second is immediate-proximate and is based on the physical alone (Adolf and Sanmartin 2009, 210–11):

> Aerial bombing of towns and cities, atomic bombs and terrorist acts were shocking developments in warfare because they erased these long-held lines of demarcation between killing and killing-free zones. Gang warfare, police brutality and lone wolves shooting up schools and workplaces are historical forces, among many others, threatening killing-free zones considered militarily. Within twenty years of the first deployment of nuclear weapons, regional and world bodies created nuclear-free zones, and places for asylum and sanctuary exist in most cultures in some form. Nation-state neutrality, neutral-zones enforced by peacekeepers, buffer zones created to avoid war-triggering skirmished between conflicting states, the list of nonkilling zones with distinct but comparable histories goes on.

Obviously, the same line of thinking, study and action applies to physical nonviolences of these and other kinds. The tremendous number of participants and conditions required for any item on this very topically limited list of locations—to which physically instituted nonviolence by location is tied and enforced to be an actuality—is breathtaking. Scholars and activists of nonkilling, nonviolence, and peace have their work cut out for them, which includes the beneficial roles they can play in world affairs.

A third type of physical nonviolence, in addition to the two types of location-based nonviolence, is to be found in nonviolent direct action, or "NVDA" (Zinn 2001). The difference lies in the distinction between conditions and participants, with the latter being best understood as comprised of individuals or groups acting socially and collectively. Within these contexts, physical nonviolence refers to active or passive efforts between individuals and groups, as well as within groups, to transform situations without recourse to violence. Passive physical nonviolence is, as can be surmised from the above, the vastly preponderate norm of human (and all animal) behavior, regardless of how attention-grabbing violence in all its forms can be. Institutionalized passive forms of nonviolence (structural nonviolence) will be contrasted with institutionalized passive forms of violence (structural violence) below. Here, our focus is primarily on active forms of nonviolence, such as NVDA, compared to institutionalized forms of active violence. While some of the most famous early instances of NVDA date back to Christian martyrs of the first century CE resisting Roman oppression, and extend to earlier centuries through other cultures, recent history illustrates that all nonviolences have long traditions behind them, overlooked at great loss.

With the proliferation of nuclear capabilities since the 1940s, and arguably for the first time since the origin of our species, what has been dubbed the "survival of the peaceful" of our primate ancestors in *Peace: A World History* now applies equally to humanity as a whole (Adolf 2009). Actualizations of this bio-genetic and cultural imperative could not have been accomplished without deterrence and détente, and they would not have taken the forms that they did without two concurrent types of anti-nuclear movements, NVDA and mass nonviolent action, both based in forms of physical nonviolence. The difference between NVDA (generally assumed to be effected by an individual or small group) and mass nonviolence is not only numbers, but more importantly, dynamics, as suggested in the monumental three-part study of nonviolent action by Gene Sharp (1972, 1974, 1976). Instead, we turn our gaze to the humble historical origins that set anti-nuclear NVDA rolling.

A year after Dorothy Day and the Catholic Workers in New York refused to participate in civil defense drills aimed at preparing citizens for nuclear war, a pioneering anti-nuclear group—as much about individual consciences as collective consciousness—was formed by longtime peace activist A. J. Muste, former Navy commander-turned-Quaker Albert Bigelow, and others (Roberts 1984). Their Committee for Nonviolent Action (CNVA) established the basic patterns of physical nonviolence as NVDA, which are still largely in place today, holding non-stop protest vigils, and purposefully subjecting themselves to arrest for trespassing or obstructing traffic through their sit-ins at nuclear-related government facilities across the United States (Bennett 2003). In the 1960s and 70s, the CNVA organized two cross-continental Walks for Peace, bringing the issue of nuclear arms reduction literally door-to-door. These early anti-nuclear NVDAs were inspired by the NVDAs of Gandhi and the civil rights movement, but differ as to the objects toward which they were directed: nuclear weapons factories, storage facilities, and launch sites. This difference marks them as doubly transformative physical nonviolence: transforming both the means and the ends.

NVDA of questionable nonviolence broke new grounds in the 1980s, when eight activists broke into a Pennsylvania warhead facility, damaged specimens, and poured blood over documents. The more emphasis that physical nonviolence places on the physical, the less nonviolent it becomes. This action in turn inspired similar plowshare actions around the world, echoing the Biblical admonition to turn "swords into plowshares." A compelling argument has even been made for employing plowshare actions as a counterterrorism measure, and perhaps an alternative to terrorism altogether, even if the distinctions between such acts, sabotage, and the criminal destruction of property have yet to be worked out (Hastings 2004). The "Plowshare Eight's" destruction of property and their confrontational intentions were condemned by many peace activists, yet in actuality neither the original action nor any of the hundreds of plowshare actions that have since been taken have been against individuals. The value of nonviolent direct action confronting overwhelming opposition lies more in making a point than making a difference. However, when nonviolent direct actions reach critical mass, the point becomes the difference. The value of mass nonviolent action, in contrast, lies in its awareness-raising mobilization and the political influence such mobilization engenders (Adolf 2009, 203–4).

Structural Nonviolence: Legal Systems and Codes of Conduct

Positing "structural nonviolence" as a field of study, a form of activism, and a basis for developing organizational goals compliments a powerful tradition in peace studies, namely the critique of "structural violence," which ranges from systemic inequalities to total disenfranchisement. Johan Galtung proposed this view, and it has been practiced by Petra Kelly with her notion of participatory democracy that simultaneously changes political goals from outside and inside the system, among many others (Galtung 1969; Kelly 1988). Structural violence is generally understood as institutionalized forms of discrimination and oppression that prevent particular individuals or groups from actualizing their full potentials based on power asymmetries that its victims are often not in a position to change. Another way to think of structural nonviolence in the terms used above is as a kind of passive violence, for example, as with the actions of bureaucratically removed decision-makers compared to those of field soldiers. The correlate structural nonviolence, then, can be understood as institutionalized forms of analogous opportunity generation and empowerment that enable all individuals and groups to actualize their full potentials, despite power asymmetries that even those in power are unable to change. The trappings of classical or neoliberalism can be escaped by stressing that structural nonviolence can be instituted within or transform any political and economic system. "Totalization," a notion that may rightly frighten anyone sufficiently cognizant of twentieth century history, may prove to be inspirational for the twenty-first if it is applied to structural nonviolence. Three didactic historical examples make this clear: citizenship in ancient Rome, legalism in ancient China, and codes of conduct throughout the ages.

Citizenship in ancient Rome, along with the privileges that it afforded within that empire's legal and other systems (economic, social, etc.), was as precious an issue to peace then as it is to nation-states today, given that it is a source of equivalent opportunity for those who have it, and an instrument of exclusion for those who do not: those without citizenship have no say in the very processes that exclude them (Sherwin-White 1979). Muslims in Europe, Hispanics in the United States, and Asians in the Middle East are but a few examples of those without substantial opportunities to address processes that serve to exclude them (Buff 2008). As the Roman Empire grew and consolidated its hold on people and territory, citizenship became and remained for centuries a bargaining chip used by Romans to transform rebellion into integration, to a point. The word "social" that we attach to "justice" today stems from one group of rebellious, aspiring Romans called the *Socii*, who were awarded citizenship as a nonviolent appeasement policy by the Roman legislature around 200 BCE. Again, the close resemblances with our contemporary immigration and amnesty debates are not coincidental. Should there come a time when demands for legitimization through citizenship threaten to become violent, as state responses to citizenship's absence already are, we know that there are structurally nonviolent means with proven historical precedents to solving the problem. There are also close resemblances between this structurally nonviolent mode of conflict resolution and one proposed and practiced in Ancient China at roughly the same time.

The functions and dysfunctions of citizenship as a nonviolent means to the end of total structural violence are possible, under modern regimes, only within viable legal systems. The upshot is that for any practical world citizenship to be instituted there must be a viable global legal system, which does not yet exist. Unless the idea of citizenship is universally discarded and replaced with a better bargaining chip, which is unlikely, our only option is to continually optimize existing inclusive mechanisms that do not concomitantly exclude, and tailor them for specific conditions, participants, and motives. A model to be improved upon can be found in the work of Han Fei (ca. 280–233), a Han-era prince who used this theory in building a pragmatic political philosophy of peace that made law the formative and decisive force in shaping individual behavior and social norms (Watson 2003; Robinson 2003). The cornerstone of his school of peace is the legal code, which he argued should be precise, publicly available, and the final word on everything for everyone. In the words of a modern scholar, the "legalist's" law code was thus set up to be the "all-powerful instrument which makes it possible to guide everyone's activity in the direction most favorable to the power of the state and the public peace" (Gernet 1999, 81). Accordingly, the law itself is authority, not the individual identities who apply it, who from high to low are bound by it and motivated by its punishments for disobedience and rewards for compliance, which are the basis of legalist morality. Legitimacy, peace, and power, then, rest in legally prescribed and delimited positions, not in the people who hold those positions. Legalism became Imperial policy with the Qin Emperors, whose chief minister Li Si (ca. 280–208) competed intellectually and politically with Han Fei, eventually killing him and 500 scholars in the name of the law.

The actual laws of different national traditions that prohibit and punish violence of different (but usually not all) kinds, and the human and other resources allocated to enforce or uphold these laws—from police to peacekeepers—all point to nonviolent codes of conduct dating back millennia. The famed oath of the ancient Greek physician Hippocrates, still invoked today, did more than make medicine a profession distinct from magic: it provided one of the earliest known Western codes of nonviolent conduct by both prohibiting violence and committing to seeking justice (Miles 2005). Likewise, the often-disparaged practice of Sophistry— which originally meant being skilled in arguing all sides, not the derogatory obscurantism it denotes today—replaced armed conflict with debate, prevented violence by compromise, and expedited reconciliation through agreement. The open, critical dialogue practiced by the ancient Greek Sophist Protagoras has proved invaluable to peace and conflict resolution throughout history, up to and including The Hague Conventions of 1899 and 1907, where humane wartime and peacetime modes of conduct were codified (Scott 1909). Think now to the myriad organizations we have today, from student bodies to professional associations and businesses that are in a position to extend the tradition of nonviolent codes of conduct into the present. Now imagine a future in which they do not extend that tradition, and they instead encourage the opposite.

Intellectual Nonviolence:
Philosophy and Conscientious Objecting

Philosophies of nonviolence that do not combine the abstract with the practical remain incomplete, just as nonviolent actions or movements that do not provide philosophies that can be understood and adapted by others also do not actualize their full potential. The love of wisdom to which philosophy refers encompasses not only sagacity, but also sound judgment and informed deeds, which together comprise the wisdom the wisest in history have sought (Sternberg 1990). It is at the intersection of these three elements that we can situate many of the traditions of intellectual nonviolence of the past, which have been and remain fruitful grounds for new and renewed traditions in the present, and for the future. On these points, what may be called the pragmatism of Richard Rorty's and Howard Zinn's intellectual nonviolence stand as exemplars (Rorty 1982; Zinn

2001). Rationality unites them all, despite its shortcomings, just as spirituality, physicality, and structurality united the three previous varieties of nonviolence with others like them.

One school of ancient Greek lineage, Stoicism, centralized nonviolence in its way of thinking and, some three hundred to five hundred years later, became the philosophical foundation for a highly violent Roman government. The Stoic philosophy has often been unduly limited by commentators as a personal and not a social doctrine, but this is inaccurate (Sellars 2006). Named after the Athenian porticos (*stoa*) where its founder, Zeno (333–264 BCE) taught, Stoicism is generally seen as the superseding counter-philosophy to Epicureanism, which propagated the absence of pain as the paramount peace, and a rational nonviolence—akin in some ways to Daoism's spiritual form—as the means to achieve it. Stoics rejected the passions (lust, greed, anger, etc., later called vices) where Epicureans rejected pain. While individual Stoics did engage in warfare (most famously, Roman Emperor Marcus Aurelius wrote his paradigmatically Stoic *Meditations* while on campaign), collectively they held that the surest path to inner and social peace was not through withdrawal but self-discipline. This self-discipline was grounded in both active and passive nonviolence, and in the view that solidarity with fellow practitioners could bring peace to the world. The effect of Stoic thinking can be traced to the Latin word *virtu*, which originally referred to manly courage in battle, and was only later associated with the nonviolent virtues of moderation and magnanimity. This significant semantic shift is reflected in the work of Panaetius (189–109 BCE), who argued that no one can be virtuous as long as they participate in or even condone violence, physical or otherwise. Stoicism, the former slave Epictetus (50–130 BCE) claimed, could bring "friendship in families, concord in cities and peace in states" (Arrianus 2010, secs. 2.13.40–41). The limited concord and peace achieved by Stoicism is due to the Roman addition of selfless duty to self-discipline, which made Stoicism a favorite pose and the unofficial code of the powerful and their acolytes.

Bringing this intellectual foundation of nonviolence into an analytical and practical process, the Englishman Jeremy Bentham (1748–1832) presented pleasure and pain as the forces governing all human activity, and their properties as gauges of and guides to individual, social and collective decision-making (Everett 1969). Pleasure and pain can be quantified in terms of extent, intensity, duration, certainty or uncertainty, proximity or remoteness, fecundity (the probability of an act causing an ongoing sensation), and purity (the probability of an act yielding a contrasting sensation), and this analysis aids in forming qualitative opinions, strategies, and tactics, which are utilitarian only insofar as they are as nonviolent as possible, and preferably involving no violence at all. Applying this "hedonic calculus" to war, Bentham ranked it low on the utility scale as a "mischief," and highest on the pain scale, indiscriminately menacing all members of the community (Bentham 1879, 215). In countering then-prevailing notions that all must invariably obey the natural laws of nations, Bentham the legalist coined the term "international law" to convey utility-based consensus. However, Bentham the economist did not apply this principle directly to nonviolent transformation. By doing so, distinctive definitional and analytical potentials thus emerge: in a general sense, transformative nonviolence is always useful because it minimizes pain; in particular cases, intellectually- sourced nonviolence can always be comparatively evaluated by properties of pain and pleasure to develop optimal, conditional strategies and tactics of action, and to continually learn from their implementations.

Conscientious objecting, found in Stoicism and utilitarianism, is based on rationality, and is more commonly associated in modernity with Mennonites and Quakers—two of the major "peace churches" that both emphasize the logic of Christ's law of love and the practicality of the nonviolence he preached, as well as his spiritual message. In the case of Mennonites, it was their reasoned arguments and not their theological ones that led to the first nation-state laws sanctioning conscientious objecting. Similarly, Quakers drew upon on pacifist principles in founding Pennsylvania, the first modern state so established among a series of similar social experiments worldwide (MacMaster 1979; Butselaar 2001; Gibble 2006). A new kind of nonviolent nationalism materialized in England in World War I as purely secular conscientious objectors extended the spiritually motivated pacifism of peace churches to include economic, moral, and political motives. The *No Conscription Fellowship Manifesto* recognized different motives for objecting (spiritual, physical, and intellectual) to war in general, or to World War I in particular, but also, and maybe more importantly, united these motivations under a single banner of defending nonviolent individualism against violent nationalism (Atkin 2002, 3). And Bertrand Russell, the man who first proved that one plus one equals two using symbolic logic, also articulated and practiced an intellectual nonviolence in lectures, articles, letters (Griffin 2002) and books, including *The Philosophy of Pacifism* (Russell 1915). Once again, these are but a few passing references to prominent proponents of intellectual nonviolence, but what is missing is an account of the everyday intellectual nonviolence that permeates the lives of most people.

Conclusion: Ten Verities of Transformative Nonviolence

The analytical import of making distinctions between varieties of nonviolence goes hand in hand with practical considerations, or not at all. If nonviolent strategies and tactics do not come about in a vacuum, neither do the conditions in which they are deployed. Actually, of the four categories of nonviolence surveyed, only one can genuinely claim to maintain—rather than transform—the status quo: the structural category. Still, even structural nonviolence is incrementally or suddenly instituted in response to changing conditions and participants in order for constancy to become the only change. Without the presence of structural nonviolence to some degree, none of the other forms of nonviolence may have come into being as they did, if at all, and therefore all were at least implicitly designed to transform. By becoming the new conditions in which new participants act, and influencing those participants with or without their knowledge, in the end, structural nonviolence also has its greatest effect as a slow-speed transformative force. Even resistance alone is not transformative; transformation only arises when the object of resistance is successfully overcome. And so, what we have discovered is that there is presently no such thing as transformative nonviolence "itself," and perhaps there never can be.

In its most potent forms, transformative nonviolence is a contextually-determined and weighted component of spiritual, intellectual, physical, structural, and other nonviolences. Nevertheless, the following ten verities of transformative nonviolence, gleaned from the long history of nonviolence, may prove instructive in improving the effectiveness of all nonviolence—spiritual, physical, structural, intellectual, or otherwise—which is the objective of the present volume:

Transformative nonviolence can be distinguished from nonviolent ways of life;

Transformative nonviolence seeks to change situations for the "better" when what is "better" is highly contentious and/or prized;

Transformative nonviolence also seeks to change situations by keeping certain of its conditions, participants, and motives the same, while altering others;

Transformative nonviolence cannot be effected on its own, but only as a component of spiritual, structural, physical, intellectual, and other varieties of nonviolence;

Transformative nonviolence has been effective since prehistory, throughout history, and continues to be effective today;

Transformative nonviolence's pasts can and do inform and improve its use in the present and future as a general strategy, and in particular tactical applications;

Transformative nonviolence cannot be effective without considering the conditions, participants, and motives it is used for and against;

Transformative nonviolence is never the only solution, nor is it usually a last-resort solution to any given problem;

Transformative nonviolence is limited only by our knowledge of, capabilities in, and willingness to use it as conditions, participants, and motives require; and

Transformative nonviolence is virtually limitless in its potential conceptualizations, applications, and benefits.

These ten verities of nonviolence, and the varieties of nonviolence upon which they are based (those existing, as well as those yet to be discovered and implemented), offer a renewed transformative framework for engaging our pasts, presents, and futures, alike. This transformative

nonviolent paradigm, predicated upon coordinated pluralities of nonviolence of proven effectiveness, rather than a single generic or hegemonic
concept, further yields pragmatic points of connection between theoretical insights and practical applications of holistic nonviolence. In short,
the variety of transformative approaches to nonviolence provides strategies
and tactics toward constructive local and global change for a world and a
species that direly need it: *ours.*

2

Historicizing Nonviolent Protest

The Role of the French Revolution

Micah Alpaugh

The trans-Atlantic age of revolution in the second half of the eighteenth century created a new age for the politics of protest. Emerging ideas about popular sovereignty led to the establishment or upswing of several innovative—and in most cases physically nonviolent—forms of contention, including political demonstrations, mass-meetings, and petition-campaigns, whose influence remain paramount in how social movements are made today. Building upon the acts of both British protesters, particularly in the "Wilkes and Liberty" campaigns of the 1750s and 1760s, and the movements of pre-revolutionary America, French revolutionaries would push the new paradigm of democratic contention the furthest, attempting to establish for themselves a regular and explicit voice in their country's governance.

Focusing on Paris, the capital and center of the Revolution, my attempt to chart the full corpus of protester methods and movements has led to the surprising finding that most protests remained demonstrably nonviolent. Based upon an event database drawn from a wide reading of Parisian newspapers, pamphlets, personal journals, correspondence, and governmental reports, by my count, over 85 percent (483 of 566) of all group protests in Paris during the Revolution (between 1787 and 1795) did not employ physical violence. What's more, over 95 percent avoided property destruction, and over half of all cases did not engage in verbal threats of violence. Instead, Parisian protesters much more commonly sought rapprochement, influence, and agreement with the French government, only rarely turning to violence after other means had failed.

As is evident with even a cursory glance at the historiography, my story does not mesh easily with ongoing emphasis historians have placed on French revolutionary violence. The "Marxist interpretation," which dominated the historiography for much of the twentieth century, highlighted the Revolution's role as an important predecessor for insurrectionary struggles around the globe (Lefebvre 1939; Soboul 1958; Rudé 1959). While such later movements increasingly utilized nonviolent tactics, Leninist dogma saw "revolution" as a necessarily violent phenomenon. "Revisionist" interpretations of the French Revolution since the 1960s, usually centered under neoliberal and/or neoconservative ringleaders, turned the theme of violence against the revolutionary tradition in order to discredit it, seeing violence as inherent in or essential to revolution itself (Furet 1981; Baker 1990). Less ideological writers, meanwhile, have commonly fetishized revolutionary violence as one of the more saleable aspects of its history, in so doing often distorting or embellishing its role (Dickens 1859; Schama 1989). Perhaps, given the continued convenience of the theme of violence, no historians have systematically looked for alternative explanations for the course of revolutionary protest.

A focus on nonviolence cannot be limited to a debate on violence, of course, but also requires an expanded examination of the rich fraternal and universalistic side of revolutionary practice and thought—categories only beginning to receive more thorough treatment from historians (Gross 1997; Reddy 2001). Influenced by expanding definitions of concepts such as public opinion, sociability, equality, and fraternity emanating from Enlightenment-era discourse and revolutionary experimentation, protesters set out to interact with and influence revolutionary authorities on a par unimaginable with earlier regimes. Parisian protesters, across numerous campaigns, and with uneven though often successful results, sought to expand new and developing forms of political interconnectivity between the state and the people. Such movements created emotionally charged spaces for mass gatherings projecting themes of ecstatic union and fraternity dear to the radical cause; the fact that these repeatedly drew tens of thousands of participants—often participating despite the very real risk of personal harm—can largely be attributed to the inclusive political vision revolutionaries succeeded in projecting.

Though not adhering to an explicit ideology of nonviolence, French revolutionary protest movements exhibited many of the tactics and ideas today associated with the practice of nonviolence. Though willing to resort to physical violence in extreme circumstances, these movements largely centered around what Barack Obama in his Nobel Peace Prize address 220 years later declared as the "need to develop alternatives to violence that are tough enough to actually change behavior" (Obama 2009). Collaborative protests that engaged in dialogue with local and national authorities appeared to hold this kind of promise for Parisian protesters. While such nonviolent protests sometimes did contain some violent elements—such as threats in the form of catcalls, intimidating petitions, or by carrying weapons—the restraint from physical violence that was shown by Parisian protesters, even when protester demands were commonly rebuffed, was evident and was commonly noted. In the most thorough theorization of peaceful protest during the Revolution, François Lanthenas (1793), a moderate assemblyman in the ruling National Convention, wrote how "it is very seldom useful, as the measurement of true courage, to resort to force, or to violence" (4). Even if "one has reason to believe that violence could accomplish in little time that which one desires, even then one should hesitate. Force appears, in all times and to all men, an odious thing" (7). Instead, Lanthenas detailed "discussion and persuasion" as the means to "complete revolutions," looking to develop associational life as "a force which each of their individual members could not cultivate on their own" (17).

In examining the rise of demonstrably nonviolent French revolutionary protest tactics, a case study of the first republican movement of June through July 1791 is warranted. Following King Louis XVI's unsuccessful attempt to flee the country (most likely to join a counterrevolutionary army wanting to reinstall the Old Regime), radical Parisian individuals and associations banded together for a series of mass-meetings, petitions, and political demonstrations that challenged both the monarchy and its supporters in the National Assembly. Until an incident of physical violence brought National Guard intervention on July 17, in what became known as the Massacre of the Champ de Mars, the movement utilized only physically nonviolent tactics, and sought to elaborate an alternative and more democratic paradigm featuring substantial popular input in major decision-making.

The republican movement of 1791 drew from the multiple conduits of associational life developed in Paris over the first two years of the Revolution. Several of the principal protests of 1789 sprang from the gardens of the *Palais-Royal*, a popular promenade outside the jurisdiction of the Paris police where ordinary Parisians could buy political tracts, listen to orations, discuss politics in the cafés, and sometimes draw others into dissenting acts. Some of the first political "clubs"—directly adopting the English term for debating societies—sprang up in the apartments above the central garden, and would soon spread across the capital, particularly after the Palais's police-exempt status as a private domain was revoked in August 1789. An additional associational channel developed through the capital's sixty districts at locales for Estates General elections in spring 1789, yielding a shift in control of local government and policing for the city with the Bastille insurrection. Though hostile to relatively lower-class elements taking control of the streets, the middle-class local assemblies still continued (with dubious legality) discussions and debates on issues of political interest in common meetings.

In spite of repeated protester attempts to build a collaborative relationship with legislators, the movements of 1789 did not institutionalize any regular, direct, and peaceful means for Parisians to voice their opinion before national authorities. Parisian contention in 1790 turned more towards establishing a recognized, systemic structure for dissent and dialogue with legislators, which could allow for significant protests without recourse to physical violence. Multiple campaigns attempted to expand mass Parisian influence by establishing direct conduits for popular sovereignty, first through enhancing the political role of the established network of electoral districts, and then through building a thorough network of popular clubs (also known as *sociétés populaires*) across the capital. On January 11, 1790, the District des Prémontrés asserted that the National Assembly had no right to make municipal law, and called for a municipal constitution including devolution of power from the Commune to the sixty districts, with each allowed to meet *en permanence* (permanently).

All "active citizens" (adult males with sufficient means to qualify as voters) would thus be able to actively involve themselves in the governing process. Such a plan gained wide popularity in Paris: following late-February and early-March meetings between the districts, forty-eight of sixty districts agreed in principle to meeting en permanence, which would have regularly convoked the bodies for debates, petitions, and potentially protests. Unadvisedly, however, Parisians then sought national legislative approval: on March 23, Paris Mayor Jean-Sylvain Bailly presented the plan to the National Assembly, declaring that "permanence is the only means for Parisians to exercise their rights as citizens." Conservatives in the legislature quickly defeated the measure, and punitively broke up the districts of Paris into forty-eight redistricted "sections" (Garrigues 1931, 147–58).

While the National Assembly did not want Parisians taking a formally active role in the governing process, in November 1790 it partially reversed itself in allowing all persons—both "active citizen" voters and "passive" non-voters—an explicit right to assemble and discuss political issues. While illicit sociétés populaires already existed in several neighborhoods, now a concerted network arose under the leadership of the *Club des Cordeliers*, a particularly influential local society on the central Left Bank, which would play a substantial role in the crises of 1791. While many of the earlier clubs remained relatively elite in their composition, the popular societies took on a more socially diverse character, giving voice to many who lacked the membership fees most other clubs required. This multiplying of associational power would soon create advantages for Parisian popular movements: on occasions when more elite organizations became too moderate to back a movement, protesters could turn to the typically more radical popular societies.

Over the first months of 1791, popular radicals became more skilled at deploying concerted waves of protest, though at first the popular societies, clubs, and sections would play only a peripheral role. The first of the year's demonstrations came in four February marches organized by Parisian market-women attempting to prevent the king's elderly aunts from departing France, which many radicals suspected would signal flight of the rest of the royal family. While the question of their leaving also occupied the sections, clubs, and popular societies of the capital in the days preceding the protests, most groups appear to have concluded that there was little that could be done legally to prevent their departure. Basing their argument on tradition and precedent rather than legal right, however, market-women in the Palais-Royal—as they had done a year and a half earlier in the October Days—rallied thousands for two demonstrations at the princesses' château at Bellevue on February 12 and 22, opposing their departure. Two additional marches, featuring between twenty thousand and thirty thousand participants sought out the king's brother, the king, and the National Assembly to intervene, presenting petitions before the last two. All authorities, however, maintained the princesses' legal rights, and allowed their voyage to Rome.

Not resorting to force in order to resolve the developing crisis of royal emigration, radical Parisians instead continued nonviolent direct action to prevent actions they feared would lead to the departure of the king, and to a subsequent counterrevolutionary invasion of the capital. On April 18, carriages gathered to transport the royal family to Saint-Cloud Palace on the outskirts of Paris for Easter, which many thought would be a staging-ground for a flight eastward into German principalities. The clubs appear to have played a central role in mobilizing a massive counter-protest: famed author Cholerlos de Laclos, in a speech at the *Jacobin Club*, explicitly asked national guardsmen not to obey rightist orders issued by their commanders (*Histoire du 18 avril* 1791, 4–5). The Cordeliers simultaneously spread the message through the popular society network, accusing Louis XVI in one widely posted circular of having taken communion from a counterrevolutionary priest, and more generally "thus preparing the French nation for the factionalism which the enemies of the Rights of Man would so like to exercise against us" (Buchez 1835, vol. 9, 408). Parisian crowds filled the *Jardin des Tuileries* to form a human barrier, making common cause with many national guardsmen who disobeyed orders from their commander, the Marquis de Lafayette, to let the royal carriage pass.

Both the king, in an address before the National Assembly, and the conservative Department of Paris the next day, unsuccessfully attempted to bring Paris opinion around to support his departure. In an unprecedented call for a referendum—possibly the first modern use of such voting—the department asked Parisian sections to deliberate and vote on whether "we [should] ask the King to persevere in his first intention of going to St.-Cloud, or should we thank him for staying in Paris, so as not to trouble public tranquility?" (Fontana, Furlan, and Saro 1997, 546–547). With the department having badly underestimated the radicalization of the Paris sections, the latter roundly called for the king to stay in the capital. "The Department," wrote one onlooker, "which believed it could win over the Parisian sections to its opinion, wound up being inextricably submitted to theirs" (Fontana, Furlan, and Saro 1997, 547). Protester opinion on the matter could no longer be dismissed as belonging to a radical minority, but rather widely spread throughout the capital.

Lafayette responded to the referendum's failure and the increasing crisis in governmental authority by resigning his post as head of the National Guard. This provoked an immediate outcry across the capital, among radicals as well as conservatives, and gave rise to the largest string of group protests the Revolution had yet seen. The Parisian sections and local National Guard units quickly amassed the first large Parisian wave of petitions and demonstrations concentrated on a common grievance before a governing body, attempting to ensure that the Municipality of Paris would not accept Lafayette's resignation. Parisian groups presented 112 such calls, including from 25 of the city's 48 sections and virtually all National Guard battalions, unanimously calling for Lafayette to remain. One journalist described April 22 as "a day of great crowds: the corridors, the stairs, the courtyard, the square of the Hôtel de Ville were covered with armed or unarmed citizens" (*Journal des clubs* 1791). On April 23 and 24, marches of Parisian National Guard units repeatedly appeared on the square outside the Hôtel de Ville, asking the Municipal officers to watch them from the balcony as they took an oath to the *patrie*. The demonstrations did not directly confront authorities, however, and instead tried to coax the commander back into power, and dissipated only when it "appeared that Lafayette would retake his functions as Commander-General" (Archives municipales de Marseille, 4 D 43 69). Such protests show an increasing willingness by popular organizations to make repeated displays of direct action before those in positions of power, and thereby play an active role in resolving revolutionary crises.

Though the two months following the April protests remained largely quiet, the attempted—and almost successful—flight of the king to join enemy Austrians on the night of June 20 led activist Parisians to push forward with their most radical demands. A republic, long regarded as impossible due to France's highly stratified social hierarchy, now looked achievable, given the abdication of its high aristocrats from responsibility and power. The king, stopped on June 21 in the eastern French town of Varennes, not far from the German frontier, would be returned to Paris on the 25th, but the future role of the monarch and the course of the Revolution remained hotly contested for several weeks thereafter. The more radical Parisian political bodies sought to leverage their power in favor of a republic, and settled upon physically nonviolent, collaborative tactics as the most likely means of success.

Influencing the National Assembly quickly became the primary objective for the popular society network in the crisis. The Cordeliers on the first day after the king's flight sought to exert influence on the legislature, adopting a petition to the deputies announcing the king had "voluntarily abdicated," and calling for the legislators to declare a French republic (de Cock 2001, 867). Instead of sponsoring a violent insurrection, the Cordeliers asked legislators to calmly "without worry and without terror" vanquish "the phantom of royalty" (de Cock 2001, 168). Through coordinated action, the final anti-Royalist revolution could happen nonviolently.

The Cordeliers and the popular society network mobilized for a major demonstration. On the evening of June 23, radical orator Anaxagoras Chaumette called for the popular societies to "surround the National Assembly with public opinion" (Bossut 1998, 76). Early the following morning, June 24, the Section du Théâtre Français sent invitations across the capital for a 10 a.m. meeting in the Cordeliers proposing "a very interesting discussion on what form of government a free people deserve" (Reinhard 1958, 117).

Wide adhesion to at least a loose republican cause appears to have been agreed upon and, to make their opinion known, that evening a demonstration in four different columns gathered across the capital, totaling upwards of 30,000 participants. At the prompting of the Cordeliers, the protesters converged on the Place Vendôme, just north of the National Assembly. The demonstrators aimed to have a newly adopted petition read to the assembly calling for Louis' removal. In the king's place, the popular societies called for the new order to be determined in joint consultation between the assembly and sections across France, specifically asking the assembly to delay deciding whether or not Louis XVI would be reinstated until the views of the eighty-three departments had been heard. Word spread among assemblymen, however, that the protest was "too republican," and assemblyman Pierre Peloux unflatteringly described in his next letter home how "measures were taken to stop this insurrection" (Archives municipales de Marseille, 4 D 43 97). Legislators rather placed an emphasis upon "ceasing all alarms, and maintaining order and public tranquility" (ibid.). The demonstrators, facing into the cannons of the National Guard, were barred from proceeding the short distance from the square to the assembly's hall. Wary of acknowledging Parisian opinion, and not wanting to publicize their plan, legislators never allowed the "Petition of 30,000 Citizens" to be read before the assembly, and the Cordeliers received only a minimal response from its president four days later. One demonstration alone would not be enough to sway elite political opinion.

The return of Louis XVI to the capital on June 25, the day after the demonstration, offered another opportunity for mass-action. Parisian authorities took extreme measures to ensure that the event passed without tumult: though returning from eastern France, the march of the king—surrounded by tens of thousands of provincials "escorting" his carriage back to Paris—skirted the radical eastern sections of the city to reenter down the western edge of the city along the Champs-Elysées. Throughout town, authorities famously posted placards warning that "Those who applaud will be bayoneted; those who insult the King will be hung" (ibid., 97). Another notice, however, struck a more conciliatory tone, "invit[ing] all citizens to maintain the peace, good order and harmony that have reigned in the capital since the moment that the departure of the King became known" (Municipalité de Paris 1791). Parisians, gathering in crowds of several tens of thousands, used the event to make a great display of passive disobedience, leaving their hats on in insult as the carriage passed, and remaining silent except for scattered cries of "The law, the law!" highlighting Louis's repudiation of the new French constitution as he fled (*Patriote français*, June 26, 1791).

Parisians' use of physically nonviolent protest largely meshed with much of their rhetoric, stressing their already achieved sovereignty, won in the uprisings of 1789, and thus their legitimate say in the national legislative process. The National Assembly, after delaying motions regarding the king for over two weeks, began to move forward with his reinstatement in mid-July. A petition apparently circulated by the Cordeliers and signed by 100 citizens on July 14—the second anniversary of the fall of the Bastille—declared that "the French named their representatives to give them a constitution, and not to establish an abjuring chief on the throne." Petitioners reiterated their cause that the deputies, in the name of "sainte liberté," wait until the views of the French departments (which had not yet been consulted) be heard before any decision regarding the king. Signed first by "Le Peuple" above the individual signatures, the petition declared that, on an issue that concerned the entire nation, the assembly had the duty to consult its opinion. Though read before the assembly, the petition met a cold reception: applause from the visitor's gallery brought recriminations from the assembly's president, and deputies called for and received a reading of the 100 signatures, among whom "the names of several widows and unmarried girls" brought condescending smiles to several legislators' faces (Archives parlementaires 1787, 312). The assembly, unmoved, passed to the day's business.

Both protesters and legislators explicitly saw themselves locked in a battle for control of "public opinion." Deputy Boniface Castelanet on the morning of the 15th, directly before the vote that would reinstate the king, describes the necessity of "fixing soon by decree the still-floating opinion of the public," believing it essential to "adopt that which will be most prudent for achieving the Constitution" (Archives municipales de Marseille, 4 D 43 108). Protesters, meanwhile, declared themselves to be signing a petition "conforming to public opinion," in order to influence the assembly. In an act of direct democracy, an ensuing deputation could then address the body "in the name of all the signatories" (*Journal du soir*, July 16, 1791). The cleavage between representative and direct democracy, never entirely resolved in the Revolution, now led to elites and popular radicals clashing for control of the revolutionary movement. While not swayed to their cause, certain legislators did recognize the changed nature of Parisian protest. The actions of the previous days, Castelanet wrote, had been well-ordered: "While the people have been agitated for several days, they have not been driven to excess," and the movements passed "without the worry that such considerable gatherings naturally inspire" (Archives municipales de Marseille, 4 D 43 108).

Efforts by petitioners to speak in the voice of "the people," not surprisingly, required unprecedented levels of local organizing. One shopgirl in Faubourg Saint-Denis later remembered how designated men went "from store to store, with a petition that needed to be signed, demanding that Louis XVI be judged." Similar "petitions and motions" were said to "circulate in all corners of the capital" (Monnard 1989, 66). While it is uncertain who paid the printing costs, in early July anti-royalist pamphlets were distributed free of charge to people's homes, with others handed out to passersby in the streets and squares. Radicals looked both to pull Parisians into the public sphere of print, and to rapidly mobilize their support in protesting.

Restrictions on citizens' right to petition the National Assembly, which passed in May, paradoxically appear to have helped mass-mobilization. The assembly's decree against collective petitioning allowed only for individually signed petitions, disallowing orators from speaking in the name of their full constituencies. A petition claiming to represent wide public opinion, thus, would be most effective if it possessed tens of thousands of signatures. Particularly if ceremonially done, this offered a new means of protest unknown in earlier phases of the Revolution, and a tangible proof of widespread opposition to the assembly's measures.

Parisian protesters pressed forward despite the assembly's resistance. The body's disregarding of the July 14 petition, paired with the passage of decrees on July 15 promising to reinstate the king if he accepted the Constitution, sparked massive gatherings in the neighborhoods around the Palais des Tuileries and Palais-Royal. Three thousand to four thousand demonstrators led by six Cordeliers officials marched from the Champ de Mars to the assembly the afternoon of the decree, though were not allowed to read their petition before the assembly. Plans for another, larger march and petition-signing at the Champs de Mars on July 17 coalesced. That night, a Cordeliers demonstration marched from its Left Bank headquarters to a session of the *Société des Amis de la Vérité* (Society of the Friends of Truth) at the Palais-Royal in which the two groups, together numbering several thousand, adopted a measure calling for Louis XVI to not be recognized as king. Agitators interrupted nearby theatre performances, and with many spectacle-goers swelling the ranks, three to four thousand people made a 10 p.m. march from the Palais-Royal to the Jacobin Club. Following an address in which the Cordelier orator declared both clubs' hostility towards the king, the Jacobins disbanded, as a petition by law could not be presented by a "collective body" such as a club before the National Assembly or any other governmental organization.

In spite of the fast pace of events, Parisians took a day before the mass-protest to consolidate and expand their movement. July 16 saw a second daytime assembly at the Champ-de-Mars to popularly ratify the next day's petition, and another evening march by the Cordeliers through the Palais-Royal, publicizing the next day's protest. More groups became involved: the sections of Paris also joined the petitioning, presenting their own decree to the assembly calling for the dethroning of the king. Plans were distributed calling for each group involved to gather under their own banners at the Place de la Bastille the next morning, from which point a coordinated march would be made without arms across town to the Champ de Mars.

The leadership of the republican movement, both in theory and action, appeared to desire a peaceful and ultimately conciliatory protest campaign. With the National Assembly's decree carrying the proviso that the king was "suspended from his functions until the completion of the Constitution," which would occur in early autumn, some Parisians believed his ultimate removal could still be achieved (*Grand récit* 1791, 1). The petition of July 17 declared "A King who quit his post to set himself at the head of a foreign army against the Nation has abdicated the throne," and, despite Parisian radicals' perturbation with the assembly, persisted with a plan that would have given them exclusive nationwide power. The protest appears to have failed more out of authorities' political differences with the protesters than through mistaking their aims. At least some in the assembly appeared to recognize the altered nature of Parisian protest: one assemblyman wrote of how the republicans planned a protest that would be "peaceful, without arms" (Déposition 1791, 9).

As protesters planned for the mass petition-signing, the forces of reaction planned as well. On July 16, conservatives in the assembly pushed through a decree requiring the Municipality of Paris "to inform immediately against all law-breakers," while also "giving orders with care to maintain public tranquility" (*Archives parlementaires* 1787, 365). The faction also requested a circular to be sent to the provinces, to counteract the rise in republican propaganda. Some individuals went even further: Assemblyman Guillaume-Barthélémy Boery, writing to his constituents the same day, described the Jacobins and their allies as in "open rebellion" against the assembly, while cryptically describing the national authority as "surrounded by the unshakable patriotism of the Parisian National Guard." Declaring the protesters "misled by foreigners and the factious," and framing them as attacking the "decreed and established government," the move towards suppression could be a quick one (Archives départementales [July 16, 1791], 49).

On July 17, the protest did not go as planned. Though protest leaders sought to win municipal neutrality by informing city officials of the times and places for the demonstration and petition-signing, from early on, protesters met strong resistance. Parisian national guardsmen blocked the Place de la Bastille to prevent the formation of the planned march. Most protesters, undeterred but lacking a planned alternate gathering place for the demonstration, haphazardly made their way across town to the parade field. Organizers persisted with calls for the petition-signing event to be conducted "peacefully and without arms" (Lacroix 1908, 663). With the discovery of two unknown men hiding under the table where the petition was being signed, however, certain protesters appear to have given in to rumors that these unknowns were government spies and, fearing their movement infiltrated, proceeded to hang them. This act of physical violence invited the intervention of a suspicious municipality as soon as word of the event reached the Hôtel de Ville: Bailly immediately issued an order to send guardsmen to the field, authorizing "them to take the most rigorous measures, if they are necessary" (Archives nationales de France, CC 24). With Lafayette in the lead, national guardsmen met scattered rock-throwing as they arrived at the field, at which point they quickly opened fire, killing scores of protesters (Andress 2000).

With authorities now able to ascribe violence to the movement, repression was thorough. Parisian authorities immediately declared martial law. The motives among certain repressors may have been cynical and opportunistic. "Calm and tranquility are perfectly reestablished," wrote the assembly's deputation from Marseille on July 19, and with the question of the king settled "we think that there's no probable obstacle to the coming conclusion of our glorious Constitution" (Archives municipales de Marseille, 4 D 43 115). Repression of the republican movement made further discussion of the king's flight taboo, repressing the political memory, and allowing national politics to continue on the trajectory national elites had been attempting to establish. The king could now be reinstated, and further radicalization of the Revolution, for the time, averted.

Notwithstanding its bloody ending, the republican movement's prior restraint from physical violence remains its most striking quality. At least until the discovery of "spies" under the petition-signing table at the Champ de Mars on July 17, the campaign became the first Parisian movement of the French Revolution to be conducted exclusively through physically nonviolent tactics. Of twenty noted street protests in Paris between the king's flight and the massacre, only a hat-makers apprentices' strike that was not directly related to the crisis during the first week of July involved physical violence, and even then violence only arose when the National Guard used force in an attempt to disperse them. Instead, likely realizing the usual negative response of revolutionary political elites to the use of physical violence, Parisian protesters adopted more peaceful methods to bring them closer to national power figures. The mass meetings, petitions, and demonstrations together dominated Parisians' physically nonviolent four-week protest campaign, and typified most protest tactics employed across the Parisian French Revolution, in general.

Despite the massacre, predominantly nonviolent protest tactics would return during the second republican movement of 1792. Before the demonstration-turned-insurrection of August 10 of that year, when the king's soldiers fired upon Parisian marchers after signs of a truce had been given, thus igniting an open battle, over 80 percent of street protests did not involve physical violence. The sections, with their local power apparatus behind them, superseded the popular societies to lead the movement, and actively worked with the National Assembly to establish the First Republic. Developing an increasing dialogue with authorities, featuring regular petitions before the National Assembly after April 1792, Parisian contention (if unevenly) developed increasingly effective conflict mediation processes. Under the collaborative order of the early First Republic (September 21, 1792 to September 20, 1793), seventy-seven of eighty-one Parisian protests did not employ physical violence. Popular violence never did predominantly "win out" over more peaceful solutions for revolutionary Parisians, and only waves of state repression in 1795 ended the protesters' significant influence over national politics.

The prevalence of seemingly "nonviolent protest" in the unexpected setting of revolutionary Paris may be of value to the study of nonviolent protest elsewhere, particularly in pre-twentieth century contexts. Aside from a limited number of recent exceptions, such as work done by Jonathan Schell (2003) and Antony Adolf (2009), peace studies histories have largely focused on Gandhian and post-Gandhian traditions, in some respects underestimating trends already developing previously. Nonviolence can be more than just a doctrinal position; it can also inform conscious attempts to adopt alternatives to violence, especially in situations—such as in revolutionary Paris—where violence can easily occur.

Many of the limitations and possibilities of the French Revolution's nonviolent tactics remain with protest movements today. In the twentieth century, still, campaigns relating to Indian nationalism, American civil rights, and South African anti-apartheid efforts have struggled in dialectic with both violent opponents and supporters. Nonviolent practice in most campaigns is not adopted in absolute terms, but rather pragmatically defined in response to real-world situations. Nelson Mandela, for example, spoke of nonviolence as "a tactic to be used as the situation demanded," believing his adherents still needed to "defend themselves when attacked" (Mandela 1994, 277). Both Mohandas Gandhi and Martin Luther King Jr. also retained uneasy partial alliances with more violent arms of their movements. The potential for violence places added impetus upon dialogue and peaceful negotiation.

Notwithstanding certain limitations of nonviolence during the revolutionary period, the possibilities opened by the democratic movements of the eighteenth century may be more profound. The age represents an important point of expansion in the history of nonviolent protest, contributing both the intellectual justification for such movements—popular sovereignty—and many of the tactics through which to conduct them. Political demonstrations, which are perhaps the most common collective protest tactic employed today, developed due to French revolutionaries' privileging of "The People" as the embodiment of their movement, and Revolutionary protesters' use of demonstrations to express opinions diverging from those of legislators. Though their nonviolence was relative and not adopted on absolute terms, their tactics offered strategies that others would push further. The French Revolution—a consciously universal movement that many of its proponents believed would lead to the freeing of all humankind—helped establish a template for democratic change that, over the last two-plus centuries, popular movements around the world have often followed.

3

"I Was and Am"

Historical Counternarrative
as Nonviolent Resistance in the United States

Jenice L. View

Between 1846 and 1946, the US government participated in over 130 wars and violent struggles, most directed toward North American populations and populations that became part of the ascending American empire (see Collier 1993). At the midpoint of this century came the US Supreme Court decision upholding racial segregation in the form of "separate but equal" public accommodations, which had the effect of codifying superior treatment for whites (*Plessy v. Ferguson*, 163 U.S. 537 (1896)). Concurrently, public education became available to nearly all children, and with it, the challenge to define a common curriculum across segregated school systems. The 1994 US Department of Education report entitled *Education Reforms and Students at Risk: A Review of the Current State of the Art,* details the history of separate and unequal schooling for children of color as encoded in law, justified by pseudo-science, and reinforced by social mores. The curriculum offered to the children in segregated, under-funded schools was decidedly Eurocentric, celebrating the victories of elite Europeans in the Americas. Social experiments in education—such as the early years of Hampton Institute and Indian boarding schools—were designed to "kill the [Indian, African, Mexican, Asian], save the child," or otherwise create a reverence for European culture, manual labor, and second-class citizenship (Buffalohead and Molin 1996; Anderson 1988). The structural and cultural violence (Galtung 1969; Galtung 1990) promoted through schooling during the period of legal racial segregation would now be considered bad pedagogy, if not an outright violation of human rights (Ho 2007).

It could be argued that in response to governmental and mob violence, and to schooling designed to "kill" their cultural identities, people of color of the period maintained a posture of nonviolent resistance, strategizing that formal education—theirs and that of others—would liberate them from racialized oppression. They hoped the story-telling—or counternarratives—of their heroes and sheroes, and the revisionist histories of their labors and sacrifices to build the American empire, would compel respect from rational members of the academic elite and lead to more equitable political and economic policies.

In particular, heritage curricula have been promoted for nearly 100 years as counternarratives to the hegemonic academic texts that ignored the histories of people of color. In light of the electoral victory of Barack Hussein Obama as the first African American president of the United States of America, the value and purpose of such commemorations as African American/Black History Month and other heritage months (Native American History Month, Latino/a History Month, Asian Pacific Islander History Month, etc.) might, at worst, be challenged as irrelevant. At best, the triumph of progressive cross-racial grassroots political organizing will be trivialized by the instinct to add Obama's face to a poster financed and distributed by a multinational corporation, serving the dual purpose of "celebrating" African American history and appearing patriotic.

Yet, the true spirit of these counternarratives suggests that if there is such thing as a canon, and if it is to have any instructional or cultural value, its value is derived from the extent of its inclusivity—a monocultural history of the United States having been discredited by the vast historical scholarship generated by multiculturalists, interculturalists, feminists, social historians, and the like. The ideologies that supported incomplete and inaccurate histories of people of color—and therefore spawned the corresponding history months—did not magically vanish on November 4, 2008. Recent legislation in the state of Arizona to ban "ethnic studies" courses for "promoting resentment toward [white people]" is a case in point (Amster 2010b; Cooper 2010). Nor have textbooks or public schools in the United States achieved a state of critical consciousness whereby the histories of people of color are infused throughout the curriculum with any degree of equity (Apple 2000; Zinn 2003). A regulation considered in the state of Texas, designed to dramatically alter the state's social studies and history curriculum standards and to serve as a "counterbalance to liberal-leaning academics" (Fox News 2010), was driven by a conservative political agenda that some argue is a "slippery slope . . . toward a racist purge across the United States and Canada" (Lee 2010). As the primary driver for commercial textbook manufacturing and distribution in the United States, the impact of the Texas decision is likely to be massive and to extend for more than a decade. Fierce cultural debate continues in the United States, and K–12 classroom teachers are caught in the exchange, especially as they are penalized for any instruction that ignores or subverts standardized tests (PBS.org 2007; Berry, Hoke, and Hirsch 2004). This chapter critically examines the history of heritage curricula and activities, arguing for their continued strategic use to overcome racialization and internalized oppression, as well as to promote nonviolence and human rights in classrooms.

The Origin and History of Heritage Activities

Heritage months and activities were prompted by the varied histories of the people in North America. The theft of indigenous lands and genocide in the Americas began with the arrival of Christopher Columbus from Spain in 1492 and continued through the end of the nineteenth century with the Massacre at Wounded Knee, considered the last of the major battles between the US government and indigenous peoples in North America (Brown 2001). Among immigrants to the United States, only Mexicans and Mexican Americans can assert a historical claim to US territory, as almost all of Texas, New Mexico, Arizona, California, Nevada, and Utah was part of Mexico until the United States occupied the capital and then annexed half of Mexico during the Texan War of Independence in 1835–36 and the Mexican-American War of 1846–48 (Huntington 2004; Martinez 1976). African Americans were also unwilling immigrants to the Americas due to the transatlantic slave trade beginning in the fifteenth century in South America, and with the first Africans arriving in the British colonies in 1619 at Jamestown. The nineteenth century witnessed the immigration of Chinese, Japanese, Korean, and Filipino immigrants to Hawaii and the mainland as oppressed laborers for US corporations (Chan 1991). Just as the American empire was expanding and the labor market was flooded with newly manumitted Africans following the end of the Civil War, public education became available to nearly all children, and with it, the challenge to define a common curriculum.

At the same time, the Reconstruction era following the Civil War invested African Americans with a sense of possibility (Franklin 1995; Du Bois 1995). Three amendments to the US Constitution were ratified to end slavery, protect the citizenship rights of formerly enslaved Africans, and award voting rights to African American men. Sixteen African Americans were elected to federal government positions, and several were elected to state government positions throughout the South. The federal government formed the Bureau of Refugees, Freedmen, and Abandoned Lands (known commonly as the "Freedmen's Bureau") to provide food, medical care, education, and resettlement to a largely landless population of formerly enslaved Africans. The hope of reparations for the evils of slavery and equal rights was crushed by the Supreme Court's *Plessy v. Ferguson* decision in 1896, which legalized "separate but equal" public accommodations, or American-style racial apartheid for all people of color. The fifty-year period between *Plessy* and the Supreme Court decision ending school segregation in *Brown v. Board of Education* (347 U.S. 483 (1954)) is of course known as the Jim Crow era.

In addition to the formal curriculum of these segregated schools, all people of color during the Jim Crow era faced a not-so-hidden curriculum in public imagery and popular media that denigrated their people and communities as lazy, dirty, ugly, ignorant, and inferior to all people of European descent (including the despised European immigrants of the early twentieth century). Formal, government-run schooling was deliberately designed "to achieve the dominant group's need for [people of color] to accept their place and not offer too much resistance" (Gresson 2008, 65). Educational policies mirrored the political and economic attitudes of creating a "colonized" or "re-enslaved" labor force (Takaki

1993, 265; Blackmon 2008). Galtung's theories of structural and cultural violence accurately describe the intentions of formal public schooling in which "resources [were] unevenly distributed . . . [;] the power to decide over the distribution of resources [was] unevenly distributed" (Galtung 1969, 171); and the "symbolic sphere of our existence—exemplified by religion and ideology, language and art, empirical science and formal science—[was] used to justify or legitimize direct or structural violence" (Galtung 1990, 291).

Nevertheless, African Americans and other groups historically oppressed by the federal government—indigenous/native peoples; other people from lands taken by force such as Mexico, Hawaii, the Philippines and other Pacific and Caribbean Islands; and industrial, agricultural, and manual workers from other countries encouraged to come to the United States to work under conditions mirroring enslavement—also sought to correct distortions of their own histories that portrayed them as passive or helpless participants in their own oppression, and to initiate educational changes on their own behalf (Gresson 2008, 56). This section describes some of the history of broad groups, with the caveat that space prohibits the nuances of differing histories within groups—for example the "Latino" experience of Mexicans versus Puerto Ricans, or the "Asian" experience of Chinese versus Filipinos.

American Indians. By the early twentieth century, American Indian communities were nearly entirely controlled by the federal government (Page 2004, 336). Tribes were relieved by the federal abandonment of the fifty-year old boarding school model, which removed children from their families, forbade their home languages, clothing, hair, or cultural practices, and forced them to labor to maintain the school facilities, leading to sickness and very high death rates (Wilson 1998, 310–22). Similarly, they were pleased to no longer participate in the Hampton experiment at the historically Black college whose "white founder believed that blacks would be the ideal instruments of 'civilization' for Indians, whose memories of wars with whites were still fresh" (Klopotek 2009, 87). Yet, the Progressive and New Deal federal government policies were no less assimilationist in failing to distinguish between African Americans and American Indians in states that enforced Jim Crow laws (Purdue 2009, 21), and in denying

American Indians a say in the education of their children. With rare exception (Reyner and Eder 2004, 210–230; Page 2004, 356), the culture, language, and customs of Native communities were considered inferior tools for teaching American Indian children, even by some of their parents who sought the same level of academic quality for their children as white children received, preferring to teach culture and language outside of formal (white-controlled) schooling institutions.

The guiding force for American Indian communities in the Jim Crow era was resistance, cultural reclamation and preservation, and eventually sovereignty (Grande 2004, 11–29). Using a two-pronged strategy, communities focused on educating others and educating their own. In 1915, individual Indigenous scholars and organizations had persuaded the Boy Scouts of America and twenty-four state governments to designate a day of observation recognizing the contributions of the "First Americans" to the establishment and growth of the United States (Parker, n.d.). This was nine years before the US Congress finally recognized the formal legal "citizenship" of indigenous peoples on lands taken from them by force. Eighty-five years later, the federal government declared November as American Indian Heritage Month. Currently, the Washington State Legislature is pilot testing a statewide, age-appropriate sovereignty curriculum that challenges misconceptions that the US government "gave" Indians both rights and land that belonged to the United States, and that reinforces the message that tribal governments functioned as sovereign governments long before treaties were signed, with the power and authority to govern their own people and land (Edmo 2008). In many ways, American Indian Heritage Month is for "other people," while efforts such as the sovereignty curriculum are inwardly-directed.

Mexican Americans. In describing the history of formal education of Mexican Americans, Sleeter (1999, xvii) states that "schools [were] an instrument of the maintenance of colonial relationships in that they [constituted] an arm of the state through which belief systems and cultural relationships [were] taught. Public school curricula [proclaimed] the 'triumph of democracy' to the virtual exclusion of any serious analysis of the US conquest." Indeed, the segregated schools to which Mexican American parents sent their children primarily served the interests of agricultural growers and industrial plant owners to maintain a low-wage workforce (Takaki 1993, 327–8). The lived experience of discrimination and violence (Shorris 1992; San Miguel 1997, 138) caused Mexican Americans to organize for improved living conditions and equal schooling in different parts of the Southwest. Yet, unlike policies applied to African Americans, those relating to Mexican Americans varied depending on the community's political power in a given state, since the federal government did not recognize Mexican Americans as an "identifiable ethnic minority" with racialized patterns of discrimination until the early 1970s.

Throughout the Jim Crow era, Mexican Americans debated the best strategy for gaining political and economic equality, never quite knowing where they stood in the social pecking order (Shorris 1992, 152–3), but certain that all means except violence—such as school boycotts, special fundraisers, protests against textbook depictions of Mexicans and Mexican Americans, and lawsuits—were essential strategies for ensuring a quality education for their children (San Miguel 1997, 137–47). In some communities, privately run schools or afterschool programs to preserve Spanish language usage and Mexican culture offered a defense against the state-government segregated and integrated public schools. In attempts to "Americanize" Mexican American children, Anglo teachers sometimes used Mexican cultural referents to "help children feel more secure," while controlling the goals and outcomes of education (Gonzales 1997, 166). However, most Mexican Americans preferred a selective process of assimilation (San Miguel 1997, 140–1).

Not until the 1960s did a new generation of Mexican Americans broadly assert a Chicano/a identity aligned with an independent, pre-1848 consciousness. In 1968, the US Congress designated "National Hispanic Week" in mid-September, to coincide with the Independence Day celebrations in Costa Rica, El Salvador, Guatemala, Honduras, and Nicaragua on September 15, and with Mexico's Independence Day on September 16 (Killman 2006). Yet in 1976, Chicana scholar Elizabeth Martinez and the Southwest Organizing Project were compelled to publish *450 Years of Chicano History* as a counternarrative to the national bicentennial celebration of the American Revolution that ignored the genocide of indigenous peoples, glorified westward expansion, and contributed to the "invisibilization" of the racism faced by people of Mexican descent. Struggles in recent decades have included those concerning bilingual education to promote the achievement of students whose home language is Spanish, and relating to lingering legacies of the Mexican-American War over 150 years after the fact, including issues arising from contemporary movement of Mexicans across a contested border.

Asian Americans. During the Jim Crow era, the largest groups of Asian Americans were Chinese, Japanese, Filipino, and Korean Americans in Hawaii and on the mainland. By the 1920s, Chinese and Japanese communities were entering their second generation on the mainland, with the strong desire that younger people escape the back-breaking labors of their parents. For both generations, formal education and English language fluency were the pathways to improved living conditions. However, the elders held firm convictions that it was necessary also to maintain language and cultural connections to the "old country" through evening and Saturday schools (Takaki 1993, 1998). Chinese parents tried to inoculate their children to the racism of the period by reinforcing the idea of a very long history of a culture "superior" to America's; Japanese parents hoped their children would serve as intermediaries between eastern and western cultures (Takaki 1998, 213, 255–6). Rather than push local governments to accommodate the cultural and language needs of their children, Asian American parents subverted the racism by creating their own schools, while also availing themselves of the free public education denied to earlier generations.

For nearly thirty years following World War II and the internment of over 100,000 Japanese Americans, all Asian American groups generally avoided making the kinds of demands on educational institutions that were rising from American Indians, Mexican Americans, and African Americans. But in the 1970s, Jeanie Jew, president of the Organization of Chinese American Women, launched a national advocacy campaign to correct bicentennial celebrations that failed to acknowledge the role of Asian Americans in US history, such as the labor of Chinese workers to build the transcontinental railroad. The month of May was chosen to commemorate the immigration of the first Japanese to the United States on May 7, 1843, and to mark the anniversary of the completion of the transcontinental railroad on May 10, 1869. Thus, Asian Pacific Island Heritage Month was born.

African Americans. The most widely known and broadest public heritage activities grow out of African American educational experiences and scholarship. Born into the Reconstruction period were W. E. B. Du Bois and Carter G. Woodson, two of the nation's most prolific African American scholarly historians. Both received doctorates from Harvard University and both sought to establish a body of work that challenged the dominant beliefs about the intellectual and cultural inferiority of African Americans. In the 1890s, Du Bois fiercely and famously began his career by debating the philosophy of Booker T. Washington, who used the resources of northern "white" elites to create educational institutions for African Americans focused solely on manual, domestic, agricultural, and basic reading and math skills for teaching in primary schools.

Woodson established the Association for the Study of Negro Life and History (now called the Association for the Study of Afro-American Life and History) in 1915, and a year later founded the scholarly Journal of Negro History to capture the emerging body of research on Africans and African Americans throughout the diaspora. In 1926, he launched Negro History Week as an initiative to bring national attention to this historical research. He chose the month of February to commemorate the birthdays of President Abraham Lincoln and abolitionist Frederick Douglass. When Dr. Carter G. Woodson created Negro History Week in 1926, he did not intend to expand the statuary in the public square by adding African American heroes and sheroes; he intended to revolutionize education by producing more scholars, activists, artists, and businesspeople with a deep and research-based understanding of their role in global history (NAACP.org 2008). In addition, he intended to shake the foundations of academic historical scholarship by challenging its overtly expressed ideology of "white" social and cultural supremacy (Huntley 2007; Crowder 1977). In this sense, Negro History Week was a call to action, answered by eager community organizations, churches, segregated schools, and libraries (ASALH, n.d.):

When the Association [for the Study of Negro Life and History] announced Negro History Week for 1926, Woodson was overwhelmed by the response. Black history clubs sprang up, teachers demanded materials to instruct their pupils, and progressive whites, not simply white scholars and philanthropists, stepped forward to endorse the effort. Woodson and the Association scrambled to meet the demands of public history. For teachers, the Association published photographs and portraits of important black people. It published plays to dramatize black history. To serve the desire of history buffs to participate in the re-education of black folks, ASNLH formed branches to bring them into the organization.

Unlike American Indians who sought sovereign control over school-ing, or Mexican Americans and Asian Americans who wanted equal school facilities and fair treatment, but looked outside of schools for cul-tural affirmation, most African Americans in the Jim Crow era wanted the public schools to afford their children academic, social, political, and cultural equity with "white" schools. One vehicle for this equity was rec-ognition of African American excellence through the school curriculum. In the 1950s and 1960s, following the international anti-colonial and anti-apartheid movements and the Southern freedom movement led by African Americans, there were growing efforts to reclaim and define the culture, history, and education of all people of color in the United States through school curriculum and public heritage activities.

The Problem with Heritage Months

One problem with heritage months relates to "ownership" of the stories that are told. Apart from the obvious fact that "those who have power over educational institutions are those who can decide how culture [and history] is taught and which cultures [and histories] should be val-ued" (Ryoo and McLaren 2010, 105), there is the "ownership" of stories within a given group. The example of post-apartheid South Africa offers important insights to American heritage months. The United States may believe itself to be different from South Africa for having defined itself as a democracy during the Jim Crow era, and countless examples of people of color throughout history serving in the US military and striving for social and political inclusion suggest a "commitment to work together for a common destiny" (Zegeye and Harris 2002, 260) despite Jim Crow's structural and direct violence. Yet the similarities between post-apartheid South Africa and the post-Jim Crow United States persist. Much like South Africa's four racial categories, twelve "native" ethnic classifications plus myriad immigrants, eleven official languages, and its four major religions (Zegeye and Harris 2002, 241), the United States has always been a multicultural, multilingual, multi-religious nation, prior to the arrival of the Spanish, the British, the French, and enslaved Africans of various cultures and nations. In much the same way that black and colored identities in South Africa have changed in recent times following the end of apartheid (Zegeye and Harris 2002, 243), each of the groups in the United States struggles with identity, representation, and political and economic power within and outside of the official media and curricula. "Diasporic and hybrid identities, borders and margins . . . challenge homogenized and monolithic notions . . . that obliterate class, gender, region and sexual orientation differences between people" (Zegeye 2002, 343) ostensibly of the same "race," and therefore, the question remains: which Black/Latino/Asian Pacific Islander/American Indian story should be told?

Another problem with heritage months stems from the general problem with history instruction in kindergarten through twelfth-grade (K–12) classrooms: most history teachers have insufficient content knowledge and very little instruction in history teaching methods (Ravitch 2000; Liu et al. 2006). Young, "white," middle-class teachers (Branch 2001; National Center of Education Statistics 2009) that are poorly trained to teach traditional American history may be particularly challenged to teach critical multicultural history using a human rights lens (View 2010, 156–7) and may instead hurt students of color, low-income children, and children whose first language is not English (Weintraub 2000, 181).

Specific to heritage months is their institutionalization. Initially perceived as a symbolic victory in the latter part of the twentieth century, it could be argued that the recognition of heritage months by the federal government is akin to asking permission, since the president is required by congressional resolution to make an annual proclamation declaring the start of Black/Women's/Asian Pacific Islander/Latino/American Indian Month. The current symbolism suggests that the history of people of color is recognized at the discretion and through the charity of the federal government. There are, however, more important problems with the current practice of heritage months.

At the time of the eightieth anniversary of Negro History Week, several African American writers and thinkers offered analyses of the evolution of Woodson's vision. *New York Times* writer Gerald Early (2006) presented the four most common critiques: that Black History Month is not taken seriously by the nation, given its assignment to the shortest month of the year; that African American history ought to be discussed throughout the year, not just during one month; the month reduces African Americans to a sub-history contingent on the larger narrative of European history; and that Black History Month is divisive, part of the fragmentation and multiculturalization of American history, where every group must have its own version of history and cannot share a common one.

Early discharges the "nation's" selection of February as the shortest and therefore least significant month by pointing out Woodson's deliberate choice of a month that recognizes the birthdays of president Abraham Lincoln and abolitionist Frederick Douglass, two towering figures in the history of Africans in America. However, the other critiques might easily be offered regarding all of the heritage months. Certainly, the corporatization of heritage months has been soundly decried by historians and social critics as companies use heritage months to market products and services to people of color (see Franklin et al. 1997; Martinez 1997). These same corporations would not likely finance a critical analysis of the impacts of contemporary corporate labor and environmental practices, yet that is exactly what Carter G. Woodson would have expected as an outcome of studying history (Goggin 1993, 141).

The populations that may have the most to gain from heritage months sometimes lose sight of the original intentions and create irrelevant, if not bizarre expressions of celebration, such as parties and beauty contests (Keels 2006). In addition, people of color who are celebrities may use heritage months as an opportunity to profit as token representatives of their people at "white"-dominated organizational celebrations (Keels 2006). The focus on positive, uplifting stories about people of color negates the complex history of racialized violence in the United States and sanitizes the complex humanity of individuals within that context, creating both bad history and bad psychology (Kaplan 2006).

K–12 classroom teachers, left to their own devices, may also confuse the original intentions of heritage months: If intended to celebrate the accomplishments and possibility of oppressed people, classroom activities fail to offer the depth and complexities of individual contributions, particularly in the early grades. If intended to expand the pantheon of heroes and sheroes, heritage month lessons tend to contribute to celebrity culture by focusing on a handful of comfortable and safe personas, rather than combative or controversial figures in US history. If intended to celebrate the triumph over adversity and oppression, classroom activities minimize the contributions of the organizations and social movements from which the individuals emerged and which are responsible for effecting and sustaining social change. As a result, young people fail to gain much sense of self or learn much about their own heritage—or that of other groups—based solely on the information passed down during school-based heritage month activities; the continued ghettoizing of heritage ensures that they are not getting much information the rest of the year, either (Hamilton 2006; Early 2006). Furthermore, the solutions to contemporary institutionalized violence against children and youth of color in the form of "pedagogies of surveillance" (Giroux 2007, 5)—such as police brutality, disproportionate rates of arrests and prison convictions, disproportionate rates of school push out and expulsion, and military recruitment—are seldom found in heritage month activities beyond the charge to individual children to ask "what would Dr. King or Cesar Chavez do?"

An unpublished informal survey of schools in the Washington, DC metropolitan area probed classroom practice and outcomes (View 2007). Teachers and students were asked to reflect on the most recent Black History Month instruction at their schools. When second grade students in a multiracial class in northern Virginia were asked what Black History Month is, typical statements included: "to celebrate black people that were shot and killed a long time ago;" "to celebrate the famous leader that changed the law;" "when black people have done something good and die and we remember them;" and "when people care about black people." Students seemed to have no knowledge of other heritage months, listing instead "Veteran's Day," "Memorial Day," and "Presidents' Day." When asked who or what they learned about this year for Black History Month, most students replied they did not know, or listed Dr. Martin Luther King Jr. or Rosa Parks. Two notable responses were "to let freedom to all the people," and "to trust black people and to let them on the bus." Finally, when asked who or what they learned this year during Black History Month that they had never learned before, most students stated, "I don't know." Three notable responses were: "I learned how to be nice and work forever;" "I learned that to be nice and respectful with them and be friends," and "I didn't learn anything new."

In a similar informal teachers' survey (View 2007), one Washington, DC teacher responded that Black History Month "is a month in which famous African Americans of the past are honored. February is a month to reflect on the past injustices and reflect on how a nation overcame them." This teacher celebrates Hispanic Heritage Month and makes a point of introducing her students to Women's History Month because "it is important for my students to understand that women were considered property in the past. Women have struggled as many other ethnic groups to fight for equal rights." This teacher taught about Frederick Douglass for the first time in 2007, partly to prepare her second grade students for a field trip to his Cedar Hill home in Washington, DC. Her "biography pie project" was a cross-curricular project to teach students art, math, and language arts skills. To the extent that her students had access to early elementary trade books about lesser known African American organizers (such as Fannie Lou Hamer, Ella Baker, and Bayard Rustin), scholars (such as John Hope Franklin and Shirley Graham Du Bois), scientists (such as Louis Latimer and Marjorie Stewart Joyner), and cultural innovators (such as Katherine Dunham and Anna Deavere Smith), their biography pies may have expanded student knowledge of African American heroes and she-roes. However, the resources for expanding this vocabulary remain limited and students tended to produce pies with African American entertainers and sports celebrities.

What Heritage Months Could Be

Dr. Audrey T. McCluskey, associate professor of African and African American diaspora studies and director of the Black Film Center/Archive at Indiana University referred to Black History Month as "a cheap version of reparations that makes no demands" and that "has become a substitute for real action" (Keels 2006). The same might be said for other heritage months.

Meanwhile, the educational experiences of children and youth of color in the early twenty-first century manifest structural (Galtung 1969; Garcia-Reid 2008), cultural (Galtung 1990, 293), symbolic (Herr and Anderson 2003) and epistemic (Ryoo and McLaren 2010, 106) violences, some of which are the continuing legacies of twentieth-century Jim Crow schooling, and some of which are promoted as market-based, neo-liberal fixes for schools that are "failing" to produce young adult consumers and producers who are globally competitive (Fitzsimons 2002; Giroux 2007). To what extent can heritage months resist these "violences"?

The "real action" implied by McCluskey's statement is a threat to the more conservative forces governing schools and school systems, in much the same way that Woodson's Negro Week was an audacious gauntlet thrown at the Jim Crow curriculum of the early twentieth century. For example, teaching all of the heritage/history months would occupy six of the typical nine- or ten-month school curriculum (February, March, May, September, October, and November) and would effectively infuse the entire curriculum with the multicultural history of the United States. Taught accurately, it would also have the effect of presenting a steady stream of stories of the institutional, structural, and mob violence used to create the United States's multicultural history.

A less comprehensive approach can still pose a challenge to government-run schools: Karen Salazar, a former high school teacher in Los Angeles, California, was fired for teaching from a district-approved text in a manner that was characterized as "brainwashing students" by the African American principal and Latino deputy superintendent (Hill 2004). Similarly, the state of Arizona passed legislation in May 2010, the purpose of which is to teach public school pupils "to treat and value each other as individuals and not be taught to resent or hate other races or classes of people [or] promote ethnic solidarity" through ethnic studies courses (Ariz. Rev. Stat. § 15–112). This is a continuation of earlier legislation to cut funding to any public school whose courses "denigrate American values and the teachings of Western civilization" (*Democracy Now!* 2008). The radicalizing of heritage months is an act of reclamation and self-determination, recognized by groups such as Black New Yorkers for Educational Excellence as a way to teach "truth and critical thinking" to students of color (Black History Now!, n.d.). While the language of Arizona's H.B. 2281 protects "courses or classes that include the history of any ethnic group and that are open to all students; courses or classes that include the discussion of controversial aspects of history; . . . and instruction of historical oppression of a particular group of people based on ethnicity, race, or class," the decision about whether a teacher is "promoting resentment" rests with the state board of education and not with the communities whose histories are being taught. The challenge, then, in Arizona and elsewhere, is to knit together the theory, research, and practice of heritage months in useful ways for public school classroom teachers.

Making theory accessible. Critical race theory (Ladson-Billings and Tate 1994; Delgado and Stefancic 2001) is one framework that can be part of this bridge: working in partnership, academic and popular historical researchers can produce the counternarratives that would offer classroom teachers a richer palette for designing heritage month activities (Brayboy 2008). Similar to the Washington State sovereignty curriculum, the Mississippi State Legislature passed a bill in 2007 to encourage civil and human rights education in all public schools throughout the state (S.B. 2718). Ideally, the counternarratives that emerge from these efforts would be part of the required curriculum for all students in the states and would offer fresh ways for classroom teachers to examine history. Similarly, the theories of multicultural education (Banks 1995), critical pedagogy (Freire 1970), transcommunality (Childs 2003), and transnational theories (Franklin et al. 2007), encourage teachers to look for and learn from the struggles against oppression by people throughout the world. But, it is the task of social justice oriented academics to make these theories more accessible to classroom teachers, particularly those lacking the resources, imagination, or courage to reach beyond the assigned curriculum and texts.

The need for more classroom-based research. Wineburg and Monte-Sano (2008) suggest that the historical consciousness of all students in the United States has been expanded by the practice of Black History Month: in a survey of 2,000 high school students in public schools in fifty states, students listed four African Americans on their list of top ten "famous Americans." However, more research is needed to document the impact of the teaching and learning of history—particularly the counter narratives offered during heritage/history months—of all people of color, and one would argue that naming famous people is not equivalent to having a deep understanding of the context shaping the historical significance of those individuals. In particular, the proponents of culturally responsive curriculum and instruction (see Gay 2000) need more studies such as the literature review by Hanley and Noblit (2008) of how these theories are practiced in classrooms. In addition, it is important to document the academic and social impact on "white" teachers and on students who are taught multicultural histories (Goggin 1993, 156).

Infusing history throughout the curriculum. The obvious placement of heritage activities is in social studies, history, and language arts courses. However Ortiz-Franco (1999, 222) urges the teaching of ethnomathematics to "increase an appreciation for the mathematical achievement of other cultures . . . and challenge the dominant perception of students and parents that only western culture created mathematical knowledge." Similarly, classes in science and physical education have room for multicultural history.

The history of "white" allies. Throughout the development of the United States, people of European descent have publicly resisted the ideology of "white" superiority, accepted the leadership of people of color, and even died for the rights of people of color. Curiously, this history is seldom told, particularly in the early grades. A complete story of human rights would include these counternarratives, as well.

Transformative practice: teaching beyond the test. It is at the level of K–12 classrooms that heritage months have the most meaning. If children learn about the full range of histories and human rights struggles from an early age, they are better prepared to avoid misinformation and the repetition of historical injustices as active adults in a democracy. Individual posters of courageous people are insufficient tools for mobilizing young students toward human rights action; a more likely motivator is teaching and showing students the histories of organized resistance to oppression, particularly for people of color from cultures that respect more interdependent models of education (Fryberg and Markus 2007). Similarly, the most likely way to challenge the individualism of neo-liberal education and the imagery of a heroic and solitary individual resisting oppression is through the collective effort of teachers.

The vocabulary of classroom teachers can expand to restructure the knowledge base about cultures. For example, Banks (2007, 86–7) insists that students should be taught

> how the concept of the west is a Eurocentric idea and how different groups in American society conceptualized and viewed the west differently. [To] the Mexicans who became a part of the United States . . . , the territory that Mexico lost to the United States . . . was Mexico's north. The Indian groups living in the western territories did not view their homelands as the west but as the center of the universe. To the various immigrants from Asia . . . , the land to which they immigrated was not the west but the east, or the land of the "golden mountain." By helping students to view Eurocentric concepts such as the west, the discovery of America, and the new world from different perspectives and points of view, we can increase their ability to conceptualize, to determine the implicit perspectives embedded in curriculum materials, and to become more thoughtful and reflective citizens.

In another vocabulary example, when teachers refer to American Indians throughout the school year, they can convey that: American Indian people prefer to be identified by their nation name; American Indian people do not live in tribes; American Indian culture differs by nation and in time; the Pilgrim-Indian image may be false; certain symbols are derogatory to American Indian people; the Haudenosaunee and other nations practiced early models for political democracy; there is a Native legacy in world commerce; and American Indian peoples maintain a contemporary and rich cultural heritage (Haukoos and Beauvais 1996).

Heritage months offer teachers a pathway toward transforming their own pedagogy and the entire school curriculum. Two or more teachers can engage in small group study (Martinez 1997) and can build libraries and imagery of groups of people working for change with materials that supplement state-approved text (Menkart, Murray, and View 2004). Two or more teachers can implement heritage month activities that are age appropriate and engaging, and which move beyond the mass-produced worksheets, the "I Have a Dream" speech competitions, the inspirational speaker for a school-wide assembly, and the food/music/dance festivals.

For teachers of younger children (kindergarten through seventh grade), some activities that hold the promise of a deeper understanding of resistance to oppression include: encouraging children to form questions about American Indians, African Americans, Latinos/as, Asian Americans, and whites for the purpose of conducting group research; learning about labor history; writing reviews of book club materials; writing children's books about lesser-known events, organizations, and people in history; holding a mini-conference with many presenters rather than one speaker for a school-wide assembly; creating a history timeline of the local community; conducting family and community oral histories on involvement in social movements; and inviting parents as guest speakers to help design curriculum (Lee, Menkart, and Okazawa-Rey 2006; Gonzalez et al. 2001).

Teachers of older children and youth have a broader palette of activities, including critical media projects in which students produce counter-knowledge through the manipulation of media tools (Morrell 2008), youth participatory action research in which students research, learn, and share their family histories and epistemologies (Cammarota and Fine 2008; Duncan-Andrade and Morrell 2008), and cultural modeling activities in which teachers use the diversity of students' home languages and their funds of knowledge to understand and deconstruct literary (and, perhaps, historical) text across cultures (Lee 2001). At the deepest level of resisting structural violence through the study of multicultural history, students would learn about and openly examine—if not critique—the historical and contemporary practice of capitalism (Macrine, McLaren, and Hill 2009).

Heritage Months and the Practice of Nonviolence

There remains the question of how the inclusion of accurate stories of physical and structural violence in the curriculum serves the cause of reducing physical and structural violence in society, in peacemaking, and in securing human rights. In describing research on genocide in Africa, Vambe, and Zegeye (2008, 776) suggest that "historical exceptionalism . . . based on the conscious politics of non-disclosure of facts" feeds the conditions for continued genocide by failing to present complex stories that lead to layered social, political and educational responses. An extensive study of contemporary US social studies and history textbooks suggests that justice is not served by sanitizing the history of racialized violence; rather, treating acts of violence against people of color and anti-racist whites as "aberrational, or temporary exceptions to the narrative of American democracy" (Brown and Brown 2010, 57) only serves to sustain the ongoing structural, cultural, and epistemic "violences" manifest in schooling (Ryoo and McLaren 2010, 107).

Heritage months, much like an ethnic studies course that uses materials and pedagogies that honor the full telling of people's histories, will likely challenge these constructions of violence and thus promote nonviolence in the process. While not necessarily arguing that the inability to honor heritage months is a human rights violation (see Ho 2007), United Nations human rights experts have argued that it is the state's "responsibility to respect the right of everyone to have access to his or her own cultural and linguistic heritage and to participate in cultural life. Everyone has the right to seek and develop cultural knowledge and to know and understand his or her own culture and that of others through education and information" (United Nations 2010). This would include the cultural knowledge and linguistic heritage of those "whites" whose stories are omitted from the traditional narrative of American history.

For example, the Peace and Justice Studies Association (n.d.) identifies many of the core values and beliefs held by its members. These include four values that might have particular meaning for K–12 educators: active nonviolence as a positive force for social change, critical analysis of institutions and social structures, societal transformation toward justice, and innovative and effective pedagogy. By practicing these beliefs and teaching the full range of histories of all of the peoples in the United States, teachers can contribute to deepening democratic practices and peacebuilding by promoting justice aimed at transforming the range of potential "violences" into opportunities to cultivate critical instincts aimed at the practices of nonviolent alternatives.

Helping every teacher to become a "peace teacher" (Cook 2010) by utilizing the proposed heritage month activities only begins to provide school experiences that teach students to become agents of human rights. Unlike the sweetened, iridescent yogurt intended to entice children to consume dairy products, a peaceful resolution to cultural conflicts is not saccharine, commercialized, and smooth; instead, the tartness and grittiness of authentic yogurt is healthier for the body, as are curricula that tell children the truth about historical injustices and attempts at their resolution. Parents, teachers, and administrators with courage will stand up to the structural violence of Arizona H.B. 2281 and Texas-approved textbooks in ways big and small, beginning with an honoring of heritage months in truthful, well-rounded ways. Without a critical consciousness and an appropriate selection of resources, teachers may only create more elaborate and equally un-politicized versions of existing heritage month commemorations. To make school curricula inclusive and less prone to replicating history's myriad "violences" takes more than school-based collective efforts to own and produce history. The consequences suffered by Karen Salazar (Hill 2004) highlights the risks to teachers in some jurisdictions of using history curricula as a tool for liberation and peacebuilding, but at least these efforts are a start.

4

Traditional Indigenous North Americans, Nature, and Peace

Pat Lauderdale

Power, status, authority, money, and property are intimately related to the absence of peace in our world today. A traditional North American Indian framework responds to related problems and the absence of peace. It contains an emphasis on decentralization via the deconsolidation of power by grassroots communities and government, the preventative processes related to violence within community, and an emphasis on equality before efficiency. Lasting peace is contingent on our understanding nature and all of the rest of our relatives. Respect for diversity, community, and the care of nature are central to civil law and peace.

Introduction

When will the time come to consider the idea that the human animal cannot have lasting peace without understanding nature and all of the rest of our relatives? Vine Deloria (1992) stresses that "if all things are related, the unity of creation demands that each life form contribute its intended contribution. Any violation of another entity's right to existence in and of itself is a violation of the nature of creation and a degradation of religious reality itself." Nature is viewed as part of human life, not separate from it. From this perspective, you can't experience a walk in nature as if it is external to you. Different North American indigenous peoples living in quite diverse cultures and speaking many different languages provide us with lessons about peace via learning from the interrelatedness of nature. They practiced many forms of nonviolent resistance against genocide and ethnic cleansing.

It is important to note that most scientists remain perplexed by the fact that they have not uncovered or discovered jails or prisons where indigenous people lived and learned about the diversity of life in North American. Most scientists usually turn to other places in the world where indigenous peoples existed since they have not been able to account for the lack of jails or prisons in North America prior to 1492. Traditional North American Indians created complex, yet clear paths to peace. These paths did not lead to simple social techniques or punitive moral standards for a nation, which empirically have led to more violence in and outside of prisons or penitentiaries. Even by the early twentieth century, Smith and Roberts (1954, 121) noted that "[i]mprisonment is not a usual form of legal sanction at Zuni, and it is imposed only for the purpose of holding an offender temporarily pending trial or for the purpose of compelling him to perform labor in situations in which he is unable to pay a fine or damages." They also noted that the premeditated killing of another human "seems originally to have been, in our terms, a 'civil' rather than 'criminal matter.'" The perpetrator was to be held liable for damages to the family of the victim, but not for any kind of retribution at the hands of the body politic. This process was not simply a way of paying the perpetrator's way out of trouble, since it included the very difficult attempt to restore the community. Other indigenous peoples in North America included banishment of the perpetrator as a possible sanction; however, here again the type of retribution present in most modern cultures was not present. The role of the modern state in most nations now is intimately related to the exacerbation of violence.

Civilization: Diversity, Spirituality, Community, and Interdependence

Ironically, most modern forms of the state make strident claims about their high level of civilization, yet civil law is rarely the order of the day. Criminal law and criminalization persist or expand with their symbiotic relationship to violence. Even the presence of the old idea of penitence has largely disappeared and spirituality is typically viewed as a nonsensical form of new age thinking or old age superstition. Yet, spirituality and ritual remain central to traditional North American Indian cultures, not separate from practical everyday life. The relationship with spiritual forces is a primary idea, the creation of the world is related to childbearing, and both genders are represented in their belief systems, as well as by male and female shamans and healers. Traditional North American practices led to respect for diversity and interdependence of all living things rather than simply tolerance, and it did not lead people down the path of homogenization or sameness. These notions stand as a useful foundation for a critical examination of fundamental concepts such as individual responsibility, group rights, time, peace, diversity, nonviolence, and nature. We also need to consider the deep problems arising from rigid social hierarchies if we truly want to embrace diversity and peace (Werlhof 1997; Oliverio and Lauderdale 2005; Lauderdale 2008).

Respect for diversity was central to civil law and peace, especially in the history of early contact between indigenous peoples and Europeans. Cooperation, respect, kinship, and the fundamental role of spiritual values and ceremonies were embodied within the education and caring for indigenous youth. Paul Le Jeune, who was "studying" indigenous life in North America in the 1600s, has been represented alternatively as a missionary, ethnographer, or colonizer. He had his work cut out for him since he did not know how to respond to indigenous people who did not punish children, who encouraged women's independence and decision making, and who had a horror of authority imposed from without—who, in Le Jeune's (1633, 242) words could not "endure in the least those who seem desirous of assuming superiority over the others, and place all virtue in a certain gentleness or apathy. . . . They have reproached me a hundred times because we fear our Captains, while they laugh at and make sport of theirs."

Despite numerous violent attempts of holocaust proportion to destroy indigenous people in North America, some of these people and important parts of their traditional knowledge persist. This knowledge includes fundamental ideas about cultural values and social organization based on learning the lessons of nature, which appear central to making or keeping the peace. While issues concerning the relatively small size of most indigenous nations and their homogeneity are important considerations, it is important to note that despite comparable size and homogeneity of numerous modern subcultures or similar groups, they typically do not possess the social organization or cultural values of the North American indigenous peoples who lived symbiotically with nature. Another important issue concerns the kinship (rather than tribal) structure of many indigenous cultures. Ideas emerging from this structure are not used as a simple social technique or as a punitive moral standard for a nation. Instead, the ideas include a respect for diversity rather than simply tolerance.

This indigenous framework needs to be rediscovered both for modern and indigenous communities. For centuries, traditional North American Indian socialization practices worked to maintain balance within their societies. Yet, colonization and imposed Western structures, values, and beliefs have displaced major indigenous political and spiritual structures, creating disharmony within many American Indian communities. Mandatory boarding schools, laws to prevent spiritual practices, and imposed political structures have resulted in stripping some American Indians of their cultural identity, their languages, their sacred ceremonies, and other cultural values and practices needed to maintain healthy societies. With displacement of traditional indigenous practices have come fractionalization and an increase in crime, arrest, and incarceration rates in American Indian communities. The traditional North American indigenous framework needs to be explicated via a critical examination of fundamental concepts such as individual responsibility, group rights, community, time, and nature and their relationship to peace and nonviolence.

Peacemaking

Many traditional North American Indian peacemaking processes are grounded in a "horizontal" system of justice in which parties are not labeled as adversaries, and the peacemaker is not presumed to be neutral but is selected from within the community based upon her or his abilities to restore peace. Contemporary restorative justice perspectives share with peacemaking a focus on restoring relations and community (Lauderdale and Gray Kanatiiosh 2006). However, there are key distinctions because mediation is often a one-time service, while peacemaking is a way of life; mediation often ignores cultural values, while spirituality is central to peacemaking. Emma LaRocque (1997) questions whether mediation and healing circles are using North American Indian traditional methods of justice. She writes: "Have they, in fact, fallen prey to contemporary . . . and even New Age notions of healing, forgiveness, and offender rehabilitation?" (1997, 85). Mediation usually is based on the decisions of one decision maker, yet peacemaking is based on community consensus. The Navajo peacemaking process, for example, is one in which community members related to both parties are frequently involved in the search for peace. It is strikingly different from US legal programs that are based on a "vertical" and adversarial process, where participants are treated as "plaintiff" and "defendant" or "offender" and "victim," and a presumably neutral arbitrator metes out decisions that are often determined by narrow procedural matters rather than substantive issues of justice. Moreover, the desire to achieve nonviolence in most alternative dispute resolution frameworks ignores the intrinsic problem with the concept of power. In fact, the power of nonviolence can become an oxymoron.

On the other hand, the peacemaking process tries to engage in a "teaching" process in an attempt to reach a new conception of shared reality and responsibility that "gets beyond excuses" (Nielsen and Zion 2005). Justice is viewed in these cases as akin to a "ceremony" in which the peacemaker tries to help offenders understand their current circumstance in light of interconnections, traditional values, mutual respect, and community well-being. We might learn invaluable lessons from considering the wisdom of the elders, rather than leaving their knowledge in bookcases or mentally shelved, or referring to elders as simply old people. And when an elder discusses beauty in the peacemaking process and points out that it means harmony, we might see that some useful New Age ideas often emerge from old age wisdom.

Most traditional North American Indian laws (or law-ways) focus upon problem solving, community participation, and sharing of resources. US law too often concentrates on punishment by the state rather than providing space for victims and offenders to give voice to their concerns (Zunes 2009). Peacemaking processes usually are perceived as more open than the larger criminal justice system because the experiences of participants are afforded more value. The peacemaking process can be viewed as a version of restorative justice that provides an alternative to models of retributive justice.

Among the diversity of North American Indians, there also is a tradition of community healing programs. The Hollow Water Ojibway Community, for example, created a community circle healing program. They wrote (in Ross 1995, 19):

> The use of judgment and punishment actually works against the healing process. An already unbalanced person is moved further out of balance. What the threat of incarceration does do is keep people from coming forward and taking responsibility for the hurt they are causing. It reinforces the silence, and therefore promotes, rather than breaks, the cycle of violence that exists. In reality, rather than making the community a safer place, the threat of jail places the community more at risk.

The dominant US justice paradigm furthers imbalance and disrespect, for it does not seek to restore or heal the offender, the immediate family, friends who are also victims, or the entire community that is unbalanced by the transgression (Ross 1996; cf. Amster 2010a). A common practice for most traditional indigenous peoples is to live in accordance with traditional teachings while retaining balance by respecting and protecting each other and the rest of the natural world (see Krech 1999 for a divergent perspective). These circles of justice consist of interrelated processes and socialization practices that provide a multi-dimensional system of checks and balances that work in unison to retain diversity and harmony within communities and nations. Preventative mechanisms for conflict are found within the traditional teachings, for example, in ceremonies, songs, dances, stories, kinship relations, and healing and warrior societies. Despite the cultural diversity among North American Indian nations, most traditional practices have emphasized civil rather than criminal sanctions. The goal of traditional indigenous justice is to promote peace, heal the network of relationships, and eradicate political, spiritual, and emotional injustices (Lyons 1992, 38).

Power versus Connectedness, and Forms of Civil Law

Power, status, authority, money, and property are intimately related to the absence of peace in our world today (Lauderdale and Harris 2008). How does a traditional North American Indian framework respond to the absence of peace? Is an emphasis on decentralization, i.e., the deconsolidation of power by grassroots government an important factor in explaining the relative peacefulness of North American Indians? Should we pay attention to the emphasis on equality before efficiency? How can we achieve peace without modern law and prisons? Can we ignore the lessons of nature?

Critically, where power is increasingly concentrated, the hegemonic forces that prescribe rules and laws and proscribe certain conduct often create intractable problems. Here, concentrated power leads to a concomitantly greater role in the promotion, revision, and maintenance of violent categories, labels, and violence. Where power is more diffuse, deviance may still persist, but it is more likely to be construed positively as is the work of certain geniuses, artists, musicians, scientists, or leaders. And where power approaches complete diffusion, ostensible problems might come to be seen as "diversity" and not as abnormal, immoral, or unlawful (Lauderdale and Amster 2008).

North American indigenous jurisprudence, which emerged from a symbiotic relationship between law and underlying transformations, has emphasized sanctions that are restitutive or basically of a civil law character (Lauderdale 1997). The majority of the known collections of ancient law and legal systems are characterized by a feature that distinguishes them from systems of contemporary jurisprudence: the proportion of civil to criminal law is striking. One of the distinct characteristics of most indigenous cultures especially prior to colonization was the lack of repressive punishment as the mode of control or domination.

Civil law is not a revolutionary concept emerging in "modern," post-industrialized nations or postmodern discourse. An examination of many indigenous societies shows us that efforts to achieve equality before efficiency are not unique, nor are egalitarian policy solutions a modern invention. Indigenous confederations and nations in North America, such as the Iroquois (Haudenosaunee), Cheyenne, and Laguna, had flexible leaders who possessed policymaking power that led to the implementation of what modern states claim under the rubric of "social justice." The Iroquois Confederacy, which included the Mohawk, Onondaga, Seneca, Oneida, Cayuga, and later the Tuscarora nations, can be seen as a model for civility in modern political forums such as the United Nations. The Haudenosaunee are notable for their avoidance of punitiveness and an emphasis on discipline as the mode of social control. The people who created this confederation focused foremost upon the welfare of the young, and the complementary nature of all life forms was also central.

Indigenous Indian culture embodies a practical as well as sacred symbiosis, reflected in interpretations of the spiritual in everyday lives, relationships, and social institutions. The kinship of traditional indigenous North Americans emphasizes the welfare and education of youth. The raising, educating, and training of youth is an intrinsic part of tribal life. In contrast, most "modern" contemporary education of youth in non-indigenous societies is dominated by formal, external social institutions such as schools, day-care centers, juvenile prisons, or orphanages. Paula Gunn Allen (1986) notes that young women and men in indigenous cultures are trained according to their individual interests and inclinations without resort to bureaucratic instruments of "higher education" that claims to measure fundamental human characteristics. Young people learn useful skills not only for themselves but also for the civil society. The leaders of the society, for example, are often those who demonstrated an early competence for work that had leadership qualities. Gender specific roles, behaviors and rituals are also taught; however, in most North American indigenous societies, the division of labor between women and men is more practical in that people's inherent inclinations and abilities are encouraged rather than suppressed. This understanding is reflected in the youths' training.

The constitution of the Iroquois League has become part of the vision of human liberation movements around the world. In nations such as the

Cheyenne, as well as the Iroquois confederacy, the selection of leaders and/or the system of governance was a central role of the matrons. Oliverio (2008, 17) suggests "there is a deep reason for the American Indian saying that a society is not conquered until the hearts of the women are on the ground." And, Allen (1986, 213) maintains that

> feminists too often believe that no one has ever experienced the kind of society that empowered women and made that empowerment the basis of its rules of civilization. The price the feminist community must pay because it is not aware of the recent presence of gynarchichal societies on this continent is unnecessary confusion, division and much lost time.

Allen also notes that men learned to cook since they were often away hunting or fighting, and there were also women represented among those considered warriors. Of course, for traditional peoples the concept of warrior had little to do with war; rather, the closest indigenous concept focuses upon the obligations and responsibilities of the young to their community. There were girls who were raised as boys if, for example, a family only had daughters. The relevant point here is that despite the great differences among the Indian nations, most of them did not have a sharp division of roles, and the diffusion of hierarchy appears to be a central part of learning and teaching in traditional ways.

Barbara Gray Kanatiiosh points out that Haudenosaunee traditional teachings are found within the *Kaienerekowa* (Great Law of Peace), the words of *Karihwiio* (the good message), *Ka'shatstensera* (the power), and *Skennen* (the peace) (Lauderdale and Kanatiiosh 2006). The teachings of the Great Law of Peace help people understand the concepts of love, unity, peace, equity, coexistence, cooperation, power, respect, generosity, and reciprocity. The teachings include reaffirmations of the kinship system, duties, ceremonies, and societies that promote Karihwiio, the good message, which is necessary to heal the body, the spirit, and to maintain diversity and harmony. Haudenosaunee traditional teachings explain how peace is maintained by preventing injustices to the natural world and by protecting the future generations yet to be born.

Prevention and Restoration

Gray Kanatiiosh notes that restorative justice is dependent on the foundational, traditional preventative structures and practices that work together
to create justice and prevent injustice. Focusing only upon the restorative
aspects of justice without incorporating the preventative mechanisms creates injustice, since it breaks the Circle of Justice and leaves individuals and
the community without the necessary cultural foundational structures to
heal and prevent conflicts. Colonization has, for many peoples, destroyed
or displaced these essential foundational traditional teachings (Lauderdale 2008; see also Goldsmith and He 2008). Traditional teachings are
preserved in, a "tribal encyclopedia" that is maintained by "keepers of the
tribal encyclopedia." The keeper, who is a traditional civil leader, is called
a *naat'aanii*. The word describes someone who speaks wisely and clearly,
and a naat'aanii is someone who is respected for her or his ability to solve
problems. The keeper can help identify and provide invaluable insights
concerning the traditional teachings found within ceremony, prayer, and
in the foundational narratives and stories. Frank Pommersheim (1995)
emphasizes the importance of narratives by suggesting that stories are not
extrinsic niceties, but are basic life forces needed to establish and preserve
communities, and to develop a common culture of shared understandings
and deeper, more vital ethics.

    The Haudenosaunee, for example, follow narratives that contain
foundational principles, norms, practices, and structures: (1) the *Tsi kion-
tonhwentsison* (creation story), (2) the story about the creation of clans,
(3) the *Ohen'ton Kariwatekon* (Thanksgiving address), and (4) the *Kaienerekowa* (Great Law of Peace). Their Great Law of Peace contains traditional
laws, political and spiritual principles, and the spiritual/political structure
of the Haudenosaunee confederacy (Lauderdale and Kanatiiosh 2006).
The duties and responsibilities of each person in the society are given
and reaffirmed when the people come together for ceremonies and social
activities. The Great Law also reaffirms the sacred ceremonies, songs,
and dances, as well as the clan system that contains a system of checks
and balances that depends not only on people not wanting to commit

transgressions, but on people understanding and having the will to prevent others from breaching the peace.

The kinship or clan system is one example of an important structure that contains duties, protocols, and practices that function to maintain justice. This kinship functions to maintain justice in many ways. Kanien-kahake Doug George-Kanentiio (2000, 70–1) writes: "A clan in former times took care of all of its members from the time they were born until they died. Housing, food, health care, education, and employment were administered by the clans. Criminal acts and family disputes were also adjudicated by the clan elders. Clans controlled marriages and ceremonial activities, and they selected political representatives." The collective nature of the processes is the fundamental point here.

There are many concrete practices that suggest the reasons for the absence of internal violence (cf. Zinn 2002). Traditional, indigenous justice practices are multidimensional and contain a balancing process, which is dependent on observable practices and social structures that function as both preventative and restorative mechanisms in the maintenance of justice. A synergistic, recursive model reminds us that the comparative and historical analysis of theories and practices of justice is a relevant alternative to most philosophical treatises and jurisprudence on what justice should be, especially with regard to its relationship to peace (Lauderdale 2008).

Colonial imposition of laws and forms of government, the loss of lands, and policies to assimilate North American Indians have caused many of the traditional indigenous justice mechanisms to become lost or damaged. Today, numerous tribal courts exist that only replicate Western beliefs and practices in an adversarial system of justice, instead of using traditional indigenous justice methods and values. Such tribal courts and forms of governance comprise a form of internalized colonialism. These types of courts cause disharmony within the community, as they do not preserve cultural traditions, nor do they heal the community. This type of replication of imposed laws, practices, and ideas has seeped into many aspects of North American Indian governments. Many tribal codes currently are merely restatements of federal and state law and are devoid of indigenous knowledge, values, and norms. Such tribal codes suggest that the great circle of justice needs to be restored within American Indian communities before other people try to borrow and implement ostensible Indian restoration practices. An important part of traditional codes is their grounding in tradition and an intimate connection with nature.

Traditional teachings, socialization practices, and organizational structures that once worked to prevent social injustices can be replanted. Some of the traditional indigenous teachings contain the seeds of how people can once again live in *skennen* (peace) or *Hozho* (balance and harmony). Prior to colonization, "law" in North America was relatively direct and accessible to indigenous North Americans since it was based on concrete notions of the individual and collective good, rather than on a modern abstract ideal imposed by a nation-state (largely for political purposes), and to which people must conform (or be punished) in order ostensibly to have security and private property (cf. Zunes 2009). It is critical to remember that for most North American Indians, the "law" was accessible to everyone, since the oral tradition allowed it to be carried around as part of them, rather than confining it to legal institutions and inaccessible experts who largely control the language and the cost of using the law.

The path that traditional North American Indians also still follow is through the oral transmission of knowledge. The (often ignored) precision of oral knowledge partly is created by carefully telling the stories over and over again. We are all here today because our ancient ancestors were precise in orally recounting those stories. If nothing else, this tradition will help remind us of the increasing problems in written forms of law— especially those aimed at peace—about which legal specialists routinely disagree regarding contradictions in legal statutes or the exact meaning of written laws.

Social diversity (the recognition that humans are part of nature, and not separate from it) and harmony are essential to peace. From the indigenous perspective, peace requires a communal approach in the sense that preventative and restorative mechanisms and practices need to be distributed throughout the community for there to be healing and justice. Alfred Taiaiake (1999, 144) writes that "the goals that flow from our traditions demand an approach based on undermining the intellectual and moral foundations of colonialism and exposing the internal contradictions of states and societies that promise justice and practice oppression." Communal restorative justice has the potential to reduce social and economic injustice, and it can continue to limit the impact of imprisonment, especially imprisonment that is directly related to unemployment, debt, suicide, and innumerable diseases (Lauderdale and Kanatiiosh 2006).

Life, for traditional Indians, is more about learning than receiving a "formal education;" life is more about healing and peace than war or conflict. Gustavo Esteva (1998) stresses that from many traditional perspectives, no one can learn for you or heal you. Taking charge of learning instead of being educated, or of healing instead of being cured, reflects the continuous exercise of dignity and autonomy that characterizes most traditional indigenous peoples.

Business Sense versus Good Sense

For contemporary real estate developers and most business people, time is money; however, for indigenous peoples, time may be more relevant to consensus, since consensus is often more important than material gains. In his work with prairie Dakota, Randy Hanson (2002) notes that these North American Indians see and learn that everything comes from the earth, and that only recently was something invented (nuclear weapons) by human animals that threatens everything that lives on this earth. Those indigenous peoples point out that the threat of nuclear destruction was created by a society that claimed it was quite civilized and not primitive. Hanson (19) stresses that for many indigenous peoples, the contemporary problem may be how to "embrace the tar baby of new global capitalism as a means of economic self-determination but not let that step become the thing itself, not let economic development become the predominant justification."

Indigenous peoples have been resisting the negative phases of globalization for centuries in the western hemisphere, and for millennia in Africa and Eurasia. Globalization is a process that is deeply connected to the first invention of states, over 5,000 years ago (Lauderdale 2008b). This process includes a series of economic, cultural and political changes typically viewed as increasing interdependence, integration, and interaction between people and organizations throughout the world. Globalization, now often cloaked under the guise of neoliberalism, claims to increase peace, yet the claims are couched in abstract and indirect terms, and the empirical data are a conundrum (Lauderdale 2009). And new expenses for education and authoritarian corporate structures have been introduced, while funding for peace studies and the humanities is cut more deeply. Neoliberal absolutism is the order of the day as academic teaching and research—initially reorganized and redefined around higher education—morph into a focus on higher investment and the profitability of the transnational education industry. In addition, evaluation models based upon private business practices are increasingly being implemented in the academic sphere. Good research is now defined as research that generates revenue from various sources, including nefarious ones.

Common sense rather than good sense increasingly has become synonymous with business acumen. Neoliberalism is often touted as bringing an increased standard of living and prosperity to poor countries, and further wealth to rich ones, yet another perspective suggests that globalization often perpetuates the long history of plundering and profiteering. Indigenous peoples are very familiar with these experiences: forced cultural assimilation; the export of artificial wants, both material and symbolic; and the destruction or inhibition of local and global democracy; along with the erosion of peace, interconnectedness, community, ecology, and cultures (Shenandoah 1987). Slogans about peace in our time are reduced to defining it as the absence of war. And claims concerning great civilizations are rarely connected to being civil and peaceful.

Conclusion

The majority of traditional indigenous ideas for peace are relatively direct and accessible, since they are based on concrete notions of the individual and collective good, rather than modern abstractions imposed by the nation-state as the ideal to which people must conform (or be punished) in order to have stability, security, and material goods. The laws of peace are accessible to everyone because the oral tradition allows it to be carried around as part of the human experience, rather than confined to legal institutions. Oral traditions in indigenous life can stimulate, develop, protect, and deliver knowledge in a systemic manner. Jurisprudence based on oral traditions has continued to preserve much of the diversity and respect for nature. Deloria (1992) suggests that within the traditions, beliefs, and customs of the peoples are the guidelines for preserving life and the future of all nature. We are instructed to learn from nature rather than try to control and "develop" it for various ends. In contrast, modern claims of progress and civilization as part of the domination of nature is a conundrum, as is the view that nature is backward or primitive. In this context, the term "primitive" is a result of different types of anthropocentrism and ethnocentrism. Nature has never been backward.

In general, contemporary philosophers continue to emphasize "the state of nature" from which humans must separate themselves in order to dominate it. The issue of nature becomes unduly narrowed to the concept of human nature, which in turn raises questions about race or utopian naturalism. Pseudospeciation, the view that leads people to define their own species as superior to another in order to dominate others and often to extinguish life for narrow political and economic purposes, is not a lesson taken from nature. The care for and examination of nature provides lessons that can demonstrate the relevance and importance of peace through diversity. A deep understanding of diversity and the meaning of all of our human and nonhuman relatives reveals ideas and methods of practicing responsibility and for ensuring the existence of future generations. Traditional indigenous knowledge of peace through diversity is useful in adapting to change. The old saying that the only constant is change can be deeply understood from such a perspective.

Despite varied attempts to destroy indigenous people, important parts of their traditional knowledge have persisted. Cultural values and social organization based on learning the lessons of nature are central to this persistence. Issues concerning the relatively small size of most indigenous nations and their homogeneity are important considerations. Despite comparable size and homogeneity of numerous modern subcultures or groups, they typically do not possess the social organization or cultural values of the indigenous peoples. Peoples who lived symbiotically with nature still have important lessons that we can learn. Again, it is significant that anthropologists and archeologists remain perplexed by their failure to uncover or discover any jails or prisons in indigenous places in North America. Different indigenous peoples living in quite diverse cultures and speaking many different languages did not find such a lesson as imprisonment from learning about the complexities of nature. What animal other than the human animal resorts to prisons to such an extent as that found in most modern societies?

One of the most interesting features of traditional indigenous peoples is their substantive reliance on the interrelatedness of nature. Today's appeal for and acceptance of global diversity is severely limited when it is built within the constraints of modern nation-states, which often view diversity as deviance if it does not conform to modern norms and definitions, especially those norms connected to markets and money. Traditional indigenous knowledge can't provide all the answers to current problems, however it can provide us with ideas on how to improve our questions and, therefore, improve our potential to provide more equitable, less oppressive structures from which to approach problems that fracture or destroy peace (Dietrich 2005). While United Nations (UN) Secretary General Boutros Boutros Ghali welcomed indigenous people from across our earth for the "International Year of Indigenous Peoples" in 1992, and UN officials wrote many good words on paper, we might consider devoting every year to learning the lessons of peace contained in diverse indigenous knowledge. The UN's words remain on paper, on those old leaves, and the issue now is how to make those words becomes reality. Law on the books never seems to be the same as law in action (Inverarity, Lauderdale, and Feld 1983; Fitzpatrick 1992; Lauderdale 2008), yet words about peace have the potential to become peace in action. In contemporary terms, it also seems important to note that the following comments are not clichés, but rather are declarations gained from long, traditional experiences that were often attempts to prevent genocide. "Peace cannot be kept by force; it can only be achieved by understanding," as Albert Einstein once famously said. (Or, in the oft-repeated words of an anonymous author: "Peace is the marriage of the people and the planet, with all attendant vows."

To illustrate the point further, I conclude with an old story about the role of nonviolence (Oliverio and Lauderdale 2005, 214):

Interpretations of the bestselling book in the world, the Bible, are myriad and often conflicting. Some interpreters focus upon the Old Testament and call for "an eye for an eye." Others rely on the New Testament and say to "turn the other cheek." Part of this confusion stems from ignoring the historical and political context of the words. Those people who call for revenge usually are in the majority when responding to acts of violence that are labeled as terrorism, and often are portrayed as strong. Those who say "turn the other cheek" usually are portrayed as weak. Yet, consider the political and historical context of this adage. At the time that Jesus was alive, it was a common practice (and an important norm) for dominant people to slap the poor or the oppressed with their right-hand across the left cheek. The left hand was defined as dirty, profane, and used for activities such as cleaning oneself after defecating. To turn the other cheek meant to put the dominator or oppressor in a position of having to slap others with their left hand, a position that was profane for the dominant party. "Turn the other cheek," in context, can be seen not as being weak but as an act designed to alert oppressors to their own misuse of violence. It also was an act of self-defense.

I would suggest that as we go forward, we likewise consider the "old ways" of our elders and the traditional indigenous paths to peace.

Part Two

Nonviolent Movements

Nonviolence does not merely think, reflect, and envision—it *acts*. As a set of principles, nonviolence is probably best understood as a way of resisting oppression and challenging exploitative uses of power. Campaigns of nonviolence have been used to throw off dictators and secure rights for the masses throughout history. In the modern era, nonviolence has played a prominent role in movements for civil liberties, environmental justice, social equity, and an end to warfare. The prevailing mindset in many of these instances includes equal parts strategic and moralistic invocations of nonviolence, informed by the implicit recognition that many of the forces being opposed are predicated on violence, as well as the realization that it would be prudent both politically and ethically to model the opposite.

There is another aspect of nonviolence that is perhaps less well-known, namely its constitutive side. In addition to being used reactively in opposition to dominant norms, nonviolence is a proactive force that can be deployed as both a means and an end, prefiguring the existence of a better world even as it works to alter the one(s) we now have. Properly construed, nonviolence can serve as a tool for undoing repression and injustice, as well as for building a society free of structural violence and inclusive of all of its members. Social movements equally embrace the preventative and transformative attributes of nonviolence, and the chapters in this section accordingly reflect that dualistic sense of the concept.

Stephen Zunes begins by exploring the role of nonviolence in the global struggle for democracy, and further provides a real-time sense of the complexities involved while offering a cautionary tale for actors across the ideological spectrum. Zunes brings his cogent policy analyses and keen personal insights to bear on nonviolent insurrections around the world, which constitute a "remarkable upsurge" in "'people power' movements that have overthrown authoritarian regimes in over two dozen countries over the past three decades." Hallmarks of these nonviolent movements include massive noncooperation and dramatic public acts of mass resistance, often including a broad range of nonviolent tactics such as strikes, boycotts, mass demonstrations, contestation of public space, tax refusal, destruction of symbols of government authority, refusal to obey official orders, and the creation of alternative institutions for political legitimacy and social organization. "In contrast to armed struggles," Zunes observes, "these nonviolent insurrections are movements of organized popular resistance to government authority, and (either consciously or by necessity) they eschew the use of weapons of modern warfare." Nonviolence adherents worldwide can play a primary positive role in the rise of global democracy largely "through example," recognizing the inherent "need for nonviolent action in the United States and other Western nations" as a significant aspect of the larger struggle—making the narratives we develop in the process all the more crucial.

This is the essential point picked up by Tom Hastings: how do we create and communicate positive exemplars of nonviolence in action? In his unique style, Hastings uses play and polemic to mirror the deadly serious teachings in his analysis of the successes and pitfalls of nonviolent campaigns. Noting the "deterrent value of a robust non-violent image," Hastings opines that nonviolence, "especially when presented with joy and creativity, can spark sympathy" and serve to diminish the pervasive sense of fear that is "the precursor to most violence." For Hastings, that moment of "jiu-jitsu" represents "the beginning of the power of nonviolence," and offers us an opportunity to flip the militaristic desire for "peace through strength" into a transformative one based on "strength through peace," instead. As a matter of principle and practice alike, the core of nonviolence is the empowerment of ourselves, each other, and those with whom we may find ourselves in adversarial situations. In this end, it is this story that is the one we need to tell over and over again.

In a chapter that exudes both political insight and personal transformation, Supriya Baily chronicles the nonviolent campaign of women in an Indian village struggling for equity and respect. As Baily describes it, this "subgroup of relatively marginalized women working to create a culture of positive peace . . . used their voices to navigate relationships of power to engage in acts that built bridges of collaboration, integration, and cooperation for both the long- and short-term health of the community." Part of the motivation for this in-depth depiction of nonviolence at the scale of a single community comes in the recognition "that women are being called upon to actively exercise their influence over violent situations" more frequently and in a range of contexts and locales. Baily highlights the work of "unheralded peacemakers," those "who are working on a daily basis to build a culture of peace without labeling it as such, who are working to dismantle age-old prejudices, and who are ensuring a safer future for their communities." In this manner, we come to understand nonviolence as a powerful touchstone not only for engaging macroscopic political concerns in hostile environments, but equally as a force for promoting just and sustainable relations at all levels of engagement.

Randall Amster extends this basic premise further by focusing on the ways in which cooperative resource management systems can yield peaceful societal structures. Amster takes an expansive and holistic view of nonviolence, one that is based explicitly on "a universal respect for both self and other," the inherent "unity of means and ends," the fostering of "cooperative and mutually beneficial outcomes," and the recognition that "everything is interconnected, not merely in a superficial manner but on a deeper level that reflects the collected wisdom of humankind." Applying these tenets to the collaborative water sharing system known as the "acequia" found in various forms around the world, Amster strives to develop a working model of "nonviolent, cooperative resource management" that stands in marked opposition to "the prevailing logic of 'resource conflict'" as a leading cause of violence and warfare. In this view, the articulation of working models of "resource cooperation" and "the cultivation of nonviolent alternatives" can point the way forward toward the just and sustainable outcomes that are, in the final analysis, the overarching aims of nonviolent resistance.

5

Nonviolent Civil Insurrections and Pro-Democracy Struggles

Stephen Zunes

The past thirty years have witnessed a remarkable upsurge in nonviolent insurrections against autocratic rulers. Primarily nonviolent "people power" movements have overthrown authoritarian regimes in over two dozen countries over the past three decades, have forced substantial reforms in even more countries, and have seriously challenged other despots. The targets of these movements have been monarchies, right-wing military dictatorships, Communist regimes, colonial rulers, occupation armies, and more. They have been both pro-Western and anti-Western. They have been Christian, Muslim, and atheist. They have been both Socialist and free-market capitalist. They have been modern industrialized states and some of the poorest nations on the planet. What they have had in common is that they had lost the support of the vast majority of their people, and the nonviolent democratic opposition movement, despite internal differences, was able to develop sufficient support to force the old regime from power, either by successfully pushing through gradual liberalization over a period of months or a few years, or by forcing a tyrant to flee in the face of massive noncooperation and dramatic public acts of mass resistance.

In contrast to armed struggles, these nonviolent insurrections are movements of organized popular resistance to government authority, and (either consciously or by necessity) they eschew the use of weapons of modern warfare. Unlike conventional political movements, nonviolent

99

campaigns usually employ tactics outside the mainstream political processes of electioneering and lobbying. Tactics have included strikes, boycotts, mass demonstrations, the popular contestation of public space, tax refusal, destruction of symbols of government authority (such as official identification cards), refusal to obey official orders (such as curfew restrictions), and the creation of alternative institutions for political legitimacy and social organization.

Not all nonviolent pro-democracy movements have been successful, of course; several have been suppressed, as in Burma and China. What is surprising is not that some of them have failed—as have many violent insurgencies around the world—but that so many of them have succeeded. What recent history has repeatedly shown is that the most effective means for democratic change has grown out of broadly-based nonviolent social movements, such as those that have toppled dictatorships and forced democratic reforms in such diverse countries as the Philippines, Chile, Bolivia, Madagascar, Nepal, Czechoslovakia, Indonesia, Serbia, Mali, Ukraine, and elsewhere. Even the relatively conservative Washington-based Freedom House has produced a study which, after examining the sixty-seven transitions from authoritarian regimes to varying degrees of democratic governments over the past few decades, concluded that they came not from foreign invasion, and only rarely through armed revolt or voluntary elite-driven reforms, but overwhelmingly came through democratic civil society organizations utilizing nonviolent action and other forms of civil resistance, such as strikes, boycotts, civil disobedience, and mass protests (Karatnycky 2005).

Largely as a result of these nonviolent civil insurrections, the number of countries under dictatorial rule has declined by half. In the late 1970s more than two-thirds of the world's countries were under autocratic rule; today they total less than one-third. Not all of these transitions to democracy have been complete. In a number of countries, the political systems have turned out to be democratic in structure, but not in practice. Yet, even imperfect democracy affords a political opening whereby coherent political forces can work for enacting policies they wish to advance. Democracy, therefore, gives an opportunity to challenge the excesses of national and global capitalism; to empower local communities; to openly defend the rights of women, minorities, and the poor; and to eventually gain political power. Without democracy, it is far more difficult. In effect, the establishment and defense of liberal democratic institutions is a necessary, if not sufficient, path toward building a just society.

Conversely, while successful violent revolutions have often initially been more effective in overturning the power of traditional elites, reforming archaic social systems, and establishing greater economic equality, the authoritarian structure and martial values that come to the fore during armed struggle have tended to result in simply establishing a new form of authoritarianism that creates its own brand of unaccountable elite rule and injustice.

Whenever governments are challenged by their own people, they tend to claim that those struggling for freedom and justice are traitors to the nation and agents of foreign enemies. In previous decades, opposition activists challenging US-backed dictatorships in Latin America, Southeast Asia, and elsewhere were routinely labeled as "Communist agents" and "Soviet sympathizers." Today, pro-democracy actors within US client states in the Middle East are depicted as "Islamic fundamentalists" and "Iranian agents." Similarly, opposition activists in countries with autocratic rulers opposing US hegemony have been labeled as "supporters of Western imperialism" and "American agents"; these governments and their supporters point to the nonviolent civil insurrections that toppled the corrupt and autocratic regimes in Serbia in 2000, in Georgia in 2003, and in Ukraine in 2005 (following efforts by incumbent rulers to steal the national elections) and claim that similar plots are in the works to topple their own regimes, as well.

In reality, however, the limited amount of financial support provided to opposition groups by the United States and other Western governments does not cause nonviolent liberal democratic civil insurrections to take place any more than the limited Soviet financial and material support for leftist movements in the Third World in previous decades caused armed Socialist revolutions to take place. As Marxists and others familiar with popular movements have long recognized, revolutions are the result of certain objective conditions. Indeed, no amount of money could force hundreds of thousands of people to leave their jobs, homes, schools, and families to face down heavily armed police and tanks unless they had a strong, heartfelt motivation to do so.

Support by foreign governments of such pro-democracy movements is arguably legal, since a nation's sovereignty ultimately rests with the people, not a particular regime (Ackerman and Glennon 2007). Unfortunately, support for democratic change has been given a bad name in recent years as the US government has used support for "democracy" as a rationalization for interventionist policies that have caused enormous suffering, and which run counter to basic principles of international law, most notably in Iraq. So-called "democracy promotion" has been compromised by the simultaneous effort to advance a strategic and economic agenda against governments that resist hegemonic designs. In many respects, the United States has done for the cause of democracy what the Soviet Union did for the cause of Socialism. Not only did the George W. Bush administration, in particular, give democracy a bad name in much of the world, but its high-profile and highly suspect "democracy promotion" agenda provided repressive regimes and their apologists an excuse to label any popular pro-democracy movement that challenges them as foreign agents, even when led by independent grassroots nonviolent activists, claiming that they are somehow part of an effort by the Bush administration and its allies to instigate "soft coups" against governments deemed hostile to American interests and replace them by more compliant regimes.

Support for nonviolent pro-democracy struggles from foreign governments has been quite limited. There have been some efforts since the 1980s by US government-funded initiatives, such as the National Endowment for Democracy (NED), the International Republican Institute, and other groups to promote civil society efforts, though these have been largely restricted to institution-building initiatives primarily geared toward small, middle class secular elements, and not toward mass movements capable of launching large-scale nonviolent action campaigns. Such funding has at times helped a number of opposition groups cover some of the costs of their operations, better enabling them to afford computers, Internet access, fax machines, printing costs, office space, and other assets. Assistance from foreign governments has also helped provide for poll watchers and other logistical support to help ensure free and fair elections. Some congressionally funded bodies have provided seminars and other training for opposition leaders in campaign strategies. What is controversial about some of these endeavors is that they have been directed primarily at helping conservative, pro-Western parties with a free-market orientation, and generally not parties of the democratic left. Nor are they aimed solely at pro-democracy struggles challenging autocratic regimes. Indeed, US agencies have also backed opposition parties in countries such as Venezuela, some of which sided with the putschists who attempted to overthrow that country's democratically elected government in 2002.

Some opposition groups in some countries have welcomed US assistance, while others have rejected such aid on principle. There is no evidence, however, to suggest—even in cases where this kind of limited US support for opposition organizations has taken place—that the US government or any US-funded entity has ever provided training, advice, or strategic assistance for the kind of mass, popular nonviolent action campaigns that have toppled governments or threatened the survival of incumbent regimes.

In a few cases, some funding was provided to opposition groups with the express purpose of "regime change," such as the decision under the George W. Bush administration to fund various Iranian opposition groups, a policy since rescinded under Barack Obama's administration. Most of these groups were led by exiles who had virtually no following within Iran or any experience with the kinds of grassroots mobilization necessary to build a popular movement that could threaten the regime's survival. By contrast, most of the credible opposition within Iran capable of forming the basis of a successful nonviolent resistance struggle, and which did launch the uprising that commenced in June 2009, has renounced this US initiative and has asserted that such intrusions have simply made it easier for the regime to claim that all pro-democracy groups and activists are paid agents of the United States.

There have been some cases where support from foreign governments has been beneficial to nonviolent action campaigns, such as the limited Western financial support—usually through NGOs and quasi-independent foundations—provided to pro-democracy movements in Eastern Europe. While the incumbent regimes tried to make political capital out of such foreign interference, Western governments were seen in that region largely in positive terms after decades of Communist repression. The history of Western intervention in most other parts of the world, however, including support for some horrifically oppressive dictatorships, has so severely damaged the reputation of Western powers that such outside support can be—and has been—used to discredit the pro-democracy movements. Indeed, given the clear economic and strategic motivations for regime change, and the tendency to take sides in internal disputes within the opposition, such efforts are generally counterproductive.

There are some limited actions that foreign governments can perform to support nonviolent struggles in other countries, such as defending the rights of nonviolent activists, supporting a free and independent media, and using embassies as meeting spaces for activists. However, there is little the United States or any other foreign government could do directly to support a nonviolent uprising. Large bureaucratic governments accustomed to projecting political power through military force or elite diplomatic channels have little understanding or appreciation of nonviolent action or any other kind of mass popular struggle. Despite the historic tendency for autocratic regimes and their supporters to blame popular insurrections on foreign powers, no authentic popular uprising can be created by a foreign power. In particular, there is little evidence to suggest that the United States or any other foreign power understands the kind of alliance-building and strategic training necessary to foment a nonviolent civil insurrection. Foreign governments have historically promoted regime change through military invasions, coups d'état, and other kinds of violent seizures of power that install an undemocratic minority. Nonviolent "people power" movements, by contrast, make regime change possible through empowering pro-democratic majorities.

Unfortunately, some "leftist" critics of nonviolent pro-democracy movements parallel right-wing supporters of US intervention in that both denigrate the power of individuals to overthrow oppressive institutions, and instead appear to believe that such social and political change can only come through the manipulation of foreign powers. For example, despite President Ronald Reagan's insistence that the popular armed insurgencies that challenged repressive military-backed dictatorships were the result of a Soviet "hit list," the reality was that the revolutions in Nicaragua, El Salvador, and Guatemala were homegrown popular movements. While the Soviets provided a limited amount of assistance, and obviously wanted to take political advantage of toppling a pro-American regime and replacing it with a revolutionary movement that would be friendlier to its interests, the oppressed peasants and workers of those Central American countries were not simply following the dictates of Moscow. Similarly, claims that the United States is somehow a major force behind contemporary popular movements against dictatorships in Iran, Zimbabwe, and Belarus, or that the United States was somehow responsible for the successes of previous movements in Serbia, Georgia, or Ukraine are equally ludicrous. This attitude appears to validate those who disingenuously credit Reagan's dangerous and militaristic Cold War policies for the fall of Communism in Eastern Europe, and denigrates the millions of ordinary people, from Polish dockworkers to Czech playwrights, who faced down tanks for their freedom. Similarly, it validates those who try to make the priests, union activists, peasants, students, and others who have been martyred in their struggle for freedom in El Salvador and Guatemala appear to have simply been agents of the Soviet Union.

In reality, every successful popular nonviolent insurrection has been a homegrown movement rooted in the realization by the masses that their rulers were illegitimate and the current political system was incapable of redressing injustice. By contrast, no nonviolent insurrection has succeeded when the movement's leadership and agenda did not have the backing of the majority of the population. This is why the 2002–2003 "strike" in Venezuela's oil industry failed to bring down Hugo Chávez, while comparable disruptions to economies elsewhere have often forced out less popular leaders.

In addition, it is important to remember that the vast majority of successful nonviolent civil insurrections have not been against dictatorships opposed by the US government, but dictatorships supported by the US government. Right-wing autocrats toppled by such "people power" movements have included Ferdinand Marcos in the Philippines, Suharto in

Indonesia, the Shah of Iran, Jean-Claude Duvalier in Haiti, Augusto
Pinochet in Chile, Chun Doo-hwan in South Korea, and Gaafar Nimeiry
in Sudan, to name only a few. Still another problem with this kind of
simplistic reductionism is that when nonviolent civil insurrections do
succeed in bringing democrats to power in countries previously under
anti-American dictatorships, the new and often inexperienced leaders are
faced with plaudits from the American right, and suspicion from the European and North American left. This could lead them to wonder who their
friends really are and reinforce the myth that those of the right, rather
than the left, are the real champions of freedom. The conspiratorial thinking and denigration of genuine popular movements appearing increasingly in some circles serves to strengthen the hand of repressive regimes,
weaken democratic forces, and bolster the argument of American neoconservatives that only US militarism and intervention—and not nonviolent struggle by oppressed peoples themselves—is capable of freeing those
suffering under repressive rule.

Both the Right and the far Left have effectively colluded in delegiti-
mizing the power of individuals to make change and to portray the United
States—for good or for ill—as the only power that can make a difference
in the world. A number of governments, most notably Iran, have claimed
that such efforts are part of a CIA attempt to launch some kind of "soft
coup." Some Western bloggers and other writers critical of the George W.
Bush administration and understandably skeptical of US intervention in
nations in the name of "democracy," have naively accepted such claims.
These theories have in turn been picked up by some progressive web-
sites and periodicals, and even by some in the mainstream press, which
then repeat them as fact (see, e.g., MacKinnon 2007). In short, not only
is it naive to assume that an external power could provoke a revolution
of any kind, it also should be apparent that the US government does not
know the first thing about fomenting a nonviolent civil insurrection. As a
result, the dilemma for US policy-makers—and the hope for those who
support democracy as a matter of principle and not political expediency—
is that the most realistic way to overthrow the world's remaining autocratic
regimes is through a process the US government cannot control.

Capacity Building, Third Party
Intervention, and Other NGO Support

A more promising form of external support has come from foreign non-governmental organizations, most of which reject direct or indirect government funding, and which offer workshops on the history and dynamics of nonviolent action to pro-democracy and anti-occupation activists, though this phenomenon has thus far been quite limited and fairly recent. Such groups as the Serbian-based Centre for Nonviolent Action and Strategies (CANVAS) and the US-based Albert Einstein Institution, International Center on Nonviolent Conflict, and Nonviolence International have worked with pro-democracy and anti-occupation activists from such countries as Egypt, Western Sahara, Palestine, West Papua, the Maldives, Guinea, Zimbabwe, and Iran. Even in these cases, however, a number of regimes facing popular opposition have gone as far as to claim that certain small independent NGOs and prominent nonviolent activists from Europe and the United States who have provided seminars and workshops for opposition activists on the theory and practice of massive nonviolent resistance were somehow working as agents of the George W. Bush administration.

Ironically, most of these activists and NGOs happen to be highly critical of US foreign policy and follow a strict policy of not giving specific advice to opposition groups. Virtually all such seminars and workshops come at the direct request of opposition organizers themselves; these NGOs tend not to seek out specific groups to assist. Virtually all of them have a strict policy of refusing support from the NED or any other government-funded entity.

The American and European groups that share generic information on the history and dynamics of strategic nonviolence with civil society organizations in foreign countries are not unlike the Western private voluntary organizations that share environmentally sustainable technologies and agricultural techniques with farmers in developing nations. Both offer useful tools that, if applied consistently and effectively, could improve the quality of life for millions of people. There is nothing "imperialistic" about it. Just as sustainable agricultural technologies and methods are more effective in meeting human needs and preserving the planet than the conventional development strategies promoted by Western governments, nonviolent action has been shown to be more effective in advancing democratic change than threats of foreign military intervention, backing coup plotters, imposing punitive sanctions, supporting armed rebel groups, and other methods traditionally instigated by the United States and its allies. And just as the application of appropriate technologies can also be a means of countering the damage caused by unsustainable, neoliberal economic models pushed by Western governments and international financial institutions, the use of massive nonviolent action can counter some of the damage resulting from the arms trade, military intervention, and other harmful manifestations of Western militarism.

Development based on Western models usually means that multinational corporations and the governments of wealthy capitalist countries end up exerting a large degree of control over these societies, whereas appropriate technologies allow for genuine independence and self-sufficiency. Similarly, unlike fomenting a military coup or establishing a military occupation, which both rely on asserting control over the population and potential political opponents, successful nonviolent civil insurrections are necessarily based on a broad coalition of popular movements and are therefore impossible for an outside power to control. Another difference between these people-to-people educational efforts and US intervention is that, unlike the NED and other government-backed "pro-democracy" efforts, which often focus on developing conventional political initiatives led by pro-Western elites, these workshops on strategic nonviolence are primarily designed for grassroots activists unaffiliated with established political parties who seek to make change from below.

Historically, individuals and groups with experience in effective nonviolent action campaigns tend to come from leftist and pacifist traditions that carry a skeptical view of government power, particularly governments with a history of militarism and conquest. Conversely, large bureaucratic governments accustomed to projecting political power through military force or elite diplomatic channels have little understanding or appreciation of nonviolent action or any other kind of mass popular struggle.

Indeed, what would CIA operatives know about nonviolence, much less grassroots organizing?

Much of the support for pro-democracy struggles follows the tradition of transnational advocacy networks, which Margaret Keck and Kathryn Sikkink define as "networks of activists, distinguishable largely by the centrality of principled ideas or values in motivating their formation" (Keck and Sikkink 1998, 1). In the late twentieth century, and particularly since the end of the Cold War, transnational advocacy networks have functioned as force multipliers for both violent and nonviolent struggles. In writing about the latter, Keck and Sikkink (1998, 200) observe:

> Complex global networks carry and reframe ideas, insert them in policy debates, pressure for regime formation, and enforce existing international norms and rules, at the same time that they try to influence particular domestic political issues. . . . Transnational value-based advocacy is particularly useful where one state is relatively immune to direct local pressure and linked activists elsewhere have better access to their own governments and to international organizations. Linking local activists with media and activists abroad can then create a characteristic "boomerang" effect, which curves around local state indifference and repression to put foreign pressure on local policy elites.

The "boomerang effect" describes how nonviolent direct action can be effective in cases where the resisting population has little or no direct leverage over the opponent. The ability of local actors to internationalize their struggle by forming functional alliances with third parties that have more direct leverage over the opponent and its allies is key to the success of nonviolent struggles in these cases.

Another form of external NGO support is provided through third-party nonviolent intervention. Such efforts have included the role the Shanti Sena peace brigade played in responding to the 1969 Ahmedabad riots in India, a role rooted in the Gandhian notion of using nonviolent force, rather than an armed police or the military, to prevent communal violence and other threats to public order. When US-backed terrorists known as the Contras were launching attacks across the Honduran border into Nicaragua, volunteers from the US-based group Witness for Peace found that their presence in villages and cooperative farms, which had been subjected to attack, served as an effective deterrent. Similarly, groups such as Peace Brigades International (PBI)—beginning in the late 1980s—sent teams to such countries as Guatemala, El Salvador, Sri Lanka, and Colombia. PBI would develop partnerships with local groups at the grassroots level, given that government authorities were either non-existent or working against them (Mahoney and Eguren 1997).

In the Middle East, Christian Peacemaker Teams (CPT) has engaged in nonviolent intervention in the occupied West Bank and the Gaza Strip: physically intervening when Israeli occupation forces invade Palestinian homes, providing accompaniment for Palestinian children facing violence from Israeli settlers while walking to school, monitoring treatment of Palestinians at Israeli military checkpoints and roadblocks, visiting Palestinian families facing threats and harassment from Israeli settlers, accompanying Palestinian farmers and shepherds prone to attacks by Israeli settlers, joining Israeli peace groups replanting orchards and vineyards destroyed by Israeli troops and settlers, and joining Palestinian and Israeli activists in resisting construction of the illegal separation wall in the West Bank. The International Solidarity Movement (ISM) engages in similar work, though it has a more explicit anti-occupation political orientation. These have included confronting Israeli armored vehicles and demolition equipment, removing Israeli roadblocks from Palestinian roads, participating in nonviolent anti-occupation demonstrations, escorting ambulances through Israeli checkpoints, assisting injured or disabled Palestinians in gaining access to medical care, and delivering food and water to families under house arrest or curfew restrictions. Both groups have tried to influence international media coverage, provide a sense of international solidarity for nonviolent anti-occupation activists, and serve to educate the public in volunteers' home countries upon their return.

The growth in transnational nongovernmental organizations focusing on human rights and the greater ease in real time communications also provide for an enhanced role by outside actors in support of nonviolent resistance struggles. This includes the rapid transmission of video documentation of attacks on nonviolent protesters by security forces, communiqués regarding the arrest of prominent nonviolent activists, and calls for international solidarity.

Case in Point: Iran

In reaction to the civil insurrection in Iran, which followed the apparently stolen election of June 2009, hardliners in the Iranian regime—often emulated by leftist bloggers in the West—attempted to blame everyone from the US government to nonviolent theorist Gene Sharp to various small NGOs engaged in educational efforts on strategic nonviolent action as somehow responsible for the popular uprising in Iran. The accusations appear to be based upon the rather bizarre assumption that millions of Iranians would somehow be willing to pour out onto the streets in the face of violent repression by state security forces simply because they had been directed to do so by people from an imperialist power that overthrew their last democratic government, and which subsequently propped up the tyrannical regime they installed in its place for the next quarter century.

In fact, there has been a longstanding Iranian tradition of such largely nonviolent civil insurrections against imperialist powers and autocratic rulers, and no outside power is needed to convince the Iranian people to rebel. Indeed, the idea that Americans could teach Iranians about massive nonviolent resistance is as likely as Americans teaching Iranians how to cook *fesenjan*. Most Iranians—who have traditionally been very proud of their political, social, and cultural history—would find it rather bizarre to learn that some in the West, ignorant of that very history, insisted that the protests were a result not of their own anger at an apparently stolen election and continued autocratic rule, but of Americans' instructions to do so.

In reality, uprisings like the one that commenced in 2009 have occurred with some regularity in Iran since the late 1800s. In 1890, unpopular concessions on tobacco and other products to the British led leading Shia clerics to call for nationalist protests and a nationwide tobacco strike, which succeeded in forcing the Shah (Mohammad Reza Pahlavi) to cancel the concession in early 1892. In 1905, in opposition to widespread corruption by the Qajar dynasty and allied regional nobles, as well as a series of other concessions to Russian and other foreign interests, an uprising initially led by merchants and clergy ensued that would continue for the next six years. In what became known as the Constitutional Revolution, many thousands of Iranians engaged in peaceful protests, boycotts and mass sit-ins, along with occasional riots and scattered armed engagements. The result was significant political and social reforms, including the establishment of an elected parliament to share power with the Shah and anti-corruption measures.

A CIA-sponsored coup in 1953 ousted the elected Prime Minister Mohammed Mossadegh and his nationalist supporters, and returned the exiled Shah to power as an absolute monarch. Through mass arms transfers from the United States, Shah Mohammed Reza Pahlavi built one of the most powerful armed forces ever seen in the Middle East. His American-trained secret police, the SAVAK, had been thought to have successfully terrorized the population into submission during the next two decades through widespread killings, torture, and mass detentions. By the mid-1970s, most of the leftist, liberal, nationalist, and other secular opposition leadership had been successfully repressed through murder, imprisonment, or exile, and most of their organizations banned. It was impossible to suppress the Islamist opposition as thoroughly, however, so it was out of mosques and among the mullahs that much of the organized leadership of the movement against the Shah's dictatorship emerged. Open resistance began in 1977, when exiled opposition leader Ayatollah Ruhollah Khomeini called for strikes, boycotts, tax refusal, and other forms of noncooperation with the Shah's regime. Such activism was met with brutal repression by the government. The pace of the resistance accelerated as massacres of civilians were answered by larger demonstrations following the Islamic forty-day mourning period. In the months that followed, Iranians employed many of the methods that would be used in the unarmed insurrections that toppled dictatorships in the Philippines, Latin America, Eastern Europe, and elsewhere in subsequent years: mass demonstrations, strikes, boycotts, contestation of public space, and the establishment of parallel institutions.

Despite the bloody image of the revolution and the authoritarianism and militarism of the Islamic Republic that followed, there was a clear commitment to keeping the actual insurrection largely nonviolent.

Protestors were told by the leadership of the resistance to try to win over the troops rather than attack them; indeed, thousands of troops deserted, some in the middle of confrontations with crowds. Clandestinely smuggled audio cassette tapes of Ayatollah Khomeini speaking about the revolution played a key role in the movement's mass mobilization, and led Abolhassan Sadegh, an official with the Ministry of National Guidance, to note that "tape cassettes are stronger than fighter planes." Ayatollah Khomeini's speeches, circulated through such covert methods, emphasized the power of unarmed resistance and noncooperation. In one speech, he said, "The clenched fists of freedom fighters can crush the tanks and guns of the oppressors." There were few of the violent activities normally associated with armed revolutions, such as shooting soldiers, setting fires to government buildings, or looting. Such incidents that did occur were unorganized and spontaneous and did not appear to have the support of the leadership of the movement (Shivers 1980).

In October and November of 1978, a series of strikes by civil servants and workers in government industries crippled the country. The crisis deepened when oil workers struck at the end of October and demanded the release of political prisoners, costing the government $60 million a day. An ensuing general strike on November 6 paralyzed the country. Even as some workers returned to their jobs, disruption of fuel oil supplies and freight transit, combined with shortages of raw materials resulting from a customs strike, largely kept economic life in the country at a standstill. Despite providing rhetorical support for an improvement in the human rights situation in Iran, President Jimmy Carter's administration continued military and economic support for the Shah's increasingly repressive regime, even providing fuel for the armed forces and other security services facing shortages due to the strikes. Under enormous pressure, the oil workers returned to work but continued to stage slowdowns. Later in November, the Shah's nightly speeches were interrupted when workers cut off the electricity at precisely the time of his scheduled addresses. Massive protests filled the streets in major cities in December as oil workers walked out again and an ongoing general strike closed the refineries and the central bank. Despite thousands of unarmed protesters being killed by the Shah's forces, the protesters' numbers increased, with as many as nine million Iranians taking to the streets in cities across the country in largely nonviolent protests. The Shah fled on January 16, 1979, and Ayatollah Khomeini returned from exile two weeks later. He appointed Mehdi Bazargan prime minister, thus establishing a parallel government to challenge the Shah's appointed prime minister, Shapur Bahktiar. With the loyalty of the vast majority clearly backing the new Islamic government, Bahktiar resigned February 11.

One element that contributed to people's willingness to mobilize under harsh repression was the value of martyrdom in Shia Islam. The movement's emphasis was to "save Islam by our blood." Indeed, there are interesting parallels between the legacy of martyrdom inspired by early Shia leader Imam Hossein and the Gandhian tradition of self-sacrifice. As demonstrated by their subsequent rule, the Iranian revolution's leadership—unlike Mohandas Gandhi—clearly did not support nonviolence as a principle, but recognized its utilitarian advantages against the well-armed security apparatus of the Shah's regime. While the revolution had the support of a broad cross section of society (including Islamists, secularists, nationalists, laborers, and ethnic minorities), Khomeini and other leading Shia clerics, strengthened by a pre-existing network of social service and other parallel institutions, consolidated their hold and established an Islamic theocracy. The regime shifted far to the right by the spring of 1981, purging moderate Islamists including the elected president, Abolhassan Bani-Sadr and imposing a totalitarian system.

In recent years, a new generation of Iranians is rising up in the tradition of previous generations using largely nonviolent tactics to challenge their oppression. Those out on the streets in Tehran, Isfahan, Tabriz, and other cities have not just been middle class intellectuals, but also represent a broad cross section of the poor and working class, and include both the majority Persians as well as other ethnicities. As of this writing, it is not clear whether the opposition in Iran can successfully organize a "people power" revolution of the kind that succeeded in ousting autocrats who attempted to steal elections in such countries as the Philippines in 1986, Serbia in 2000, or Ukraine in 2005, or whether—as in Azerbaijan, Belarus, and Mexico—the regime will remain in power. In any case, it is clearly a home-grown indigenous struggle. Any effort by the United States (which has allowed one—and possibly two—stolen elections to stand in recent years) to intervene will only hurt the pro-democracy movement. Given the history of US interventionism in Iran, President Barack Obama's cautious approach thus far will likely do more to help those in the current popular struggle than anything more explicit, despite oppositional demands to the contrary. The future of Iran belongs in the hands of the Iranians, and the best thing the United States can do to support a more open and pluralistic society in that country at this point is to stay out of the way.

Conclusion

Successful nonviolent revolutions, like successful armed revolutions, often take years or decades to develop as part of an organic process within the body politic of a given country. There is no standardized formula for success that a foreign government or a foreign non-governmental organization could put together, since the history, culture, and political alignments of each country are unique. No foreign government or NGO can recruit or mobilize the large numbers of ordinary civilians necessary to build a movement capable of challenging an established political leadership, much less toppling a government. It is important, therefore, to recognize that because nonviolent movements for human rights and democracy are by their nature indigenous, homegrown phenomena, they cannot be controlled by external actors.

Trainers and workshop leaders can emphasize certain strategies and tactics that have been successful elsewhere in applying pressure on governments to change their policies and in undermining the support and loyalty required for governments to successfully suppress the opposition. In some cases, local activists may try to emulate these models. However, a regime will lose power only if it tries to forcibly maintain a system that the people oppose, not because a foreign workshop leader described to a small group of opposition activists certain tactics that have been used successfully in another country at another time.

The primary positive role outside actors can play may be through example. The success of nonviolent struggles for democracy and against occupation in non-Western countries can provide inspiration for grassroots

pro-democracy groups. With the United States and other Western governments distributing billions of dollars worth of sophisticated armaments
in support for autocratic governments, providing occupying armies with
military and financial assistance, and maintaining large armed forces that
have themselves engaged in human rights abuses, the need for sustained,
strategic nonviolent action in the Middle East is no less than the need for
nonviolent action in the United States and other Western nations in opposition to such policies that help make such oppression possible.

6

Apathy, Aggression, Assertion, and Action

Managing Image for Nonviolent Success

Tom H. Hastings

> Perception may be understood as the process of selecting, organizing, and interpreting stimuli. In perceiving, we create what are called cognitive structures. Cognitive structures may be thought of as mental maps for assigning meaning to our existence and interactions.
> —Barbara A. Budjac Corvette, *Conflict Management*

Nonviolence and Image

> "The impact of these methods on the attitudes of others will vary considerably."
> —Gene Sharp, *Waging Nonviolent Struggle*

At the teacher orientation at the college where I started teaching, I asked one of the psychologists if he might be willing to come talk to my non-violence class sometime about the role of psychology in nonviolence. He looked at me blankly, asking, "What does psychology have to do with nonviolence?" I said, "Well, without psychology we have no chance for nonviolence to work at all."

If someone believes that you hate him and you will use any tactics to hurt or destroy him, he will have all the permission—and in fact, prompting—to use brutal tactics either in response or preemptively to stop you. Triggering conspecific predation in any way is maladaptive (Lopez-Reyes

1998). If someone believes you respect their personhood and only disagree about issues, they are at least inclined to let you live another day to lodge another protest. Fear is the precursor to most violence, but fear is diminished bilaterally by unilateral refrain from violence. That is the beginning of the power of nonviolence. It is simply psychologically adaptive to lower levels of fear if you'd like to survive long enough to make the other strategies of nonviolence work, as Peace Brigades International learned in Guatemala in 1985 when their accompaniment of the local nonviolent opposition candidates—several of whom had simply been assassinated the year before by the military junta—led to a cessation of overt, naked violence. Even though the lead state terrorist called them "wolves in sheep's clothing," they had already established their image internationally as absolutely nonviolent and as a group not fronting for guerrillas. None of their charges were assassinated, even though they were warned that they were targeted by the death squads that had been so active and so devastating (Mahony and Eguren 1997).

This deterrent value of a robust nonviolent image seems to be a factor in the startling advantage that strategic nonviolent struggle has over both violent insurgency and terrorism, with 53 percent, 26 percent, and 7 percent success rates, respectively (Stephan and Chenoweth 2008). Through the years 1955–65, as African Americans transitioned from nonviolent campaigns to riots and Black Panthers' threats of armed self-defense, legislative and social indices of gains stopped (Mills 1992); when the large, 100,000-member Students for a Democratic Society (SDS) devolved into bickering factions, including the violent Weathermen, SDS membership shrank and fell apart (Isserman 1992). Fear will cause sympathy to evaporate and progress to stall. Further, history reveals that most gains produced through fear will quickly evaporate unless that fear is constantly renewed (Gandhi 1938).

Battle Apathy with Images of Joy

In one of his television episodes, Michael Moore confronts the KKK. He wins. How?

No, he doesn't imitate some of the Klan-bashing mobs who scream and threaten.

No, he doesn't copy the dignified actions of the Civil Rights movement with sincere sit-ins or slow, calming songs.

No, you don't see him going to the house of the Grand Dragon, standing plaintively outside, à la *Roger and Me* and so many of his other films, vainly attempting to interview the top dog. He doesn't even self-emulate.

Instead, he brings his Love Squad, a racially mixed team of cheerleaders. They are dressed for it: cheerleading outfits, pom-poms, and they are all cute and smiling as they cancan kick, arms around each other, cheerily chanting:

"One, two, three, four!
We just want to love you more!
Five, six, seven, eight!
Even though you're filled with hate!"

Who could not love these young, chipper, smiling women, so clearly full of good will toward all? There they are, on national television, and the Ku Klux Klan members scowl impotently, likely losing sympathizers as they project churlish, childish rage at the sweet Love Squad.

Adversarial conflict is a zero-sum game at best, and often a lose-lose race to the bottom. Nonviolence, especially when presented with joy and creativity, can spark sympathy and opens a portal to victory over a bad idea or unjust practice, even as it offers validation for the humanity of the instigator of injustice. This is not compromise; it is powerful moral and political jujitsu. It destroys apathy by inviting the observer to join in the right, to belong with the good, to protect the sweet, and to be part of the fun. It also overcomes the apathy of burnout from the effects of rage-against-the-machine, from the self-immolation of perpetual anger at perpetrators of hate and violence and injustice. Those who practice the Joy of Resistance are in it for the long haul. Not the vapid joy of the ecstatic loopy but the real deep love of life that can roll right over the fires of hate and flow right into the caves of apathy, shining a love light on a struggle, inviting everyone along.

Images of Aggression and Consequences

When Rachel Corrie was run over by an Israeli Defense Force military bulldozer in early 2003, it pierced the hearts of those who teach peace and conflict studies in colleges and universities across the land. This young woman wrote beautiful and sincere pieces about wanting to help, about justice, about freedom, and about hope. She went to Palestine and Israel to help and she was murdered. Many of us in the field knew one or more of the professors who had been a part of sending her to her death. All of us were distraught. She could have been my student. I took it quite personally and still do. Indeed, at that very time I was advising a young student who looked remarkably like Rachel, and the practicum-abroad experience that she had found was with the International Campaign to Ban Landmines, in Eritrea. I was hyper-cautious in my advising, and even though this student did go to Eritrea, it was with a truckload of advice on how to proceed. I think that's when I started to get gray hairs.

The Rachel Corrie case was a classic example of image and aggression, image and sympathy, image and consequence. The alternative media showed her as she was for the vast majority of her brief life—sweet, loving, contemplative, altruistic, joyful. Mainstream media was noncommittal and had little to offer. The right wing found one photo of Rachel in black hijab, face contorted in what looked like a hateful shriek, a raging and angry jihadi wannabe. That photo, that one image, was used remorselessly by the right wing to "prove" that Corrie was no more than a dupe for Palestinian terrorists who would be slaughtering Jewish children as they slept in a little kibbutz. For many, that single image of Corrie self-slandered and slurred her short life and excused her death. With one snap of the shutter at one non-representative moment, the issue was settled. She courted what she got. She invited the worst and it happened. She chose sides, she threw in with the violent ones, and she paid the price. Oppressors usually prefer just enough violent resistance to justify overwhelming violent repression (Sharp 1973), but will manufacture the image if it is possible. Sadly, in this case, it was. A photo can be worth ten thousand lies. It was code. Did that photo show Rachel Corrie running guns, sheltering snipers, or cheering suicide bombers who massacred innocents at a wedding? No. That photo showed her in one ill-advised moment of chanting along with Palestinians frustrated at ongoing indignities and brutalities. That photo showed her anger at injustice, not her intention to support or commit terrorism, but that nuance was lost when the right wing cynically used that photo every time her case was considered.

While image should not be the arbiter of life and death, it can be. When we train nonviolent activists, we will either teach them to consider the effects of the images they produce or we will leave them bare to the winds of war, standing undefended against the manipulation used to justify violence. The semiotics of a smile or a grimace are far more powerful than perhaps they should be, but that is reality. Images that portray aggression are easily used to produce apathy. "Oh, she was one of those." How many people dismissed her death as just another combatant killed?

It is imperative to create and maintain an image of fairness and to avoid partisan overtones if we seek credibility. In 1968, the Women's International League for Peace and Freedom engaged in strong criticism of both the Soviet invasion of Czechoslovakia and the US occupation of Vietnam (Foster 1989). Without such balance, nonviolent activists can simply appear to be dupes, or tools, or even less charitably, "useful idiots." In the end, image is a function of a trained and disciplined set of individuals acting in concert with credibility to produce sympathy and even brave resistance on behalf of victims, as Nazis learned when confronted with civil but disobedient church leaders in Norway in 1942 (Jameson and Sharp 1963). Image matters a great deal.

Communicable Success

Using nonviolent communication techniques can help us avoid the image of defensiveness and its corollary, the negative attribution error. Intra-organizational communication and external communication benefit from: (1) differentiating observations from evaluations; (2) identifying, experiencing, and expressing feelings; (3) connecting feelings to needs; and (4) making and responding to requests in order to contribute to human flourishing. These skills are used in three modes: (1) honest expression, (2) empathic reception, and (3) self-empathy (Latini 2009, 20).

It is unhelpful to ignore observable fact, including behavior. It is helpful to acknowledge how those facts elicit certain feelings that are connected to needs. To validate all parties in this form of communication is decidedly enlightened self-interest. It creates a sharply human image, a transparent and compassionate portrayal of both individual and movement, and strikes people as refreshingly kind and honest, rather than brutally accusatory. This is the communicative power of music that soothes the savage breast lurking protectively in each of us. This becomes the beginning of an assertiveness that can promote nonviolent resistance to injustice, even as it lowers the levels of fear and tension that can lead to higher costs for all parties.

Speaking Truth to Power: The Peace de Resistance

"Iraqi children are totally innocent of oil power politics."
—Kathy Kelly, "Nonviolence and the
Ongoing War against Iraq"

When I give nonviolence trainings I stress that the more decades I engage in nonviolence, study nonviolence, and observe the consequences of campaigns, the more I'm convinced that nonviolent resistance is one part action, and nine parts media and training to influence others. Going out to engage in action without worrying about the recruiting, training, liaison work, coalition-building, and other aspects that bolster your power is simply ineffective. When we are fixated on individual spiritual witness or we are only concerned with burnishing our individual image to our radical compatriots, we miss the mark by a wide margin. Watching self-absorbed religious actionists sanctimoniously "speak truth to power" in ostentatious gestures of devotion is certainly more satisfying than watching masked demonstrators flipping off cops and throwing bricks, but the idea is to effect change, if possible, not to simply self-aggrandize spiritually or garner more radical credentials.

The first problem, then, is to examine speaking truth to power. Truth to the elite in power? Who cares? They aren't listening. It's long past time for us to think strategically, not like slaves to clichés. As Anne Braden reminded us just before many were about to be arrested at the White House in Washington for opposing war funding, "People are going to ask you if the president heard you. I want you to tell them, 'No, that's not who we were talkin' to. We were talkin' to the American people.'" That is the power to whom we are speaking our best truth. Failing to heed Anne's advice is a setup for failure. Understanding that our power in civil society is mostly latent and dwarfs all the other powers in its potential is our first strategic imperative. Our work is to transform that latent power into real usable power and to keep it informed and nonviolent.

This means that we have to be able to communicate to the bulk of our fellow citizens. Burning US flags will turn most of them off, as cathartically gratifying as that may be when the those flags lead invasions of foreign lands. Tossing stones through plate glass windows will certainly alienate most Americans—or Nigerians, or Colombians, for that matter. When Fox News overreached and became the media organizing power behind Tea Party assaults on town hall meetings on health care legislation, it pushed its role to the maximum and was ultimately burned badly by the kind of hate populism that created an image of gun-toting, spittle-flying, screaming know-nothings. Most of civil society was unimpressed. Fox News failed to separate its analysis of what Americans like in their Hollywood movies from what they like in their national conversations. From the other side, black-bloc types often appear to fail to understand movement-building as a precursor to success in public policy change or creation.

The program in which I teach is quite international, and this is part of what I try to impart to those who wish to have some political effect in America: you will either win the hearts and minds in the majority of our citizens or you will fail. Showing that you can speak stridently and cogently against US policies is a distant second to winning sympathy for the affected people hurt by US policy. So, when I work with Palestinian students who produce bombastic posters excoriating US policy, I ask them if they want to vent or achieve success. Most say success. I ask them to take my word for what might work a bit better in our culture, and we look at possible messaging strategies. The last thing they want to impart is that they are an inch away from donning an explosives belt and heading for the nearest pizza parlor. They need to create a far different and much more sympathetic image of Palestinians in the minds of Americans and for that they will need to be both vulnerable and diplomatic. They need to make Americans want to help. They need to help Americans understand that innocents are suffering as a result of US foreign policy and that only the citizenry can require policy change.

When children were attacked by dogs in Birmingham in the summer of 1963, that moved Americans. When Rosa Parks, a hardworking, modest, composed African American woman was arrested in December of 1955 for merely refusing to give up her seat to a white man on a Montgomery, Alabama bus, the nation reacted to that image and supported her.

In short, if we do not carefully craft a sympathetic image that motivates Americans to help, protect, save, or otherwise rescue the oppressed from the bullies of the world, we will almost certainly go down in noble defeat. It's hard work, but necessary. The image we craft is of our own making when we learn how to train our involved populace, and when we work hard with our media to help them help us help others.

Full "False Dichotomy Alert": Aggression or Apathy?

"The law of karma is actually very scientific. There is always a connection between cause and effect. It's like the light of a star, isn't it? The light that we see now was initiated so many light years ago, but there it is."
—Aung San Suu Kyi, *The Voice of Hope*

Well, we are asked in the so-called national discourse around injustice occurring someplace that Washington has deemed important to our national interest, do we want to bomb somebody or just do nothing? Our entire mission in the fields of nonviolence studies, conflict resolution, peace and justice studies, peace and conflict studies (or whatever permutation of alternative constructive conflict management you like) is to suggest, research, develop, and call for the third path: *assertion*. The difference between assertion and aggression is quite thin, but quite bright, and you need to get right up to that line if you want to be effective. Hang back and the oppressor can ignore you. Cross it and he now has his excuse to crush you. But when you come up to that line, if you step back a bit when you sense you have crossed into aggression, and if you come right back to it after any seeming defeat, you will most often win. That is assertion and that is the winning modality. The image of black citizens in Montgomery walking miles to work every day for a year, rather than ride segregated buses, was assertion at its best. They won. As one elderly woman (Mother Pollard) famously told Dr. Martin Luther King Jr., "My feets is tired, but my soul is rested." Even Montgomery whites got it eventually, and whites across the country got it almost right away.

I watched the same strategy employed by indigenous people struggling to regain their treaty rights in northern Wisconsin. They were out long hours, far past midnight as temperatures plunged, snow still in the woods, night after night, for three springs in a row (1989–91). They were abused, but no one could humiliate them. The more racist the language and the more violent the opposition to them, the more they persisted with great dignity and grace. Public polls switched to support them. They never reacted with hatred and violence to hatred and violence, and they won enormous respect. They were right on that thin bright line, never once backing down when hundreds of screaming racists surrounded small handfuls of them. The same native people would come back out the next night. I've never witnessed stronger nonviolence, better image creation, or a more swift and direct change in public opinion.

Creating an image of violent opposition, however justified, is maladaptive. Creating an image of slinking, cowering, pusillanimous retreat is maladaptive. Creating and maintaining an image of courageous assertion is most adaptive. It works, and those who understand the vectors of image and recruitment will adapt and win.

Manipulation by the Numbers

If you don't like how the mainstream media manipulates you, then learn to manipulate mainstream media, instead. What are the steps involved?

They are macroscopic steps, such as retraining the nation, as demonstrated by student leaders who engineered the nonviolent overthrow of Slobodan Milošević. Intra-movement education and training is first. We cannot expect spontaneous, nonviolent *satori* without dissemination of information on the methods.

Develop relationships with mainstream media reporters, correspondents, photographers, videographers, editors, and anchors. Help them understand that your movement desires an image, is working diligently to train and educate itself to live up to that image, and is highly motivated to help them get the story and get it right.

The same thing goes with law enforcement. If officers believe you are coming out to rock and roll, they will cheerfully oblige, much to your detriment. Work very hard to help each police liaison learn that you are nonviolent, you are not sneaky, and that you earnestly want them to fade back, in general, so your people can provide their own security and policing. Obviously, if the primary objective of your movement is, in fact, to call attention to police brutality, this is a much more sensitive and difficult task, but it can and should be done or the police will work very hard to erode your image.

Develop conversations and working relationships with those who favor violence or random property destruction. Let them vent; it's their strong suit. Appeal to their sense of movement manners, i.e., when you do all the organizing for a campaign or event and they aren't part of the hardworking planning group, they should show the respect for your efforts that you show for theirs. You share a common understanding of how tough it is to recruit and organize, and they will generally respect that. Stress that your leadership has been meeting and meeting and meeting; it has reached consensus on the tone, tenor, and practices of your events; and you will not come to their events and act against their decisions—and you expect the same from them.

There are, of course, innumerable smaller steps involved in creating the image you feel will garner at least the sympathy of the majority, if not its active participation. It involves a great deal of discipline, follow-up, relational upkeep, and anticipation. The greater the goal, the more complex and sustained your movement needs to be to overcome any image problems or erosion. The payoff is victory. You can change public opinion 180 degrees. It happens, and it's connected at least somewhat to the work you do to create and successfully defend and propagate your image to the constituencies who can do you the most good.

Image, Nonviolence, and Lifting Blocks to Progress

> In January of 1968 an invitation came from the government of North Vietnam Professor Howard Zinn and myself were invited to Hanoi to bring home 3 captive American airmen.
> —Daniel Berrigan, SJ, *The Trial of the Catonsville Nine*

In the 1980s, there was a generalized conventional wisdom that the end of apartheid would be a bloody, brutal process of slaughtering minority whites by the black majority, who had been brutalized and who were the victims of massively systemic human rights violations. Nightmarish visions of machete or machine-gun wielding blacks—like the Mau Mau (actually, Kikuyu) of a generation earlier in Kenya, featuring violence against the white occupiers (1952–60)—were the common fear. Indeed, immediately following those events (1961), the African National Congress's (ANC) shift from nonviolent tactics to the formation of the Umkhonto we Sizwe (Spear of the Nation), the military wing of the ANC, helped solidify those fears and assumptions.

But a military uprising would have been enormously costly; as soon as the ANC abandoned nonviolence, ten of its leaders were arrested and convicted in the Rivonia trial of 1961 and sent to prison. Mandela was among them, and the image of a violent insurgency served to make that movement more commonplace. Such events deprived black South Africans of worldwide status as clearly innocent victims, and instead introduced the fear of the bloodbath. As a result, Walter Sisulu, Nelson Mandela, and others languished in prison (Merideth 1997). Violence can serve to justify such long incarceration, even when the violence was begun by the ruling elite, and even when the insurgent violence is directed not at people, but at infrastructure (as the Umkhonto we Sizwe sabotage was).

Then came a new generation of young black leaders in the townships who organized mass strategic campaigns, including brilliantly crafted boycotts, both nationally and internationally, and apartheid fell. To add to the nonviolent tool kit, Archbishop Desmond Tutu helped launch a national Truth and Reconciliation Commission (TRC), which convened from 1996 to 1998, and the image of nonviolence in South Africa took on an additional layer of evolved practice right where it all began: it was in South Africa on September 11, 1908 that Mohandas Gandhi announced his first campaign of mass, nonviolent resistance against the Asiatic Registration Laws. Like the improvements to nonviolent strategies that the American civil rights movement (1955–65) achieved—such as immediately capitalizing on oppressor violence, as African American students did in Nashville in 1960 when whites bombed their lawyer's home—the South African TRC added a special tool to the box. Whites were only going to cede power in South Africa if threats were diminished. The first threat was the potential for a bloodbath, and the new generation opened a window that made the change possible without additional slaughter. The second threat was the potential for arrest of most of the white leadership for provable crimes against humanity; the white leadership demanded amnesty before stepping aside, and so it was written directly into the new constitution (Vora and Vora 2004, 301).

We see in the South African case that image can retard or accelerate forward motion toward success. Reevaluation and rehabilitation of image is a part of the ongoing work of any struggle. It's not a question of justice—for those who subscribe to the just war doctrine, violent revolution in South Africa was absolutely justified—but rather of efficacy. Convincing a dangerous oppressor that you aren't going to stoop to his tactics once you win will get that victory far faster.

Something to Hide, Fear, Crush

"Secrecy interferes with the subtle political and psychological mechanisms at work during nonviolent action. An essential aspect of the power of nonviolence is the way in which personal and group

qualities such as honesty, commitment, conviction, courage, and
integrity cause shifts of loyalty and thus undermine the power of
the opponent. Secrecy subverts this process."
—Robert J. Burrowes, *The Strategy
of Nonviolent Defense*

A movement that explicates itself and appears to engage in deliberative
dialogue with all comers is a movement that doesn't generate nearly as
much fear, and thus oppression, as do movements that are covert, sneaky,
deceptive, and which generate an image of sneering superiority. Of course,
it's all culturally relative, but still more or less generalizable. How do we
instill the desire to work hard on creating and maintaining this kind of
positive image? Gandhi used fasting as penance for failures in *satyagraha*
conduct, or he occasionally called off an entire campaign (Gandhi 1983).
Cesar Chavez did the same. It's different in every culture, every struggle.

Serbia illustrates several pieces of this puzzle. The Balkans are famous
for terrorism, often inflicted by the state, and Slobodan Milošević was an
exemplar of that. He presided over a nationalistic regime marked by forc-
ible annexations, concentration and rape camps, ethnic cleansing, and
extraordinary suppression of minorities. Both internal and external powers
attacked him violently, and he strode through with swagger and an aura
of the Serb standing alone in courageous defiance of all those who would
attack Serbs. What finally brought him down was the unexpected soft
power of nonviolence and community organizing writ large. The Serb
youth started it all, organizing demonstrations, mock conventions, humorous but highly political street theater, and a web and alternative media
presence that was infused with joyous rebellion.

They kept at it, and eventually enlisted mainstream political opposition leadership in a coalition that toppled the regime via elections, a general strike, and ultimately a takeover of Parliament. The youth movement
(Otpor!) had open offices, held frequent open public demonstrations and
actions, and was markedly different from the youth demonstrations of western Europe and the United States, in that none of its demonstrators acted
violently or covertly. None ever wore face coverings of any sort—no ban-
danas or masks to hide identities, even though the potential for police and

army capture, torture, and worse was far greater than in western Europe or the United States. I asked one of the Otpor! organizers, Srđa Popović, if any of them ever wore masks.

He laughed. "Never! We wanted everyone to know that these were local kids, nice young people who simply wanted to work for a better future."

Some of the kids were beaten, at one point, when the government became desperate and tried to declare Otpor! a terrorist group. This backfired on the government—the people knew better and Milošević lost even more popularity as his policies produced war, international pariah status for Serbia, and economic hardship for Serbs. Milošević bet that his police and soldier brutality would provoke an in-kind response and thus justify even harsher methods "necessary" to maintain domestic order. Instead, the nonviolent discipline and transparency of his civil society opponents clearly won the day. Milošević lost the loyalty of his people, his police, his soldiers, and he lost the election and his power, and was turned over to the international community to stand trial. He died in prison and the trial was never concluded, but the effectiveness of transparent nonviolence was made quite obvious in that struggle.

Another backfire case was the dioxin poisoning of Viktor Yushchenko on September 5, 2004, at a dinner with state security officers during the presidential campaign in Ukraine. Yushchenko was the clear frontrunner to replace Leonid Kuchma's unpopular regime, which was aligned with Vladimir Putin in Russia, and when Yushchenko survived the attempt on his life and resumed campaigning, sickened and disfigured, his popular support grew deeper, wider, and more fervent than ever, standing by the scores of thousands in frigid Ukraine winter weather to defend his clear victory in the vote (Åslund and McFaul 2006). Literally, the image of the nonviolent Orange Revolution was poor Yushchenko's visage, permanently aged and ravaged, and that image of innocent victim prevailed over the brutality exerted by Putin, Kuchma, and Viktor Yanukovych. Since then, Yanukovych made a comeback and Yushchenko is out, but the image of vulnerable strength was important in the success in 2005.

In the above cases, nonviolence was not a philosophical commitment for many, but rather a strategic commitment. Philosophies of nonviolence are compelling (Chernus 2004), but the clarity of commitment is more influential than philosophy or religion in these cases.

Identity as Image

"The root cause of war is this old, and now obsolete, mental division of the world into 'us' and 'them'."
—Winslow Myers, *Living beyond War: A Citizen's Guide*

Who we are in the eyes of others is the image we project, but of course that image comes across differently for everyone who reads it because, as we know from the field of constructive conflict management, no two people's perspective is identical. Thus, we try to project an image of who we mean to be, but the perception of that image is modified by each person's observational powers. Some are affected by personal trauma and cannot see that we mean them no harm. Some are affected by cultural bias and cannot trust that we have no secret hegemonic agenda. Some are professionally trained to be suspicious of all who lodge a challenger message. Some are mostly sheltered by their own narrow vision, blinkered by their struggle for survival. Many are overwhelmed by the clutter of contradictory information and are infused with media imagery that extrapolates from one version of reality into hyperbole and distortion.

How can we overcome these blocks to accurate perception of our identity? Primarily through patient persistence and ongoing outreach. For example, after I went out into the north woods of Michigan in 1985 to physically dismantle a portion of a thermonuclear command center that was part of Project ELF (Extremely Low Frequency), I used my subsequent jail time to write letters to editors of small town publications. I did an interview on the local affiliate of public radio. I met with the editor of the only daily paper in the area. Although the first reaction to my message in all cases was incredulity or hostility, careful reworking of the arguments, considerate reframing of the issues, and the simple discipline of restraint and establishing commonalities with the local people helped. It's doable, but it takes time.

Images of the United States: Exceptionalism = Fundamental Negative Attribution Error

"I was given the opportunity to address the congregation of a conservative church [in America] on the subject of the European peace movement and our objectives. I was pleasantly surprised to see the minister and her husband, the pastor, wearing 'Swords into Ploughshares' badges on their white robes. . . . I was constantly surprised to find peace the topic for discussion at church discussion evenings. The subject which most concerned these meetings was the way American arms policy causes deaths in the Third World every day, and is also one of the factors responsible for the catastrophes of famine and disease."

—Petra Kelly, *Fighting for Hope*

Petra Kelly was a German Green. The image of the United States throughout the world is vastly different from our image of ourselves. Some would call this disparity the fundamental negative attribution error. That is, when Americans make mistakes, we view them as the result of honorable intentions and pure motives, but others would call this hypocrisy or a double standard or grossly patronizing. What is so dangerous is that we are failing as a nation to correct the facts that reveal the United States to be a global hawk, a planetary predator, a militaristic corporate raptor.

How do we fix it? Close overseas bases. We have hundreds of military bases—almost 1,000 of them—on the sovereign soil of other people's lands (Lutz 2009). Stop exporting arms. We can earn income in other ways. We can earn loyalty with other methods. We will never be an honest broker of peace and a supplier of arms at the same time. Transform the military from aggressive and offensive and violent to protective, de-escalatory, and nonviolent. Never ever invade another country with violent forces.

Of course, there are many other practices and principles that can help positively change the image of the United States in the world, and many plans for doing that. I only offer the most basic, and most structural. Achieving these would dampen the damage worldwide, and would lead to many other changes that would be just and sustainable. Can a nation-state use Gandhian methods? At least we can learn that the methods that

Gandhi used to combat colonialism have a great deal of transferability to work on other issues (Chapple 1993). To the extent possible, it would be wise to attempt to alter the behavior of our nation-state as well.

Changing the image of a movement is hard work. Changing the image of a nation-state is even harder. But it is possible and desirable. The journey of 10,000 miles, says the *Tao Te Ching*, begins with one step.

Strength through Peace: Images of Resolution

> "Go out and return with a basket full of wisdom."
> —Vietnamese proverb, quoted in John
> Balaban, *Remembering Heaven's Face*

The focus of every activity of every peace and justice movement is recruitment. Even if the focus is not recruitment, it is. All decisions about movement activities ought to pass through a sieve that asks, will this activity increase recruitment? If the answer is no, don't do it unless you plan to modify it or supplement it so that it can recruit.

Isn't this reductionist? Yes, somewhat. But if this question is not central to the planning of any activity, how will the movement ever become effective? Nonviolence succeeds when mass action compels rulers to negotiate with movement representatives or risk a far worse consequence, even an existential challenge. That negotiation is made much more likely when opponents are approached from an invitational standpoint, without any loss of dignity (Terkel 1996), even as those opponents are being profoundly challenged. We see the difference in indigenous-majority Western hemisphere nations: the shift from revolutionary leftist *campesinismo* struggles to *indianismo* conflict is not existentially threatening to extant rulers (Pallares 2002). Reducing perception of danger reduces likelihood of furious response.

There is, then, a natural tension that occurs when the leadership of a nonviolent movement needs to convince others that success is possible, since success involves challenging and overcoming an opponent that is often simply fearsome. There is a natural frisson of fear and excitement at the possibility of something so dramatic as success. At the height of this tension, the drama of events can break through the typical media tendency to ignore nonviolent efforts (Harris 2002). Here is where an image of strength and power through nonviolence can generate the hope and raised expectations that social scientists say will assist recruitment (Kriesberg 2007), provided the nonviolent posture doesn't itself stray from being a dignified challenger movement and instead embrace a culturally alienating love of suffering (Groves 2000).

It is then that a tipping point of power to the movement augers success. Controlling this shifting, evolving image is how a challenger movement can break through previously impenetrable walls and trigger mass recruitment and transformative change. Leadership that is exceedingly conscious of image can ride this tension to victory, as we saw in Birmingham in the summer of 1963 and in many other cases, when the oppressor's failure to manage the image of the movement accompanied the shift. Moral leadership—via priests, ministers, nuns, rabbis, and imams—can quickly and strongly create sympathetic legitimacy (Hodge and Cooper 2004; Nepstad 2008), and that should be an integral part of movement strategy.

Employing these methods, mere protestors suddenly find themselves sitting at the negotiating table and gains are made from a position of power, as took place in 1996 in northern Wisconsin. There, civil resistance of Native Americans was so resolute, so dignified, and was articulated with such cultural clarity to the threat of a mining corporation's intentions to ship millions of gallons of sulfuric acid across the Bad River Chippewa reservation. Tribal members set up a prayer and drumming camp on the tracks, and the sheriff so admired their courage and calm that he refused to arrest them. Soon, tribal leaders were invited to negotiate and they earned major victories. On a much larger scale, in Poland, the trade union Solidarity went from outlawed status to negotiating partner as the Communist dictatorship crumbled in the face of overwhelming people power—a particularly ironic victory, since many Communist authors favored violence as the way to revolution (Breyman 2001).

These are the historical moments to which nonviolent movements aspire, when the militaristic imperial dictum "peace through strength" is flipped, and a positive "peace power" transformation produces a nonviolent mantra of "strength through peace" instead.

7

Our Actions Are Louder than Words

Gender, Power, and a Nonviolent Movement toward Peace

Supriya Baily

> For those who would drive the team of peace
> must link arms on either side,
> harness their anger against injustice,
> conquer the fears of centuries.
> Those who would run the course of fire
> must run in waves that shift their lands
> from strife to shared endeavor.
>> —David Adams, "The Dawning
>> of Peace"

Introduction

Who are the peacemakers? The role of peacemaker is well known, especially in the context of those world leaders who speak the language of peace and reconciliation and have extensive experiences to hold and exert their power in multiple domains and capacities. Other peacemakers are active in communities that value their commitment to peace, such as places of worship, schools, and progressive social institutions. Peacemakers emerge through the door of celebrity, with causes to champion, and still others research and write about the scholarly aspects of peace and maintain a sense of activism through the reflective work they do to move the agenda of peace forward. Yet, outside of these categories, there are peacemakers who are working on a daily basis to build a culture of peace

135

without labeling it as such, who are working to dismantle age-old prejudices, and who are ensuring a safer future for their communities. These
are the unheralded peacemakers.

In the movement to understand peacemaking at the grassroots level,
women are increasingly encouraged to be seen as the local arbiters of
peace by national and international entities. Yet, it appears that international organizations have done little to correct the deplorable extent to
which local women have been relegated to the margins (Hunt and Posa
2001, 39), and there is very little understanding of the role women take on
to build a peaceful community, especially in those societies that are not
under active military interventions or wars. Swanee Hunt and Cristina
Posa (2001) highlight the role of women in conflict situations like Bosnia,
Burundi, and Israel. Unfortunately, outside of those movements, there is
slim to little information on how the actions of women in local communities contribute to building a culture of peace.

In discussing the role of women as peacemakers, the goal of this chapter is not to revisit the debate between the gendered argument of men and
women as peacemakers. My only foray into that argument here is to recognize that there is an inherent battle in the feminist movement regarding whether the qualities of peacemakers are the same qualities deemed
"appropriate" for women to exhibit. This is well contested in feminist literature; my point is not to "valorize women's experiences as peacemaker"
(Forcey 1991, 350), but to present how the actions undertaken in one community, spearheaded by a small group of women at the grassroots level,
leads me to liken their actions to those of peacemakers.

Context

It is often said that "violence begets violence," but this does not always
prove to be true. Women around the world suffer all forms of violence,
if for no other reason than that they were born women. Violence is often
defined in ways that focus attention on physical pain or harm to one's
being or property, but Collins (1998, 921) suggests that for violence to be
properly understood, it must be conceptualized "as a more dynamic concept whose complexity lies in its socially embedded nature." Women are

often viewed as subservient to men and their limited status, resources, and power, contribute to the worldwide forms of violence women face.

Yet, one of the ways women have primarily sought to change their status and role in society has been through collective action. Women's collective action increased during the twentieth century, and one area that has been directly impacted by women's action has been in the work of environmental protection. Women in culturally diverse countries such as Indonesia and Canada often use civil disobedience methods to promote their causes. In fact, it has been said that women in India were using forms of collective action before civil disobedience was used by Mohandas Gandhi as a tool to defeat the British during India's struggle for independence. This history has been cited at the highest levels of Western multilateral agencies, where even the former director of the United Nations Development Fund for Women (UNIFEM) states (Snyder 2003, 620):

> Historically, women laid the roots of their development movement by mobilizing and protesting colonial policies for generations—often to preserve their capacities to provide for their children . . . ; they mobilized, first, for independence struggles . . . and then to debate their own roles in their new nations.

Though there is a history of honoring women speaking out, the context of a United Nations entity lauding these efforts continues to promote the influence of a Western hegemonic process where these organizations encourage women to speak to the new post-colonial nation-building process. This promotes a Western agenda on development such that the "strategic, temporal initiative to harness the strength and unity of the nation as a part of an ongoing, critical process of decolonization, not as recolonization" (Sefa-Dei 2005, 272) gets muddied based on whose interests are at stake. This lens of peacemaking moves the debate slightly away from the mandates of development, since there is a more iterative process at work with the women rather than an economic agenda to be solely exploited.

Within this frame, I look at how one community negotiated relationships of power as a vehicle toward their own empowerment, and as a result, found evidence of actions that emphasized the role of peacemakers in local communities. The stories and voices below draw attention to the often-understated role of bridging conflict in the community by a group of people with little power, a history of marginalization, and a clear sense of commitment to the local community in which they have spent most, if not all their lives.

This chapter stems from a larger research project to understand how women in rural India worked collaboratively to engage their communities in development efforts as a result of their participation in nonformal education programs. Using the case of one village, I explore how the changes women championed created and sustained a culture of peace in their community, developing a framework in which we come to understand how women—with limited education, power, and agency—undertook endeavors pushing them to challenge historical roles and prejudices. As a result, this opened the minds of others in their community, leading them to become peacemakers. Their struggles, their quest for better lives, and their activist spirits emerged as far away as imaginable from the world and work of peace and justice studies, yet efforts such as theirs are central to the bigger goals of building and sustaining cultures of peace. Finally, this chapter presents the voices of grassroots peacemakers, highlights the changes they made, and identifies those qualities in the women that foster a culture of peace. As the need for peace continues to grow, it is critical to our future to understand the role, importance, and trajectories of grassroots peacemakers, and the power of their actions as they journey simultaneously from disempowerment to empowerment and navigate the role and power of peace in their communities.

Situating the Case

To understand the role of a grassroots peacemaker, it is critical to understand the setting within which they live and work. India is a country of vast dichotomies where both modernity and tradition live side by side. As both the homeland of Gandhi and the setting of violent riots between Hindus and Muslims, where one can see the presence of strong female leaders and extreme cases of gender disparities, India is a complicated and complex nation. While such extremes in progress are common in most countries,

India, which faces high levels of poverty and marginalization on the one hand, while quickly becoming a respected player on the world stage on the other, makes these dichotomies far more visible, as a result.

The beauty of the village I studied is that it is a community that could be representative of so many others in rural areas around the developing world. (I have changed the names of people and their locales here in order to protect their privacy.) Sanjuktahalli is located at the outskirts of a small town, Kanthi, which has a bustling population. To arrive at Sanjuktahalli, I traveled off the main highway connecting two cities in southern India and drove through Kanthi. After passing a large water reservoir and seeing a number of buses careening around the narrow roads, I encountered Sanjuktahalli as it emerged from behind a bend in the road, rather close to Kanthi, making it more accessible and less isolated than other rural villages. On the far side of the road from the village, there were three or four little shacks selling local staples like bananas, *beedis* (local cigarettes), and peanut brittle. A few drunks were also loitering there, but were not permitted to come to the near side closer to the village.

The village sits on the crest of higher ground. At the entrance of the village is a small temple devoted to a particular deity, which is tribal in nature. (Providing the name of the god would make it impossible to keep the name of the village confidential.) About 100 feet from the temple, up a dirt road, there are two sturdy looking buildings, each about fifteen feet by ten feet in size. The first is a guesthouse for the temple, where visiting devotees may spend the night, but on a daily basis is used as a nursery school/daycare center for children in the village below the age of five. Above this, is a meeting hall, the pride and joy of the women in Sanjuktahalli, as they were responsible for every aspect of building the structure, from raising the money, to contracting the builders, to taking over and building it themselves when the contractors were in danger of going over budget and delaying the finish. The two-room building is used by the women for their meetings, for local events, and is rented out to other members of the village for special occasions.

The school is at the other end of the village, about one-quarter of a mile away. In between these two buildings, in three parallel rows, the forty or so houses of the village stand. These houses range from small shacks with dried coconut frond roofs, to brick and cement two- to three-room houses painted in bright colors, with red oxide-painted floors. The village has three wells, electricity, and no running water or toilet facilities. Behind the three rows of houses, in the dip behind the elevated land on which the houses sit, are the fields where many of the villagers work.

The Peacemakers

A small band of women worked together to improve their day-to-day lives in Sanjuktahalli. Over the course of seven years, these women came together to create a self-help group, a local group that took out microcredit loans and attended trainings related to farm labor, accounting, budgeting, trade, health, and well-being. By talking with women, the power-holders around them, and people involved in nonformal education efforts in the village, a story emerged of the measures women took on a day-to-day basis, allowing me to develop a more acute picture of their role in grassroots peacebuilding efforts.

In Sanjuktahalli, I spoke with many women, among whom was the local nursery school teacher (age 20–25); a worker at the nursery school (age 30–35); a woman whose husband was being disinherited by his parents, and was dealing with corrupt lawyers (age 50–55); a woman (age 40–45) with three children between the ages of 10 and 15; a woman (age 60–65) married to the local priest, and having one surviving son and two grandchildren; and a woman (age 45–55) married to the local electrician who was prominent in the village. The women narrated their stories over two weeks highlighting acts of peace that impacted the community around them, allowing them to live a more tranquil life with greater expectations of safety and security in their community.

Acts of Peace

In a community as small as Sanjuktahalli, every action can have either positive or negative repercussions echoing through the populace. The choices made by individuals can determine whether the ramifications of those actions help or hinder the promotion of a peaceful community. As

Amy Betit and Mary Elizabeth Lynch (2004) observe, "The qualities of peacemaking . . . can be present in any mundane situation of life, not just the big decisions. Each time that we encounter an irritation or a conflict, we have a choice to make. We can either fan the flames and stimulate the conflict to grow intense, or we can actively seek the 'message in the conflict' and work to find a peaceful and creative solution."

The actions uncovered in this chapter are a sampling of the efforts women undertook in the village to act as peacemakers. Viewed under a microscope, it can be seen that these measures improved the standard of life in the community, but as one pulls back, it is clear that these actions were small steps taken by individuals to build a culture of peace at the most grassroots level.

Collaboration as an act of peace. Deciding to collaborate was one of the first things the women quickly incorporated into their daily practice in their village. Gavriel Salomon and Baruch Nevo (2002) define the concept of positive peace as encompassing a spirit of collaboration along with integration and cooperation. Working together, the women learned that the power of their actions could reverberate further if they had the support of the group behind them.

> LAXMI: "If the group comes to know about a certain issue, we talk about it in the group, so we sit and decide. If everyone agrees, we proceed. Otherwise, no."
>
> SWATI: "We always cooperate and take them along. Even if they are against, we somehow see that they are with us."

The women were very conscious in their conversations with me about how they engaged the community in their activities, with collaboration being a central facet of their strategy. This could be seen as continuing to promote the "traditional" roles of women over men, as collaboration is often seen as a hallmark of how women work in groups. Hunt and Posa (2001, 41) have studied how social science research continues to support "the stereotype of women as generally more collaborative than men," and this might be something for us to remain aware of as we look at these women as peacemakers.

In describing the setting, I mentioned a two-room building, which was the pride and joy of the women in Sanjuktahalli. It was built to help the women run their microcredit business, but was also used to help the community (discussed below). In talking with the women about this project, as well as other development related projects, Lata said: "As we were doing all these things, [the headman might think we are] 'stubborn, leaving me and doing all these things!' But we never used to leave him. Sometimes we used to call him. If we leave him, there might be a rift in the village. We used to ask him to accompany us. We did not want any fights and misunderstandings in the village."

Cooperation, engagement of others in the community and building consensus are all hallmarks of strong peacemakers (United Nations 1992). The women in Sanjuktahalli showed an innate understanding of human relationships, and through some of the trainings they undertook, they learned practical skills to facilitate cooperative meetings.

Sharing as an act of peace. Another act of peace involved the women's sharing of their two-story building. Though the community could rent the building on a regular basis from the women, the women were also willing to open up their property and share it with those around them as opportunities were presented. In Smita's words: "[They] kept *raagi* [a type of millet], on the premises, since it was raining. The raagi would have gone [to] waste [until the threshing machine made its stop in the village], so [another member of the village] came and requested . . . the room, and we obliged."

In fact, one village leader, Gopal told me, "So much has been achieved by them. . . . [W]hen the villagers perform a marriage, or in times of trouble, all come to the community hall, eat here, cook here. If they get guests and there is no place in the house, they use this building. If there are any rituals, then they do it here and they have kept it very neat and clean. Everyone is very poor here, with very small houses. Suppose there is a marriage, there is no place for five or six people to sit . . . ; this is very useful."

The act of sharing is an attribute of peacemaking. Conflict resolution can be anchored on a number of different foundations, and among them is the ability to promote the process of "sharing of our common resources" (Murithi 2006, 32). Conflict is minimized when a spirit of sharing is already part of the culture of the community. In this instance, the women set the example in their community and perhaps caused traditional maternal practices—"characterized by such descriptive words as receptivity, relatedness, responsiveness . . . empathy and caring"—to influence others to engage in more nonviolent behavior (Forcey 1991, 338).

Eliminating stressors as an act of peace. The women also acted as peacemakers by providing tangible security. Specifically, the women took on the onerous task of changing local community norms by eliminating alcohol in their village. Krishnan's study on violence against women found that "men who consume alcohol are less likely to resolve marital conflicts without resorting to violence and are more likely to enter into situations of conflict" (2005, 772). Though alcohol is heavily taxed in the state where Sanjuktahalli is located, women talked of how their husbands might have been "at a drinking party from morning to evening" and took to keeping "a bottle under (their) pillow" and, as a result, developed a ban on alcohol in their village. The women in Sanjuktahalli were aware that the absence of alcohol in the community was one of their more well-appreciated efforts; if it was not immediately apparent, that appreciation became clear over the course of time.

This courageous act caused the community to "[spew] venom at us." As alcohol consumption was a community norm, there were no official paths for eliminating alcohol, but over time the women pronounced the ban, spoke directly will sellers to alter their practices, and stood firm in spite of every provocation on the part of the villagers. Smita explained, "They also spoke two words; we also spoke two words [i.e., a discussion was had]. . . . Anyway, the liquor was not sold here. . . . [T]hey go to the other places and use the facilities for drinking . . . , not anywhere here."

It is important to clarify that in such a community with limited resources, selling alcohol was also one way of earning a living for some women. The women in the cooperative knew that they would have to step in to help another village woman (who was not in the cooperative) find an alternate livelihood. Working together, the women taught her how to make snacks and incense sticks to alter her income potential. They also appealed to her guilt and her solidarity with the other women in the village where they said, "If a man comes and beats his wife, are you going to be a bystander? Do something else. . . . Leave this!"

The women were aware that they had not stopped all the men from drinking all of the time, but they recognized that they halted some of the more troublesome aspects of having liquor close to the village. The women said the men used to take the women's money to buy alcohol, but now, the women have started to keep most of their money in the bank, thereby limiting the men's access to the funds. They also said the men who were poor could not afford the bus fare to Kanthi to buy liquor there, so they stayed home more. Finally, for the ones who were still stubborn and went to Kanthi to drink, they were usually sober by the time they returned and were unable to cause any trouble at home since they would have to either walk back or take a bus ride, during which they would sober up, returning home more passive than if they had come from across the street drunk and disorderly.

Community improvement as an act of peace. Taking care of others less fortunate than themselves was also a facet of the work of the women in Sanjuktahalli. The women provided books, pens, and pencils for school children. The women recognized the impact of their influence in the village and this style of philanthropy earned the goodwill of others, leading to the development of a culture of peace in the community.

Other actions taken by the women were development oriented and resulted in an improved community for all villagers in Sanjuktahalli. In the first of these, the women targeted the safety of children, who faced long walks of over five kilometers on rugged highways to go to school. The women petitioned local political leaders and influenced them to provide a school right in the heart of Sanjuktahalli. This was a huge accomplishment: not only were they providing a school for the children, but the mere presence of the school influenced many more families to send their children, especially their daughters, to school. Secondly, the women were able to petition the electricity board to provide electricity to the village. Finally, they were able to use their savings as part of a collective to build two bore wells in the village for everyone's use. As Lata described it, "We have asked for homes for the homeless. So many of them are living in rented houses. We have approached them so many times; we have brought the electricity to the village. There was no water, [but] we got the water tank, we got the water facility."

The Qualities of Peacemakers

The women who manifested the four themes described above in creating a culture of peace had little formal community development education and negligible formal knowledge of peacemaking. Navigating their community, the women used their instincts to exhibit strategies that are grounded in peace, highlighting certain qualities that could be considered central to the evolution of a peacemaker.

Stuart Twemlow and Frank Sacco (1996, 164) define the peacemaker as one who would stress "the protection of the weak by the strong, powerful, and gentle warrior," and the notion of peacemaking as "the view that violence is reduced when a cross section of the community become warriors with gentle souls." In contrast, Di Bretherton and Jackie Bornstein (2003) studied the autobiographies of Nobel Peace Laureates and distinguished eight categories or qualities of peacemakers that might be present in the individual. Their categories included:

1) Optimism and faith in humanity
2) Interconnectedness
3) Recognition of the contradictory nature of things (including people and experiences)
4) Clarity that life is characterized by conflict and crisis
5) Kinship with others
6) Recognition of opposing values
7) Promoting the success of others
8) Using crises to promote peace

While the women were not powerful, influential, or traditional "warriors" in the terms of the Twemlow and Sacco model, and while they were not manifesting all the qualities of the Bretherton and Bornstein model—which almost no person or group could manifest simultaneously—the latter model better describes the qualities of the peacemakers in Sanjuktahalli.

Of the eight categories, optimism, interconnectedness and kinship with others were the primary qualities visible within the women. Delving deeper into how the authors view these categories, Bretherton and Bornstein (2003, 38) talk of optimism being manifested as a "sense that one's goals are achievable." In their view, interconnectedness differs from kinship in that interconnectedness lies in one's sense of responsibility to others, while kinship denotes a sense that no one person is more or less important than others.

Exhibiting a sense of hope and asserting a sense of optimism in humanity (ibid., 38) was seen at the micro-level, where the women talked about their confidence as evidence of their optimism. Smita talked of this in her conversations with me: "We have acquired a lot of knowledge; work goes on, but acquisition of knowledge will always happen. It will benefit us at some point [in] time!"

With a clear sense of optimism and a trust that the future would be better, the women allowed themselves to enjoy a sense of control over their futures, one that was free of conflict and strife. Maintaining a sense of hope is a critical component of how the women could be seen as peacemakers.

The second quality was the palpable interconnectedness they felt with those around them. No doubt small communities are linked by blood, marriage, friendship, and scandal. Privacy is often an unknown commodity in a small community, but what was evident here was that the women promoted a strong sense of interconnectedness with others around them. Many of the women I spoke to no longer had school-age children to be concerned about, but they were vocal in their concerns of the safety of the children in the community, who were put in dangerous situations walking back and forth to school. In the words of Gouri, an elderly woman whose own children had long left the village: "The school was a few kilometers away, for the children to go on the road would have been risky; small children, buses and lorries, ply on the road. It would have been too much for the children. So we said please make a school for us [here]. So we went to the *taluk* [local government] office . . . and brought the school to the village. It was good for the children who were studying until the class five [fifth grade]."

Finally, kinship was another quality that emerged from my conversations with these women. India is beset by divisions of religion, caste, income, gender, ability, and social status, and this is no less different in the small villages where over 70 percent of the population resides. Actions taken by the women benefited everyone in the village, regardless of differences of caste and religion, which are the two most divisive issues that separate people in the country, and which divide people in this village to some extent, as well. Allowing people to freely access the fruits of the women's labor emphasized kinship and community, promoting a more positive culture of peace.

Conclusion

Traditionally, women have been considered the fragile and "weaker" species, needing the protection of men in times of violence. This "inherently unequal dichotomy alienates women from the conditions of their own protection and frequently forces them into passive and weak positions; this, in turn, can undermine their claims to women's rights and depoliticize their actions" (Mason 2005, 739). The story articulated by this village is one where women changed the perceptions of men to see them as less vulnerable and more independent, leading to a more pragmatic view of nonviolence: "that nonviolent action is more effective than other means of action for opposing aggression and oppression, in particular more effective than violence" (Martin and Varney 2003, 215). Their nonviolent action also manifested itself through their collective action, and Amartya Sen maintains that the "the adversity of exclusion can be made to go hand in hand with the gifts of inclusion" (2006, 3). In his book, *Identity and Violence*, Sen talks of how the divisions that are drawn between people and the choice of a solitary identity leads to greater propensity for violence. Collective action by these women illustrates the power of inclusivity as a mechanism to prevent exclusion and, by default, greater violence.

Violence is not an unusual state of affairs for most of the world. The cycles of violence and hatred are regrettably a way of life for many communities, and "the attitudes and values in these societies seem to be based on self-interest, private accumulation and the competitive drive for power and resources" (Murithi 2006, 26). Yet, there are other communities where people are working either independently or collectively to provide for a group based on positive peace with a strong sense of connection to others, and a clear perception of "their responsibilities, in relation to others" (ibid., 26). The women in Sanjuktahalli were not trained to be peacemakers, were struggling for their own voice in a community that was just learning to value women's worth, and were navigating issues of power and privilege at the same time that they were trying to improve their village.

Challenges still exist. Some of the reactions of people around the women were hard to ignore, especially reactions that failed to give them credit: "They don't openly acknowledge [what we've accomplished], but they are aware of this in their minds," was a comment I heard a few times. Men and power-holders were sometimes grudging in giving credit to the women for their development-related efforts, hindering the true nature of building a culture of peace where there are still gender disparities and assumptions of male superiority. In fact, one man who was a local but who taught school in a neighboring village said: "We should not make a group for our own selfishness. . . . The first priority should be the improvement of the village. . . . They have not paid attention to the problems of the village. [The women] should work for the village."

Such criticisms, even in light of the tangible changes seen in the village, highlight the uphill struggle women face in terms of their own development. By employing the qualities of collaboration, sharing, stress elimination, and outreach to others, these women have been acting as peacemakers, helping to build a culture of peace in their community, and developing the power of nonviolence by changing attitudes in a small community.

It is also clear that the power of women at the grassroots level is spreading. In a brief news search, I found an article describing a similar group of women in northern India; one of the women is quoted as saying: "We did a lot of *dharnas* [prayers] for water two years ago. We jammed the road, went to the District Collector, [and] sat there for three hours. Everyone came. The water came for two days and then stopped. It is the first time I heard the voices of women drown out those of men!" (Sharma 2009).

In parts of the world where the struggle to make ends meet on a daily basis is a monumental challenge, that struggle does not prevent development of a culture of positive peace alongside efforts to meet basic needs

(Baily 2009). Grassroots efforts like the ones described above emphasize that operationalizing certain qualities of peacemakers can in fact work to maintain a culture of peace and promote the continued power of nonviolence. Despite collective poverty, individuals are less likely to wage war against neighbors who are storing millet for them, who are preventing husbands from coming home drunk, and who are protecting the community's children by providing better access to school. These actions emerged as part of a collective process, but the provision of training on collective action, mentioned earlier, played an important part in the women's development and their willingness to use their voice.

I have presented here a narrative of a village that was not engaged in open conflict, but that nonetheless had the active participation of a subgroup of relatively marginalized women working to create a culture of positive peace. Peace studies researchers are increasingly recognizing that women are being called upon to actively exercise their influence over violent situations. The women in this community used their voices to navigate relationships of power and to engage in acts that built bridges of collaboration, integration, and cooperation for both the long- and short-term health of the community.

8

From the Headwaters to the Grassroots

Cooperative Resource Management as a Paradigm of Nonviolence

Randall Amster

When we consider the causes of conflict, violence, and warfare, it is by now a relatively straightforward proposition that access to and control over resources are leading factors (see, e.g., Amster 2009b). While ideology, religion, ethnicity, politics, and culture are certainly part of the equation, it is also the case that most (if not all) large-scale conflicts among peoples and nations can be viewed through a prism of material acquisition. Interpersonal conflicts likewise will often possess an aspect of resource competition, including battles over more intangible goods, such as time, space, and social capital, in addition to those over wealth and commodities. In short, resources (including fuels, minerals, territories, and essentials such as food and water) have comprised a root cause underlying the appearance of violence in the world at levels ranging from the personal to the international. As Michael Klare (2002, ix) observes in his book *Resource Wars*: "Conflict over valuable resources—and the power and wealth they confer—has become an increasingly prominent feature of the global landscape [and] has posed a significant and growing threat to peace."

The general premise of this worldview is that resources are scarce and growing scarcer by the day due to population expansion, human consumption, and the planetary changes wrought by these practices.

Nations compete for control of valuable commodities under the rubric of security, and people within nations compete for resources, oftentimes out of sheer survival. This "scarcity-competition-conflict" paradigm is pervasive in academic literature and policy analyses alike, becoming something of a fait accompli in terms of its widespread applicability and seemingly obvious logic. The problem is that this narrative represents only half of the story of humankind's relationship to itself and the environment; missing from this formulation (much as has transpired with the popular version of biological evolution) is the appearance of cooperation as a crucial counterbalance to competition. In this light, the shared management of resources, both among and within nations, can be seen as crucial for peacebuilding and for the cultivation of nonviolence, a view that is often omitted from the analysis of how to confront our present crises (see Carius 2006, 4).

To illustrate the point further, this chapter focuses in particular on the essential resource of water as a source of both conflict and cooperation, and as a trigger for the appearance of violence and a touchstone for the promotion of nonviolence alike. In so doing, the discussion will be guided by the proposition that nonviolence is a set of methods and tactics for promoting political and social change, but more to the point, it is a way of "being in the world" that requires us to deconstruct the kernel of violence that potentially sits at the core of many of our relationships and practices. In other words, nonviolence is both a means *and* an end, connecting the personal and political spheres of our lives, and providing a moral compass for evaluating our interactions with ourselves, others, and the environment itself. In this sense, it is a holistic conception of nonviolence that animates this discourse, inspired by the working definition promulgated by the Metta Center for Nonviolence (2010) and reflective of what may be taken as the "best practices" in the field:

> Nonviolence is a powerful method to harmonize relationships among people (and all living things) for the establishment of justice and the ultimate well-being of all parties. It draws its power from awareness of the profound truth to which the wisdom traditions of all cultures, science, and common experience bear witness: that all life is one.

In order to reach this point of unity, however, we must first consider the various—and sometimes less constructive—pieces of the puzzle.

Water and War

Although not usually perceived as a dominant trigger for warfare, it is actually the case that "conflict over water has, in fact, been a feature of human behavior throughout history" (Klare 2002, 138). To a large extent, nearly every major conflict in recent decades has had an aspect concerning water, including seemingly intractable disputes between Israel and Palestine, India and Pakistan, and Iraq and Iran, among others. Noting that transnational river systems bring a substantial risk of "violent conflict," Klare (2002, 147, 189) concludes that "[t]he major shared systems of the Middle East and Southwest Asia—the Nile, the Jordan, the Tigris-Euphrates, and the Indus—have been the sites of conflict throughout human history; indeed many of the earliest recorded wars occurred along their banks." With demand rising and supply falling, the conflict potential in these regions is heightened; indeed, it has been observed that "water scarcity" is part of the set of factors that has "exacerbated the high level of violence between Israel and the Palestinian Authority" (Weinthal et al. 2005, 654; see also Shiva 2002, 72–74). With only about one percent of the planet's water being usable for human consumption, we are fast approaching a point where "total human usage will approach 100 percent of the available supply by the mid-twenty-first century, producing severe shortages in some areas and intensified competition for access to important sources of supply" (Klare 2002, 19).

Predictions of future war already have been rendered by powerful figures, including former United Nations Secretary-General Boutros Boutros-Ghali, who once flatly proclaimed that "[t]he next war in our region will be over the waters of the Nile, not politics" (quoted in Klare 2002, 153), and former World Bank Vice President Ismail Serageldin, who opined in 1995, "If the wars of this century were fought over oil, the wars of the next century will be fought over water" (quoted in Shiva 2002, ix). As Vandana Shiva (2002, ix) notes, however, "water wars are not a thing of the future. They already surround us, although they are not always easily recognizable as water wars." The pressures of globalization—and its concomitant forces of privatization and commodification—have served to heighten the related problems of scarcity and conflict, although as Shiva suggests they have done so in a manner that often cloaks this reality under a veil of competing ideologies and "business as usual." In this manner, water has become a decontextualized global commodity akin to what Maude Barlow (2002) describes as "blue gold," touching off a furious push by both militaristic and mercantile forces to control it in the name of either "national security" or "economic prosperity" (see Amster 2009a). Increasingly, it is difficult to separate these aims, and as Kenneth Boulding (1977, 288) once opined, the sense of "persistent struggle" underlying both of these potentially conflict-laden impetuses "often results in mutual exhaustion and even extinction."

Water and Peace

Against this grim backdrop, it might seem like a non sequitur to suggest that water—especially given its apparent scarcity and irreplaceable nature—can serve as an important tool for the promotion of peace and the practice of nonviolence. In fact, it is actually the case that "water resources . . . are so important that even adversaries must show some semblance of cooperation over them" (Ali 2007, 337), and thus "the dire impact of depletion" will often foster a profound aversion to potentially disastrous "water wars" (Ali 2007, 4). As Alexander Carius notes (2006, 9), "dependence on the same water resources can therefore create communities of diverse users and stakeholders, fostering cooperation and transcending conflicting economic interests, thereby generating advantages for all participants through the cooperative management of natural resources."

In the South Asian context, it has been observed that "the issue of shared water resources carries the highest potential for violent interstate conflict . . . yet shared water resources have actually been the source of extensive bilateral cooperation, even in the face of security crisis" (Swain 2002, 65). Likewise, regarding the Middle East, it has been contended that, "in spite of the seeming intractability of the political conflict between Israel and the Palestinian Authority . . . opportunities exist for water to serve as a source of cooperation rather than conflict" (Weinthal et al. 2005, 654). As the authors of a hydrologically informed study conclude, it is ironically the case that "the severe water situation in the Gaza Strip could serve as a source of environmental peacemaking" among the hostile entities in the region (ibid., 659), a point echoed by Carius (2006, 9), as well: "In some cases (e.g.[,] the Israel-Palestine issue), water problems offer one of the few chances for cooperative dialogue in otherwise heated bilateral conflicts." Similarly, in another conflict-plagued area, it has been argued that "water cooperation efforts in the U.S.-Mexico border region have the potential to improve U.S.-Mexico relations in many respects [and] could help to move the border from a zone of uneasy transition and human insecurity to a zone of peace" (Doughman 2002, 191).

The salient feature of these optimistic observations is that the crises of scarcity and conflict are also opportunities for mutually beneficial engagement born of necessity, but aimed at longer-term sustainability. This mirrors the notion that a potential outbreak of violent conflict can actually offer an opening for the promotion of a peaceful resolution, which recognizes the senseless waste of the former juxtaposed to the possible promise of the latter. The cultivation of a sense of shared destiny and mutual necessity can bring even ardent adversaries to the negotiating table when it is apparent that conflict will likely leave both sides "high and dry," so to speak. Carius (2006, 11) cogently assesses this potential for environmental conflicts to create opportunities for peace:

> As a mechanism for peace, the environment has some useful, perhaps even unique qualities that are well suited for peacebuilding and conflict resolution. Environmental problems ignore political borders. They require a long-term perspective, encourage participation by local and non-governmental organizations, help build administrative, economic and social capacities for action and facilitate the creation of commonalities that transcend the polarization caused by economic relations. . . . As environmental cooperation develops and societal and political stakeholders are systematically integrated in negotiation processes to protect natural goods, a simultaneous thrust is given to building trust, initiating cooperative action and encouraging the creation of a common regional

identity emerging from sharing resources. It also helps establish mutually recognized rights and expectations.

All of this can serve to point the way toward "the establishment of justice and the ultimate well-being of all parties," as noted above in the Metta Center's definition of nonviolence. By further weaving into the analysis ecological concerns over riparian habitats, water quality, and sustainable utilization, what begins as a profound crisis can slowly yield a deeper cognizance of the interrelatedness of "all living things," including both human communities and the environment itself. In the last analysis, this process of converting insularity to interconnection may well be the essence of a nonviolent worldview.

The core of what Shiva (2002, 34) has termed a "water democracy" also stands in contrast to the water piracy and authoritarianism evident in large measure around the globe, and comprises a vision that coheres in many respects with Stephen Zunes's (2009) observation that "nonviolent movements tend to create sustainable democracy" and thus bring about conditions in which "alternative institutions are created that empower ordinary people." These sentiments are echoed in the examples Shiva (2002, 126–27) cites of villages in India that have deployed a "collective decision-making process [that] has helped prevent conflicts" by emphasizing solidarity and community control, and are notably illustrated in her recounting of the "mass mobilization" against water privatization in Cochabamba, Bolivia, which demonstrated how the "corporate takeover of vital resources can be prevented by people's democratic will" (102–3). Among the basic principles contained in Shiva's democratic view of water are: "Water is nature's gift;" "Life is interconnected through water;" "Water must be free for sustenance needs;" and "Water is a commons" (35–36). This last point, in particular, is crucial in its political and economic implications, and again suggests the sort of interconnectivity and empowerment that are essential to the establishment of sustainable and nonviolent communities.

In her extensive and Nobel Prize-winning work on "common pool resources," Elinor Ostrom has devoted a good portion of her investigative efforts toward irrigation and water management systems around the world. She has focused in particular on the self-governance properties of these systems in the belief that "social capital"—which includes "the aspects of the structure of relationships between individuals that enable them to create new values"—is just as important as physical infrastructure in determining whether a given irrigation scheme will be sustainable (Ostrom 1992, 13). Key features of successful cooperative arrangements are the presence of "working rules or rules-in-use" that can be contrasted with more rigid and bureaucratic "formal laws" (19–20); the development of "conflict resolution mechanisms" that are generally "informal" and localized (74); a pervasive sense of "trust" and a "common future" (Ostrom 1990, 21); and the maintenance of community relationships in which reciprocity and interdependence can take hold (88–89). A particular exemplar of these phenomena is the irrigation culture of Valencia, Spain, and Ostrom's assessment of the forces at play there illustrates the remarkably dualistic nature of water:

> Given the high stakes, conflict over water has always been just beneath the surface of everyday life, erupting from time to time in fights between the irrigators themselves, between irrigators and their own officials, and between groups of irrigators living in the lower reaches of the water systems and their upstream neighbors. Despite this high potential for conflict—and its actual realization from time to time—the institutions devised many centuries ago for governing the use of water from these rivers have proved adequate for resolving conflicts, allocating water predictably, and ensuring stability in a region not normally associated with high levels of stability. (69–70)

This analysis is quite literally a harbinger of the collaborative management efforts and inherent nonviolence represented by one of the last true common-pool resource systems in the United States—namely, the four-century-old acequia communities of the southwest that derive, in part, from the Spanish model identified by Ostrom as ecologically sustainable and socially just.

Nonviolence Redux

Before exploring the acequia system in detail, it would be prudent to return briefly to what we mean by nonviolence. As previously noted, there are myriad formulations of the concept in both theoretical and practical terms. Yet, some basic tenets have emerged that are foundational to nearly all definitions of nonviolence. These synthesized principles include (but are not limited to) the following: (1) maintaining a universal respect for both self and other, especially those seen as adversaries; (2) demonstrating the unity of means and ends, in the sense that what we do along the way strongly defines where we are headed; (3) manifesting the inherent power of living one's truth, so as to honestly represent one's beliefs without denigrating others' in the process; (4) fostering cooperative and mutually beneficial outcomes by prioritizing relationships and the concomitant aspects of communication, trust, and conflict transformation; and finally (5) recognizing that everything is interconnected, not merely in a superficial manner, but on a deeper level that reflects the collected wisdom of humankind from indigenous cosmologies to cutting-edge sciences. Again, while there are many formulations of nonviolence, these reflect the major commonalities.

Another key aspect of nonviolence that bears mention is the linguistic conundrum of defining it primarily in opposition to violence (see Kurlansky 2008). While this is a particularly acute consequence of the English language, it is also the case that other cultures have struggled with the same challenge of defining the term more proactively than reactively. Nonviolence, particularly in the West, oftentimes appears as a set of strategies for opposing warfare or violence, and is generally associated with tactics of social protest and passive resistance (see Amster 2009c). Less evident in the popular consciousness, however, is the constructive nature of nonviolence, namely its deep roots in the material conditions of life (as reflected in both Mohandas Gandhi's and Dr. Martin Luther King Jr.'s landmark applications of the principle), as well as its educative functions as a set of moral (secular or spiritual) principles for building a world free from violence and instead filled with the positive attributes of respect, unity, truth, cooperation, and interconnectedness. In this sense, nonviolence is an expression of a world-in-progress defined by the values of sustainability, mutuality, and flexibility. It is proactive even as it rejects oppression and domination, and is decidedly forward-looking even as it draws from the wellspring of history. In its call for recognition of both diversity and oneness as equally critical virtues, nonviolence is also uniquely integrative of both social and ecological paradigms. This is the lens through which the inherent power of instructive models, such as the acequia, begins to come into sharper focus.

The River Is Flowing

"More than any other resource, water needs to remain a common good and requires community management," writes Shiva (2002, 19) in her book *Water Wars*. "Because water falls on earth in a dispersed manner," she continues, "because every living being needs water, decentralized management and democratic ownership are the only efficient, sustainable, and equitable systems for the sustenance of all. Beyond the state and the market lies the power of community participation. Beyond bureaucracies and corporate power lies the promise of water democracy" (24). Turning the prevailing logic of the "tragedy of the commons" on its head, Shiva—like Ostrom before her—persuasively demonstrates that in fact it is "the principle of cooperation, rather than competition" (27), that allows common-pool resources to survive and their attendant human communities to flourish.

One of the positive examples Shiva cites is the traditional acequia system of the American southwest, found today most prominently in the Rio Grande Valley region of northern New Mexico and south-central Colorado. This network of mostly low-tech irrigation ditches has provided water to farmers and pastoralists in a very arid area since at least 1598, making it not only one of the most sustainable resource systems in the hemisphere, but also one of the oldest and most enduring forms of governance as well (see generally Garcia and Santistevan 2008, 111–19; Rivera 1996, 747; Peña 2005, 83).

The roots of this remarkable yet little-known system are intriguing and powerful in their own right, deriving from a confluence of Spanish,

Arabic, and Pueblo Indian sources. Following the occupation of Spain by Muslim Moors, many of the adaptive irrigation practices left behind were brought to the New World, where they slowly mixed with indigenous customs and regional techniques for managing water (Rivera 1998, 5). Indeed, the word *acequia* itself derives from the Arabic term *as-Saquiya*, which translates roughly as "the water bearer," and thus the "customary law of the acequia derives from Roman, Spanish, and Arabic sources" (Peña 2005, 82). The result is an amazingly multicultural (cf. Eastman, King, and Meadows 1997, 21) and truly global system that nonetheless remains highly localized in terms of its cultural and political implementation (cf. Rodríguez 2006, 115).

While there are many common features among acequias throughout the region, each community sharing water from a particular irrigation ditch has its own unique social structure. This allows the system as a whole to survive by developing a base of shared knowledge and "best practices," while still diversifying and localizing control in ways that promote great resiliency and adaptability, as Paula Garcia (2000) has suggested: "As local, participatory democracies that manage water based on indigenous knowledge accumulated over generations in their own watersheds, acequias have important lessons for anyone interested in the sustainable, just, and equitable use of water. . . ."

Moreover, in today's geopolitical climate, the fact that this centuries-old American system possesses Arabic roots is in itself a powerful statement that could serve to promote greater understanding of the role of nonviolence in Muslim history and practice (see Amster 2010). Perhaps even more to the point are the basic principles underlying the acequia, which include: "(1) the communitarian value of water, (2) the non-transferability of water, (3) the right of thirst, (4) shared scarcity, and (5) cooperative labor and mutual aid" (Peña 2005, 82). These tenets underscore a culture of shared benefits and burdens grounded in reciprocity and equitable exchange (cf. Rivera 1996, 745), fostering respect for basic human and environmental rights—such as in the above principle number 3, where it is held that "all living things with thirst have a right to water" (Peña 2005, 83).

In this sense, the acequia is a manifestation of the nonviolent recognition that "all life is one," serving as a source not only of human sustenance but also as a series of networks that "provide habitat and biological corridors for wildlife," among other "beneficial ecological services" that comprise a significant aspect of the system's overall sustainability (Peña 2005, 84). Further, in recognition of this "web of life" ethos, acequia farmers "have organized campaigns for watershed protection and ecological restoration projects [and] are active in the sustainable agriculture movement and support local food security" (165).

Nurturing the Grassroots

Still, one of the primary critiques leveled against acequias is that they are inefficient and wasteful of water. Many of the acequia ditches are indeed primitive, earthen, and maintained by hand, meaning that they will leach water back into the earth along the carrying route. But, whereas proponents of the worldview in which "water is considered a private property right to be bought and sold" (Garcia 2000) prefer concrete canals and metal pipelines to ensure the full flow of their valuable commodity, practitioners of the acequia vision in which "water is considered a community resource" (Garcia 2000) understand, in the words of elder Joseph Gallegos (1998, 239), that "acequias are good for the land. . . . The ditches make a lot of plant life possible in what is really a cold, barren desert. More plants means that the wildlife—birds and mammals—have a home. The ecologists call this 'biodiversity.' I call it life, tierra y vida." In this lexicon, as Devon Peña (1998, 253) further elaborates, water is seen as "part of a complex ecological system. Interacting with geography, water creates the conditions that encourage the emergence of diverse life-forms. These life-forms—plant, animal, human—interact to create life regions that are based on close relationships between the various members of the mixed community." As such, the acequia can be said to constitute a genuine form of "local grassroots participatory democracy" (Hicks and Peña 2003, 457) that naturally extends the practice beyond merely human pursuits.

Even at the basic level of human sociopolitical systems, the acequia is evolutionary and potentially revolutionary in its deceptively simple workings. In essence, all of the users along a particular ditch constitute a self-governing micro-community where the principle of "one person, one vote" is often practiced in spirit, but is rarely formalized in quite such linear terms. In each acequia, a titular *mayordomo* (see Crawford 1989) is selected to serve as facilitator, overseer, and trouble-shooter, with the position often rotating among members over time. In recent years, certain state laws have required the presence of three-person *comisiónes* (commissions) for each acequia, although the power generally has remained with the community members themselves. In some instances, acequias have also found it necessary to form associations and other legalistic entities in order to cope with a rapidly changing set of rules and regulations imposed by the state, and also to be able to push back in a coherent manner against the impetus of water privatization and the attempt by outside entities to hinder, if not outright eliminate this agropastoral way of life. Despite such outward formalisms, for many acequias the old ways still hold sway, devolving upon a "deep-rooted tradition of mutual aid and communal labor" to maintain the ditches—including an annual "springtime ditch cleanup" that is both pragmatic and ritualistic—and an unwavering commitment to the principle of "local self-governance" (Hicks and Peña 2003, 453). These practices are reminiscent of Gandhi's call for *swaraj* ("self-rule"), which included an emphasis on decentralization, self-sustaining communities, and the cultivation of voluntary association (Murthy 1987).

The acequias speak directly to many of the fundamental aspects of nonviolence by promoting cooperation, mutualism, and a form of governance grounded in respect rather than fear. As Peña opines (2003, 163), "the acequias can be considered an important example of existing grassroots alternatives to top-down environmental managerialism. . . . They represent an important example of social movements that combine the principles of self-determination (autonomy) with environmental justice (sustainability)." This assessment concludes that the acequia system potentially constitutes a "new social movement for social, economic, and environmental justice" (Peña 1998, 274), with the stakes of this emergent movement being no less than the survival of indigenous knowledge, local stewardship, the commons, and "ecological democracy" (275), among other core values.

These are not matters to be taken lightly, and without a concerted effort this multicultural, sustainable, and inherently nonviolent way of life could be lost to the forces of commodification and control. In this sense, the organic processes of the acequia are being directly threatened by the implicit violence of profiteering and bureaucratization. Luckily, the acequia is firmly on the side of the "force more powerful" that is nonviolence (Ackerman and Duvall 2001), and furthermore contains within it the time-tested capacity to transform crises into opportunities and conflicts into resolutions.

Making Ends (and Means) Meet

As with any cohesive theory of nonviolence, the practices and processes of the acequia mirror its ultimate goals and visions, as well. It is not static or rigid, and does not pretend to have achieved some sort of completed utopia in which people magically get along at all times. As longtime mayordomo and *parciante* (irrigator) Joseph Gallegos (1998, 237) has observed, acequia life is complex:

> There is always some kind of acequia problem, conflict, or strange situation. These irrigation associations are not some sort of perfect heaven on earth. It would take a lifetime to write all these stories down, but let me tell you, the acequias work only because the farmers depend on each other for water. This is never an easy thing; fights and conflicts are an accepted part of the everyday life of acequias. Ditch stories are true-life tales and have lessons to teach us about mutual aid and cooperation among the parciantes. The stories show us how hard it is to keep the peace in the ditch.

This reflects the challenges faced by every human community, and acknowledging this openly is a form of "manifesting truth," and thus embracing nonviolence. As Peña (1998, 261) adds, there are many levels to the issue of managing crises and disputes in real-life situations:

> The acequia irrigation system is a cultural institution sustained by intense social relations. For the mayordomo there is always the prospect of a struggle about the ditch. To maintain the cohesion of the group of irrigators, the ditch rider must encourage reciprocity and mutual aid.

This is not easy, because the membership of ditches is changing and the law provides little refuge for the maintenance of customary practices. Nature can also take its toll. As a bad drought demonstrates, good-natured neighbors quickly get vile when water is scarce.

Crawford (1989, 223–24) likewise reflects on the subtle intricacies of heading off destructive conflicts in acequia communities:

The collective power of a ditch crew of twenty or thirty men can often be felt as threatening or dangerous, but what holds it in restraint are the conventions and traditions that have evolved out of hundreds of years of maintaining acequias—a complex social fabric binds a ditch crew together far more than the character of a mayordomo or the commissioners, recalling it to a sense of common purpose and preventing the inevitable disputes from flaring into political divisiveness or even physical violence.

Considering that the system has survived for over four centuries despite these challenges, we would do well to consider some of the tools utilized to manage conflicts and promote peaceful relations over time and in the face of uncertain conditions.

In terms of reactive means of resolving disputes, semi-formal procedures of *conciliación* (conciliation) are sometimes utilized (Rivera 1998, 33), which are generally "designed to reach a compromise . . . rather than to designate an all-out winner as in the adversarial common law process," in an effort "to preserve community harmony" (Tyler 1990, 25). Other reactive measures include the use of "informal sanctions" such as "ridicule, isolation, withdrawal of cooperation, and even the shutting down of compuertas (headgates)," as well as more formal sanctions, including "fines for water waste or for taking water out of turn" (Hicks and Peña 2003, 460). If any of this seems harsh, we might consider the sundry brutalities of the enforcement mechanisms deployed under the guise of "criminal justice" in the larger society. And the reality is that reactive resolution measures are less frequently utilized in the acequia than the proactive means of day-to-day operations, such as the "annual spring ditch cleanup; the tacit skills and experiential knowledge related to flood irrigation;

and the sharing of labor for planting, cultivating, irrigating, harvesting, and processing of crops—all these represent the persistence of acequia customary norms of mutual aid and cooperative labor" (Hicks and Peña 2003, 460).

The overarching ethic of the acequia has thus been one of "equitable, or proportional, distribution" that constitutes a "system of sharing" intended to "function in avoidance" of costly disputes and conflicts (Tyler 1990, 45). In this manner, the processes of self-regulation and mutual aid have yielded communities that are in fact well-regulated and mutually supportive. In other words, the means employed and adapted over the centuries have likewise become ends in themselves in a process that perpetually continues to evolve. The acequia, in short, achieves the nonviolent aim of "sustainable democracy" primarily by practicing democracy and behaving sustainably. The question remains whether it will still be able to do so going forward. Understanding and applying the lessons reflected in the stories being collected and transmitted could be the deciding factor as to whether the acequia survives the ravages of modernity.

Speaking Truth to the Future

One of the clichés often heard in nonviolence circles is the primacy of "speaking truth to power." While there may be a utility in this, it is also the case that powerful interests frequently will ignore such speech, twist it through the mass media, or market it back to the populace in a crassly decontextualized form. To avoid these increasingly evident outcomes, we might instead consider speaking our truths to ourselves, our communities, and our descendants. A way of life as elegant and essential as the acequia is difficult to encapsulate in formulaic terms, but it can be done less vulgarly through the telling of stories and the narration of living histories. To date, perhaps the three most significant books devoted exclusively to the acequia and its socio-cultural import are precisely aimed at keeping this narrative alive. A short recounting from each will serve to effectively summarize and animate the argument and analysis presented here, namely that the longstanding acequia system can provide us with a powerful model for promoting a paradigm of nonviolence based on the tenets of universal respect, the unity of means and ends, manifesting truth, fostering cooperation, and recognizing interconnectedness. Here, then, in a paraphrased and interlinked narrative, is how the acequia appears to those who have implicitly documented its potential as a model of sustainable nonviolence (Crawford 1989; Rivera 1998; Rodríguez 2006):

> The difference between the modern world and the world which it has almost completely displaced lies largely in the nature of relationships— namely whether they are close, local, and held among near equals; or are remote, abstract, and held between individuals and vastly larger institutions. The process of "adjudication" over these relationships, and the various regulatory steps that accompany it, creates a new hierarchy of water users—replacing an oral tradition of constant negotiation with one based on a system of legal documentation. But the main effect of adjudication is that once the process is completed, a water right becomes a commodity that can be leased or sold anywhere. This process can sweep through a community and undermine traditional arrangements that have been in place for hundreds of years, in order to convert what has been held in common to that which can be owned privately.
>
> There are few civic institutions left in which members have as much control over an essential aspect of their lives. Relatively autonomous and practically democratic, the acequias of the southwest form a web of almost microscopic filaments that have held this culture and landscape in place for centuries. In the long run, the sustainability of water quantity and quality may depend more on democratic and social processes than on technological or regulatory fixes. As a physical system, the acequia has required communal upkeep and operations, but beyond this dimension it also bonds communities through self-help, mutualism, collective governance, shared values, and oral traditions that form a distinctive regional culture. For the moment, the earthen acequias of the southwest remain and function as common property resource systems quite different from the modern, concrete-lined irrigation canals prevalent in most places. The parciante irrigators own the acequia watercourses, regulate them, police them, and maintain them from generation to generation—all the while perpetuating a sense of place and a system of direct, participatory democracy.

The story told here arises out of the struggle of acequia systems to survive in a world where water scarcity and competition are no longer local issues but part of a global crisis. This worldwide crisis magnifies the significance of the acequia as an example of a workable, elegant solution to the age-old problem of allocating water where it is scarce. The lesson to draw from the acequia system is that water is a resource best shared in a community of mutually-responsible and fully accountable stakeholders. In this context, local moral economies struggle against the hegemonic zero-sum, winner-take-all ethic of global capitalism. Acequia culture combines the sharing of river water with secular and ritual practices that unfold in shared space and that require mutual respect. People cherish and defend the surviving acequia systems not because they are a lifeless artifact from an archaic past, but rather because they continue to function in an ever-changing yet persistent form.

Concluding—and Succeeding—Thoughts

In this brief assessment of the acequia system as an exemplar of nonviolent, cooperative resource management, the prevailing logic of "resource conflict" has been problematized and its appearance of inevitability undermined. The articulation of working models of "resource cooperation" can serve to illuminate how communities based on social and environmental justice might take hold and flourish, and suggests to us a palpable locus of nonviolence-in-practice that stands in marked contrast to the dominant realism of the present. Further research can enhance this effort by uncovering similar examples from around the world, and offering comparative insights and competing visions. Rather than simply standing aghast at and in opposition to the coming age of overt resource wars, the cultivation of nonviolent alternatives can point the way forward in positive and proactive terms. While it is sometimes said that a river will follow the "path of least resistance," we might instead consider how people around the world striving to share river water cooperatively and sustainably are in fact pursuing a much-needed path of nonviolent resistance.

Part Three

Nonviolence Pedagogy

The essence of effective pedagogy is to enlighten the mind, empower learners to formulate and articulate new critical questions, facilitate the re-imagination of human relationships and the relationships between people and their environment for the common good, and fill the heart with compassion. How can this be done? Where and when should this kind of education take place? Who should assume the responsibility for such transformative pedagogy? This section focuses on nonviolence pedagogy, and is particularly critical to this volume because it unites the traditionally separate fields of peace studies and education. The contributions herein address the questions raised above in ways that are authentic and transformative to further the quest for a just and nonviolent world.

In this part's opening chapter, longtime peace educator George Lakey offers practical examples of how to use direct education to teach students about the power of nonviolence within college-level courses. Using the analogies of building the container, working with images, and strengthening the container for conflict, he discusses how he creates a safe learning environment that encourages students to take risks, revise their conceptual frameworks, try new skills, and unlearn old prejudices. He engages them in activities that empower them to listen actively, express themselves honestly, and develop a flexible mindset that facilitates the constructive resolution of conflicts. In this manner, Lakey connects the pedagogical and substantive aspects of nonviolence, providing an experiential framework for educators at all levels to utilize in their classrooms.

Picking up on this holistic spirit of pedagogy as substantive unto itself, Laura Finley challenges us to consider ways that creativity can revolutionize the practice of peace education in colleges and universities to more effectively teach both about and for peace. She describes six barriers to creative teaching and learning within the traditional higher education framework, including the specialized nature of higher education; professors' limited training in pedagogy; academic-related pressures; the rigidly hierarchical structure of most higher education institutions; and the fact that most higher education institutions still operate within a centuries-old paradigm. Finley proposes that creative peace education must be grounded in the study of human rights, multicultural education, and service learning. In the end, she reminds us that "educators at all levels must be conscious that simply teaching about peace is not enough to transform our culture. Rather, it is imperative that we teach *for* peace as well," necessitating the deployment of our full intellectual and creative powers all at once.

These essential and equally necessary dimensions of nonviolence pedagogy come to the fore when we consider the challenges of educating for peace in a world fraught with injustice at nearly every turn. Highlighting the need to articulate new critical questions and to reconceptualize the what, where, how, and why of pedagogy, Elavie Ndura outlines the essential role of multicultural education in furthering the quest for human rights, nonviolence, and peace. Anchoring her discussion in the broad vision of a united movement of nonviolence across socio-cultural differences, she establishes "building bridges of caring consciousness" as the ultimate goal of multicultural education, and as the prerequisite for creating and sustaining peaceful and nonviolent livelihoods and communities. The chapters presented in this part collectively illustrate how we can all be teachers and learners in striving to realize those aims.

9

Direct Education

Learning the Power of Nonviolent Action

George Lakey

If people learn by doing, as was famously proposed by John Dewey (1966), then how can students learn something of the power of nonviolent action within the format of a course?

Luckily, I've been blessed with teaching opportunities that gave me space to experiment. My life has seesawed between full-time activism and college teaching, so what I've learned in one context I've tried applying in another. My biggest activist influences were Mohandas Gandhi and Martin Luther King Jr., both of whom were conflict friendly, to say the least. Can a classroom be a conflict-friendly venue?

Along the way I was attracted to Paolo Freire and popular education. Freire's approach elicits the knowledge already held by participants, and encourages them to teach each other. The teacher often reframes, assists participants to connect the dots, and facilitates the solving of puzzles that emerge in group discussion—all in a tone of great respect for the participants, rather than the tone of the "know-it-all expert." Can a classroom work with an experiential methodology?

My fifteen years with Training for Change had me interacting with a variety of cultures, sometimes in the same workshop! Theory is expressed in language, but language is linked to culture. If there is a diversity of cultures in the room, how does that impact one's hoped-for clarity of theory? Can a curriculum embrace a diversity of cultures and still build theoretical clarity?

171

This chapter is a progress report in response to these questions, rather than the last word, but I'm optimistic about a door that's been opening. My Training for Change colleagues and I call the door "direct education," a pedagogical approach that builds on popular education as well as insights from newer learning technologies, including that of the contemporary psychologist Arnold Mindell (1997).

I've been developing direct education in many cultural settings around the world, and—because it is conflict friendly—the approach seems to support students' ability to navigate a multicultural environment without "walking on eggshells" or retreating into political correctness. Direct education is too new to have been tested empirically, although education experts have observed from the back of the room; this chapter therefore comes "hot from the griddle."

Most of all, direct education is rooted in Gandhi's philosophy of conflict which is described by political scientist Joan Bondurant (1971). Gandhi believed that truth can be advanced through contention and passionate encounter. He even condoned fasting unto death to support the communication of a vital truth.

Gandhi's perspective was joined by the work of Dr. King (1964), whose campaigns elicited so much turbulence that when he was awarded the Nobel Peace Prize, the Norwegians were criticized by some for linking "peace" to such a confrontational figure!

Since the 1960s, the image of Dr. King has experienced a makeover in some circles in the United States, and he is often put forward as a "day of service," nonconfrontational nice guy. Even a quick look at a standard history texts, like those of Taylor Branch, published in three volumes (1988, 1998, and 2006), demolishes this revisionist version of Dr. King.

Because direct education is conflict friendly, the pedagogy might be useful in our polarized world, threatened as it is by high levels of scarcity and resource depletion, and where students (and teachers) need to learn how to thrive in the midst of turbulence without using violence or retreating into gated security zones. While a single peace studies course cannot fully prepare anyone for such a world, a conflict-friendly pedagogy can, I believe, open the door to an empowered citizenship for the real world that young adults now face.

In this chapter I relate some pedagogical case material in detail so the reader can catch layers and nuances of interaction between teachers and students. A textured story often conveys more information than expository writing can in the same amount of space! Before the case material, though, I'll describe the careful preparation (building the container, "working the group," and working with images) that I believe enables students to engage at a level where they can learn significantly the power of nonviolent action.

Direct Education Starts by Building the Container

In the old paradigm of education, participants in learning groups are left to their own devices to create a tacit social order. An exception might be lecture halls, where massification overwhelms the human inclination to create structure and the satisfactions of familiarity. In smaller classrooms I observe participants creating some kind of order, perhaps because there's too much anxiety about fitting in if they don't. The order they create may, however, not support the maximization of their learning. A group may, for example, sort its members into highly motivated students and those who are just content to get by; the latter may resign themselves to passivity and eye-rolling.

We call an intentional social order built to support learning a "container." The metaphor of a container suggests that it might be thin or thick, weak or robust. A strong container has walls thick enough to hold even those groups undertaking turbulent work, risking conflicts in order to learn intensely.

In direct education, teachers are proactive, and in the beginning they have the job of building the container. They set up exercises for introductions, engage in icebreakers to lighten the atmosphere, set up buddy pairs or small support groups. Later, students will join in by sharing non-derisive humor, authentic conversation over breaks, cleaning up, and admitting confusion or doubt.

What does this have to do with nonviolent action? Here I make some assumptions based on my experience in multiple colleges. Few students arrive with the knowledge, skills, and attitudes of an experienced nonviolent activist. For the most part they arrive full of cultural messages about the superior efficacy of violence, the rightness of competitive individualism, and the terribleness of appearing a fool. They can float through an informational curriculum memorizing some names and factoids and still retain their armor against learning the power of nonviolent action. Learning something new sometimes requires unlearning something old, and that, for many, is experienced as a risk. We would be wise to treat it as such.

In short, to learn the power of nonviolent action, students need to risk: to revise their conceptual framework, to try new skills, to unlearn old prejudices, to admit there's a lot they don't know. To risk voluntarily, people need safety. To be safe, they need a group or teacher capable of supporting them.

Container-building is an invitation to be real. It proceeds step by step, through acknowledgement and mutual disclosure. Participants hide out and engage in pretense in the beginning of courses because they are afraid to be real. By taking small steps, they gain mutual trust and realize they are safe; they are at least a little bit accepted for who they are and what they really think.

When participants are still busy putting energy into pretense—"the good student," "the avid listener"—they have less attention for actual learning. As the container strengthens, they can relax and pay attention to the content of the class.

My experience, even in highly competitive university environments, has been that students can sometimes set aside the behaviors that reflect their insecurities, and by halfway through the semester take some responsibility for holding the container. They are then amazed to find how much they look forward to the class—and how rapidly they learn.

Working with Images

I find it useful to show many films of nonviolent struggle and use a variety of means for processing the film content. I use non-documentary films, as well as excellent documentaries like *Bringing Down a Dictator* (York 2002) and *A Force More Powerful* (2000), because non-documentaries often reach more effectively the diversity of learning styles in the class. I've gotten strong, positive responses to *Freedom Song* (Robinson 2000) (about Mississippi's Freedom Summer, 1964), *Beyond Rangoon* (Boorman 1995) (about the Burmese student uprising in 1988), and *Iron Jawed Angels* (Garnier 2004) (about militant woman suffragists in the United States), among others.

I use as many films as possible in order to counter the predominance of the pro-violence paradigm. I have talked with hundreds of students who have read books about nonviolent struggle in peace studies courses and neatly compartmentalized the information, just as Thomas Kuhn (1962) taught us to expect when a new paradigm comes along. Old paradigms are defended by framing the information that doesn't fit as "an exception." Nonviolent victories are dismissed as the exceptions to the rule that, when a real challenge comes along (usually the current war the United States is engaged in), only violence can work. Attachment to an old paradigm—especially one as emotion-tinged and daily reinforced on television and elsewhere as is violence—can hardly be expected to be dislodged by books and articles! I naturally reach for more vivid media, such as films.

Because I believe I am working with students' unconscious attachments and limiting beliefs, I find it only realistic to assist students to process the films in ways that enable them to engage as deeply as their courage will allow. I don't focus on "right or wrong answers;" the real pedagogical challenge, I believe, is for the student to be authentic. I try pairs, small groups, journal writing, storytelling, guided meditation, and more. I ask them who they identify with, what they might do in that person's situation, what might be tough for them, where they might turn for support to be more courageous than they otherwise would be.

If they don't learn something about courage in my course, they haven't learned much about the power of nonviolent action.

Working the Group: Strengthening the Container for Conflict

Every group has a mainstream and one or more margins (Mindell 1997). The mainstream of a group sets the tone and generates the behavioral norms of the group, sometimes as powerfully as does the teacher. Margins and the mainstream in a group might be defined in many ways: by gender, color, religion, political opinion, physical ability, age, by who speaks up in discussion and how, by grade point average, or sports reputation.

Building a strong container requires acknowledging margins, somehow or another. Students are wondering not only how they fit in regarding their individual characteristics, but also whether the group has space for their individual and sub-group identities. Will this be a typical mixed-gender group in which men talk 80 percent of the time? the women ask themselves. Will this be a typical mixed sexual orientation group in which all the references to relationship are heterosexual? the sexual minorities ask themselves.

One reason the unvoiced questions around the room are important for a teacher to recognize is that, in general, the more "at home" the margins feel, the more those students can learn. The less the margin students experience the group as a safe place for them, the less they can learn. There are many options for teachers to use in acknowledging the existence of margins. Acknowledging margins and differences can be expressed to the group fairly easily: "A lot of people want to do it this way, and I realize some of you don't. In this case, I think we'll go ahead with the way we're doing it now." Or: "This generalization may fit many of you, but I imagine some of you have a different experience."

Most people (and especially students) find difference to be scary. This is fortunate for us teachers. Openly acknowledging difference becomes a risk, and successfully doing so builds the container (on a group level) and conflict capacity (on an individual level). The group dynamics that exist in every classroom can be tapped by peace and conflict studies to advance our curriculum!

An activity I often rely on is the "diversity interview." I ask, ahead of time, one or more students if they would be willing to be interviewed in front of the group about a difference that is important to them. Typically I sit beside the one(s) interviewed and ask, in sequence, a series of questions that draws them out. They are in control of what they share and whether to participate in the exercise at all. Every single time I've done this the participants find it empowering, and express relief that they no longer feel invisible. The participants in the exercise get to model courage and leadership. They get the satisfaction of facing their fear and overcoming it, and they feel more connected with the mainstream, as a result. The group experiences multiple benefits from the diversity interview: the container strengthens, other margins feel safer, the mainstream gets specific useful information about "the invisible/ignored ones," and everyone has gone through a (modest) stress and survived.

The diversity interview tool builds capacity for nonviolent action, but is not serviceable as a stand-in for it. A "speak-out" comes closer to the real thing. At the University of Pennsylvania in the 1970s, I found students reluctant to acknowledge that both blacks and whites were present, even though usually about one-third of the class was African American. In that context blacks were the margin, so as the container strengthened I asked the black students each semester to participate in a specific exercise called a "speak-out." Following is a typical example.

During the mid-term weekend retreat, a dozen black students agreed to perform their speak-out on Saturday night. On a campus where blacks and whites rarely mixed socially, these black students went all out, expressing their deep anger at the racism they encountered on campus and their determination to do what it took to maintain their dignity.

The minds of the white students were blown and I had the teacher's usual concerns about how the class would reunite. After spending some time debriefing the white students, I touched base with the black students caucusing on their own in the breakout room. I found the blacks laughing deeply and congratulating each other. How was it for you? I asked. "Oh, you'll see," came an answer. "We're going to party tonight." The closing circle was barely over before hot music was blasting and the black students were calling the whites to dance with them. Of all the student parties I've been to, I've never seen a better time.

Since the 1970s, I've used speak-outs multiple times, with margins of gender, culture, sexual orientation, and religion. The tool is best used rigorously, with the teacher standing next to the group that is speaking out, asking specific questions in a specific sequence and facilitating the exercise, while the listeners sit quietly in their seats or on the floor.

Note that the exercise has the shape of confrontation: (1) no one knows what will be said, or (2) how passionately, and (3) the issues addressed are painfully real. In each of those respects the activity is characteristic of nonviolent action. Still, the activity is facilitated by the teacher, and when the container is strong enough, I've used speak-outs in the classroom as well as in the course's weekend retreat.

Two Principles that Maximize the Learning of Nonviolent Action

The classical four-step model of experiential education (Kolb 1984) works for teaching the power of nonviolent action:

> *One*: The experience (for example, watching a film, speak-out or other juicy high-participation activity).
>
> *Two*: Reflection (thinking and processing what was going on in that film or other activity, what the dynamics were, what the impact of this or that element was, what worked, what didn't, etc.).
>
> *Three*: Generalization (plugging the reflection into one's cognitive map of the world or of oneself, comparing and contrasting with other cases/activities, building theory).
>
> *Four*: Application (trying out the knowledge in a fresh situation).

When I taught "Nonviolent Responses to Terrorism" at Swarthmore College, I structured the course around a term paper assignment: each student chose a country somewhere in the world that was threatened by terrorism, and had to create a nonviolent defense strategy specifically tailored to that country (Lakey 2009). In terms of Kolb's learning model, I organized the course around step four.

I diagnosed my students to be, like most Americans, sufficiently fearful of terrorism that it would be tough to meet this challenge. Application is rooted in imagination—people can't apply knowledge to a new, unique situation mechanically. To write their papers, the students would somehow have to melt their fear sufficiently to be able to apply their knowledge.

The container-building and my coaching (and of course the course content) were all directed toward unlocking their imaginations, and as a result, most students did design nonviolent strategies. Application was abundant.

Of course the fourth step, application, can be treated as a new step one, and the cycle is then repeated—a formula for lifelong learning, or what Gandhi called "experiments with truth" (1996). Below, I'll illustrate using the four-step model in teaching for the United Nations a global group of indigenous leaders the power of nonviolent action.

But first I'll describe another fundamental design principle in direct education. Harvard sociologist George Casper Homans (1950) observed that we gain our understanding of the world through a series of successive approximations.

Homans was certainly describing how I've learned about complex phenomena. I first get a very simple and superficial picture. I then add more aspects and the picture grows. With additional angles and connections the picture gets closer to how things really work. As I play with it in varied contexts, my image becomes still more complex and I'm able to make sense of more and more of what it is I'm trying to understand.

When I first began to teach college-level courses as a young man, I didn't perceive the value of teaching through successive approximations, even though that was in fact how I learn! Instead, I identified the body of knowledge at its appropriate level of complexity for the course, and then organized the information by abstract categories that were in some way logical.

I relied quite a bit on logic.

In those days (the 1960s), most of us teachers were innocent, imagining a homogeneous world in which everyone learned in the same, linear way. Years later I discovered the joy of teaching in alignment with how I—and others—actually learn! Instead of offering students opportunities to merely receive knowledge, I experimented with ways to encourage the pursuit of knowledge.

A problem arose. For creative curriculum designing, "successive approximation" didn't stoke my imagination. I needed a metaphor. I chose "peeling the onion." It's a working class image to balance the ivory tower. It taps the kinesthetic and visual learning channels. It's active, not passive, and invites discovery.

This way of thinking about the content of a course excites me because it invites empathic imagination: what are the successive layers of approximation through which participants' understanding of nonviolent action becomes ever more accurate and complex? Then, how do we design activities that will lead to the peeling of those layers of the onion, one by one? And how can we tap into the corresponding layers of the participant's own challenges and goals? For the sake of space and convenience, I'll describe the design process applied to a very short course.

The Geneva-based United Nations Institute for Training and Research (UNITAR) held, in the 1990s, a series of trainings on conflict resolution skills for indigenous leaders from all over the world. The graduates began to complain that negotiation skills are useless when nation-states regard the minorities as politically irrelevant; instead, indigenous peoples need skills in mobilizing nonviolent power to force power-holders to the negotiating table. In 2001, I was asked to lead a three-hour strategy workshop for the indigenous leaders.

I flew to Geneva a day early so I could get acquainted with the participants and some of their own experience with conflict and nonviolent struggle. Then I made my plan: to assist them to understand the distinctions among three different applications of nonviolent action, since such an understanding could be important for their beginning to strategize in their own situations. I'll use bold type to outline the session's onion-peeling structure, and italics for the steps in the model of experiential education.

We started with an *experience* in which I stood next to the flip chart and the participants shouted out any images and associations they had with the phrase "nonviolent action." I wrote as quickly as I could. We *reflected* on the list. I circled and linked some images and then related them to Gene Sharp's (1973) definition. I didn't claim that Sharp was correct, only that it would be convenient if we used the same term for this workshop. This *generalization* step narrowed and sharpened their initial images and associations—**the first layer of the onion**.

In small groups, participants next shared cases of nonviolence that they'd heard of, including those in the histories of their own people (the *experience* step). We harvested the small group work in the whole group (*reflection*), and did some work comparing and contrasting (*generalization*), thereby reaching the **second layer** of the onion: "There are many cases in our own indigenous histories of this thing Gene Sharp calls non-violent action!"

Together with the whole group of thirty, we returned to the *experience* step, and performed a parallel lines exercise (sometimes called a "hassle line") in which we role played an intervention intended to halt abuse. (This and other tools are described in detail at www.TrainingforChange.org.)

After *reflecting* on which tactic was most effective, we *generalized* this form of action and gave it a name: "third-party nonviolent intervention," which I consider a major application of nonviolent action. By characterizing a particular kind of conflict to which nonviolent action can be applied, we introduced a new cognitive step and sharpened our understanding of this **third layer** of the onion.

The group container was growing rapidly (thanks especially to the role playing), so I grabbed the momentum and generalized some more: I explained that in addition to the application of third-party nonviolent intervention, there are two other nonviolent applications—social change and social defense (**fourth layer**).

In traditional education, this is where the process might stop. We've "covered" the curriculum goal of Gene Sharp's definition of nonviolent action, in addition to three major applications. I, however, have zero confidence that "covering" is the same as "internalizing" or actually changing the cognitive map of most of the participants. People need to work with ideas to "get" them: "We learn by doing" (Dewey 1966). We need a step of application. In this case, as frequently happens, the application is a new experience.

To achieve this step, we undertook another experience/application by going to the oft-neglected kinesthetic channel of learning. We had an "applications relay race." Relay teams raced back and forth across the room with cards—printed with their own conflict situations—to place them under categories printed in large letters on the opposing wall: CHANGE, DEFENSE, THIRD-PARTY NONVIOLENT INTERVENTION, UNCLEAR.

When the teams had all finished, with much cheering, they gathered at the wall and reflected on where they had placed the cards. I led a discussion that compared and contrasted the different choices the teams made, generalizing and sharpening our evolving theory. We reached the **fifth layer**: understanding the three applications and their relation to each other.

Finally, with the three-hour session drawing to a close, I put my finger into the pie they'd cooked, giving my own judgments about which nonviolent applications match which of their situations back home. Of course, I welcomed it when they challenged me; the challenges elicited the **sixth layer**: strategists can sometimes choose how to frame a campaign. A group may find it more useful to frame their struggle as, for example, defending something (e.g., the rainforest) rather than changing something (e.g., the capitalist system that is destroying the rainforest).

In the three hours we went from a vague scattering of images of what nonviolent action might be to a working conceptual framework that supports choices for strategy. We harnessed the classical model of experiential education, peeled six layers of the onion, and the group had fun doing it.

Practicing through Waging Conflict in the Group

Mass graves were still being uncovered and the atrocities committed by all sides were fresh in people's minds. In a 2001 course at the University of Bologna, we had twenty-two young Serbians, Croatians, and Bosnians who had been directly affected by the wars in Bosnia, Croatia, and Kosovo. The course offered skills for building nongovernmental organizations in the participants' home countries, but the university hoped that these former enemies would also find common ground. Knowing how volatile the mix was, and that I had been studying with Arnold Mindell and his Process Work colleagues, I was asked to co-teach the group.

The first part of the weekend course was the honeymoon period, where participants "made nice." On Saturday afternoon, pretense faded and anxiety began to surface. By late afternoon, the tension was thick but our three-person teaching team waited for it to be acknowledged in the group. Finally, a young Serbian man said it: "The air in here is really tough—so tense. Can't you teachers help us?"

"Let's do something about that," I responded. "Let's take a break, and when you come back we'll suggest a way forward."

During the break our team huddled. "I have an idea," I said, and quickly explained it. The others agreed and asked what their roles would be. "Two things are helpful," I said. "One is to appear confident, even if at times you are a bit shaky. The participants will need the reassurance. The second thing is to pray!"

Our participants returned and I greeted them with a smile. I started with a question. "You know how sometimes the weather can be hot and very humid, and you wish it would just rain and get it over with?"

Heads nodded. "That's what we have here, an atmosphere that needs a storm so the air can clear. So our next activity will be to precipitate a storm." Participants gave each other confused and worried looks. I continued:

This storm will have some structure to it so it will be safe. First, we'll do this activity standing within our circle of chairs. Whoever wants to start off will make some kind of statement. If you can identify with or relate to part of what the person says, move your body to where they are. Stand beside them or sit beside them even if you disagree with some of what they're saying but agree with other parts or if you can relate to the feeling that's underneath what they're saying. Maybe you are feeling nervous and it seems like they are nervous; it's fine to move to be with them and support them even if the words they're saying don't quite express your point of view.

Someone will say something different from the first statement, so, again, anybody who can relate to that can go stand beside that person. Maybe the two who have said something will argue back and forth. It's likely that someone else will take a third position, and we'll ask that person to take a spot on the floor while they say it. Again, some people will move to identify with that third position.

If the point of view that occurs to you isn't expressed, yet, take a fresh position on the floor and state it. Others may join you as you are saying it, or afterward. There may be multiple places on the floor occupied by different people.

Even if you've recently taken a place on the floor and expressed something and you hear something else that you agree with, please move to that place. We're creating mobility with our bodies here to avoid the stuckness that makes conflict sometimes boring and even destructive. Got that so far? [Heads nodded.]

Second, you'll need to express your feelings honestly, and as strongly as you'd like. Yelling is fine, crying is fine. We'll ask you not to hit each other [alarmed looks appeared], because that wouldn't be safe. If someone forgets themselves and hits somebody else, facilitators will simply step between them to stop it and we'll continue with the storm.

It was time for the other two facilitators to look confident. "Oh, and another thing: the facilitator may sometimes say something intended to express a feeling or position that hasn't yet been said, just as a way to get it out into the open. It might not be the facilitator's own view, but this is simply a way to give voice to something in the room that hasn't yet been expressed. Because the facilitator may do that again and again, what she or he says may be completely contradictory—which is fine, because the facilitator is just wanting to give voice to what otherwise might remain silent."

A worried participant spoke up. "How will we know that the storm is over?"

"You'll know, just as you do in nature with a rainstorm. But if there is any doubt—still a raindrop here or there—the facilitators will make the call. OK, please get on your feet. The floor is open to anyone who wants to make the first statement."

Only a moment passed before a young Croat launched a blistering attack on the Serbs. The storm had begun, with counter attack soon following, and decibels rising. Facilitators moved among the young people, reminding them to stand beside the person who had said something they could identify with in some way. The choreography unfolded as more points of view were expressed and participants moved from one polarization to another. Veins were sticking out in the necks of some of those yelling. Suddenly, a quiet moment came. Someone would begin to sob. Other statements, and then more yelling. When two participants moved toward each other to go head to head, facilitators intervened and reminded them to hold their places on the floor so others could join them.

The storm went for hours, with the argumentation becoming ever more complex. Oversimplifications were dropped; historical myths were shattered and left behind. Participants listened and moved, listened and moved, as a tapestry of understanding began to be woven.

Suddenly, the storm was over. Participants looked around in wonder, as if the sun had suddenly come out after a deluge. "Looks like the storm is over—is that right?" I asked.

Heads nodded. "Please get together with your buddy and share what that storm was like for you, personally."

They eagerly moved to their buddies—a comfort zone at last! The room was full of buzzing and occasional tears.

Teachers huddled, too, each of us beaming. "I know you were praying," I said, and we all cracked up, then shared how it was for us to hold the container while emotions were bouncing off its walls.

"Please bring your buddy into the closing circle," I announced. Participants circled up, looking like completely different people from their sullenness in the afternoon. "Please share in a word or phrase the state you're in just now."

"Relieved" was the word used most often, closely followed by "enlightened."

We all trooped off to dinner at the restaurant we'd contracted with. Jokes and laughter rippled among the hungry young people. Facilitators finally pulled away from the group to go back to the dorm to prepare. The next morning we learned that these former enemies had stayed at the restaurant until it closed at 3:00 a.m., laughing and sharing their lives with each other.

The Bologna story illuminates the difference between "comfort zone" and "safety." Each of us has a comfort zone, consisting of those habits, beliefs, relationships, feelings, and actions that for us are comfortable or familiar.

While a comfort zone is reassuring, it can get stuffy and boring. Humans often leave their comfort zones for stimulation and excitement. We may raft on white water, drive too fast, ride a roller coaster, date someone very different from ourselves, or see a scary movie. Some people will pay a great deal of money to become uncomfortable and climb a distant mountain or enter an exotic race.

When we leave our comfort zone many people check to make sure they'll be safe—the bungee cord won't break, the date will happen in a public place. We know that safety is a different issue from discomfort, and teachers need to keep that distinction very clearly in mind.

The young people in Bologna went to a very scary place in sharing their conflicts with one another, and not one was comfortable. They were, however, safe. To maximize learning, invite students out of their comfort zones as frequently as possible. Coupled with awareness, the experience of discomfort is crucial to learning the power of nonviolent action.

Break Out!—A Case Study

Haverford College is a small Quaker school surrounded by a large campus, in turn surrounded by Philadelphia's tony Main Line suburbs. Conflict avoidance was the culture. How, then, to teach the power of nonviolent action?

Mid-semester, I announced that we were getting on the commuter train together and going into Philadelphia's downtown to stand on a street corner and speak. Blood drained from some faces. "You've had a buddy system all semester," I reminded them, "so now is the time for you to come through for your buddy. Assist him or her to make the most of this learning opportunity."

I gave them a short time to decide their individual topic after answering some of their questions about the exercise. We jumped on the train and were soon nervously milling on a corner across from City Hall. I pointed to the milk crate we were to stand on. "So, one at a time each of you will get the chance to speak for a couple of minutes. If you feel you need to pass, you can do so. We'll do a second round," (I heard groans) "and you can always jump in then when you see that we're not dead yet." (I heard nervous laughs.)

Students chose numbers from one to thirty-five to get their speaking order, and number one began.

By the fourth speaker the group's energy started to build, and by the eighth we looked centered enough that a couple of pedestrians stopped to listen. The tenth speaker surprised himself by how long he held forth and how funny he was, and the group began to relax. One of the students who had insisted to me on the train that she would never speak—"ever!"—got up on the box. A few students engaged with bystanders after they got down from their turn. A few came to me (I stood on the edge of the crowd) with eyes glowing: "Can I speak on a different topic for the second round?"

During our second round we got our first real heckling, and the student rose to the occasion, enjoying the argument. That attracted far more bystanders, and some students had trouble gazing supportively at the speaker (as I had instructed) because they were fascinated by the diversity of people stopping to listen: business people, hippies, teens with skateboards, a priest, blue-collar workers just off from work, and assorted races and genders.

At the end of the first round I took my turn, and at the end of the second I called the event over; I then had our group circle up for a quick debrief. "In the next class session," I said, "we'll take a longer time for debrief, but tonight it's important that you do some quality journaling on what happened for you, especially with regard to conflict and courage. And be sure to check in with your buddy on the train on the way back to campus."

Most of the times that I've taught peace studies, I've taken my class to do street speaking. The students experience it as scary, just as nonviolent action often is. Consider the elements of the activity: uncertainty, strangers and sometimes crowds, sometimes police, the opportunity to give and get support, each person taking personal responsibility, and not even the leader knows for sure what will happen. The structural model of typical nonviolent action is there.

Then, afterward, the celebrating: "We did it!" "It wasn't so bad!" "My buddy made the difference!" "I can't believe I was actually coherent when the heckler came!" "Did you notice that person who stopped and listened for the longest time?" "I think we actually connected with some people!"

Street speaking as pedagogy, an exercise also available from Training for Change, delivers the experience of nonviolent power to most students. To them it feels risky, but the teacher can choose sites that have as little risk as most field trips. Students bring the excitement back to the classroom with heightened zest for learning. It is the surest bridge that I've found to assist students in relating to the Student Nonviolent Coordinating Committee (SNCC), Alice Paul, Malcolm X, Norman Thomas, the Wobblies, and other trailblazers in exploring the complexities of nonviolent action.

Direct Education: A Pedagogy for Our Times

Students, as well as adults, observe that political leaders will not (I would say *cannot*) change war-making and planet-destroying policies by themselves. The path to an empowered citizenry requires giving up conflict aversion, which in turn is marked by pedagogies that are conflict friendly. Direct education offers a structure and tools that accelerate learning for participants who will act for justice and peace. It stimulates students to learn the power of nonviolent action in a course, and in life, as well.

10

Teaching Peace in Higher Education

The Role of Creativity

Laura L. Finley

Learning can be fun
Stretch your mind in unique ways
Stress is not required
—A haiku introduction
to my classes

Introduction

Although an increasing number of universities are incorporating some type of peace education in their curricula, there is still much work to be done. One concern with peace education courses is that their focus too often is still on negative peace. Additionally, many peace education courses simply teach about peace, but not for peace. Courses that teach about peace focus exclusively on content, or what is taught. Many times, these courses fail to use innovative methods in presenting peace education. Courses that teach for peace emphasize Johan Galtung's (1996) notion of "peace by peaceful means." These courses address the three levels identified by Riane Eisler (1987): content, processes/methods, and structure. Thus, courses that teach for peace go beyond what is taught to create environments in which power is shared and cooperation, not competition, is the primary mode of instruction.

These are what Eisler referred to as "partnership" models. As Parker Palmer (1998) pointed out, education as it is currently done is full of paradoxes. It separates head from heart, facts from feelings, theory from practice, and teaching from learning. Emphasis is on the cognitive realm and, even more narrowly, on specific disciplines that are separated from one another (Gardner 1999). As is hopefully clear from my opening haiku, my philosophy of education is much different. As a collegiate peace educator working in the fields of sociology and criminology, I believe teaching and learning to be creative are arts in and of themselves.

This chapter explores the need for creativity in establishing and implementing peace education courses in colleges and universities that are not just about peace, but *for* peace, as well. I begin with a brief exploration of the dominator model, as well as other barriers to implementing peace education, and then highlight some of the many ways that creativity is beneficial, ultimately providing recommendations for universities and colleges in establishing and implementing transformative peace education courses and programs. The chapter concludes with some of my favorite creative classroom activities and projects.

Defining Peace

Peace scholars generally differentiate between positive and negative peace. The distinction is credited to Galtung (1984), who came to define negative peace as the absence of overt violent conflict. Positive peace is far more than this. It is the absence of overt violent conflict, coupled with conditions of social, political, and economic justice (O'Kane 1991–92; Reardon 1995). I agree with Ian Harris and M. Morrison (2003, 13) that positive peace should be "concerned with different forms of violence and operate[s] at many different levels of human existence." Positive peace is the recognition that various forms of violence—interpersonal, economic, environmental, institutional, and more—are interconnected. To me, positive peace embodies the notion that we must "be the change" in that it emphasizes not just outcomes, but also the methods used to achieve them.

Peace Education

Harris and Morrison (2003, 4) describe peace education as follows: "Peace education involves students and educators in a commitment to create a more just and peaceful world order. This type of education (adaptable to all ages and all sorts of settings) provides citizens with information about current policies, sharpens their ability to analyze current states of affairs, encourages commitment to various spheres of individual concern and endeavor—politics, public affairs, trade union activities, social and cultural life—and strives to promote the free will necessary to make personal choices about public policy."

I like this description because it emphasizes what I believe to be the key elements of any quality peace education program: the idea that students and educators are in collaboration, not opposition; that peace education can and should take place anywhere and with any group; and that the goal of peace education is more than just knowledge—it also compels us toward commitment to social change for human betterment.

Peace education takes many forms, some focused mostly on negative peace and others more inclusive. These range from conflict resolution or peer mediation focused at the micro level to more macro-level peaceable schools (Patti 2001). While some peace education programs focus more specifically on war and conflict, others are multidisciplinary and address broader human rights issues, both domestically and globally. Many draw from women's studies programs that have long been framed on the three Cs—care, compassion, and connectedness (Forcey and Harris 1999). Recently, peace educators have begun to include attention to the environment, as well (Harris and Morrison 2003; Lin 2006; Wals 1999).

While it sounds like there can be no downside to peace education, problems do arise in how it is implemented. Betty Reardon (1997, 21) explained that when education focuses on peacemaking, it is emphasizing negative peace and on "what should not be than to the positive possibilities of what could be. So it is that peace education and peace studies (as the field is known in universities) have been a bit of a 'downer' for all but those students who are 'positive thinkers' by nature, drawn to social action fields, or simply curious about the study of the 'impossible'." In essence, it is a discouraging experience that can leave students depressed or jaded. My field of sociology/criminology has long been accused of the same thing: when you are critiquing social structures that are the genesis for numerous social problems, students sometimes feel as though they are powerless to make change. Harris and Morrison (2003) explained that true peace education is both about peace and for peace. That is, students receive information about problems related to violence, militarism, and social inequalities at the same time that they are taught and encouraged to use nonviolent skills for social change. Ultimately, what is taught is equally as important as how it is taught.

Challenges to Implementing Peace Education

Although there has been some wonderful expansion in recent years, many schools and universities still lack peace education programs or courses. Eisler's (1987) work is also instructive in explaining the reluctance to fully implement peace education in schools and in other institutions. Eisler (1987, 2000) described two ideologies or models that influence the creation and maintenance of all our major institutions, including schools. These are "systems of belief and social structures that either nurture and support—or inhibit and undermine—equitable, democratic, nonviolent, and caring relations" (Eisler 2000, xiv). These she called the partnership model and the dominator model (ibid.). The dominator model is a model of interaction based on power over, not power with. It values competition over cooperation and domination over partnership. Authority, discipline, obedience, efficiency, and rationality are of greatest importance in a dominator system (Marullo 1993; Merryfinch 1981).

Eisler pointed out that our society generally uses a dominator model in three levels or layers: our content, our methods, and our structures. Structure refers to "where learning takes place: what kinds of learning environments we construct" (2000, xvi). Process refers to the ways we learn and teach. Content is "what we learn and teach. It is the educational curriculum" (xv).

Many of our traditional teaching methods can be summed up in one word: boring. Paulo Freire (1983, 284) referred to these passive methods as "banking education," which he described as "the art of depositing, in which the students are the depositories and the teacher is the depositor." It is a system where students are seated quietly and obediently and are waiting for their teachers to "impart truth" upon them (Finley 2003, 6).

Controversial issues may be presented, but are often done so through methods that do not allow students the chance to question or challenge; to permit such challenges means relinquishing power.

Many teaching practices allow little emotional expression, rather focusing on so-called rationality (Finley 2004). Because of this, findings from a 2002 survey indicated that students were generally not engaged in their coursework and almost half turned in assignments that did not reflect their best work (Sax et al. 2002). In addition, the majority of them felt more overwhelmed and depressed than they did when they entered college (Duerr, Zajonc, and Dana 2003). A nationwide poll conducted in December 2009 found that 60 percent of respondents believe colleges most resemble businesses and care primarily about the bottom line.

Teacher education programs are also heavily reliant on dominator models. Future educators are taught that the most important thing is to control their students. Teacher education literature posits that college professors may not have received partnership-model training, and thus are more likely to "default" to the banking model of education (Bauman 2005; Burke 2001; Cassuto 1998).

College classrooms tend to be dominator-structured. The large lecture hall, so common on large campuses (and even smaller campuses, today) creates a structure in which the professor or instructor is the "sage on the stage" and the students are sitting in nice, even rows that make it difficult to create any type of collaborative environment (Sperber 2000). The tendency to increase class sizes makes it far more difficult for professors to truly know their students, thus furthering the separation of fact from feeling (Palmer 1998). Students have very little voice in the authority structure of a typical college classroom, as professors generally select the material to be included, the methods of delivery, and the assignments to be used. Clearly, the dominator model is in opposition to one that truly promotes positive peace.

The dominator model, although insidious, is not immutable. Once we see how it has influenced higher education and the negative impact it has had, we can move on to creating a different way. As Paulo Freire (1974, 47) said, "To surmount the situation of oppression, people must first critically recognize its causes, so that through transforming action they can create a new situation, one which makes possible the pursuit of a fuller humanity."

Another Possibility

Eisler (2000) suggested that we do not have to follow a dominator model; instead, a partnership model is possible. This model would involve cooperation, shared power, and the institutionalization of mutual honoring, respect, and peaceful means of conflict resolution—what Fellman (1998) referred to as mutuality. Nancy Flowers and David Shiman (1997) asserted that, under a partnership model, peace and human rights would be the fundamental organizing principle behind our systems of education. Importantly, a partnership model would require reconsidering the content we teach, the methods we use, and the structures we create. Peace education is a natural fit with partnership education when they both teach about peace and for peace. Peace education is a way to question structural violence—the dominator model—and to create an alternate system (Harris and Morrison 2003).

The first step in creating a partnership-modeled program is to envision what that would look like. Our creativity must be tapped individually, but also collectively. Maxine Greene (1995) explained that the mind can be nurtured to think not just about what is, but what can and ought to be. Lin (2006) envisioned such a system. The pedagogy for a school based on love would include reflectiveness, tranquility and silence, learning humility and simplicity, sensitivity, direct contact with nature, direct contact with people around the world, and creativity and imagination (ibid.). Similarly, Nel Noddings (2005) argued for schools based on caring. For her, caring is more than empathy—it is moving away from the self toward being receptive to others. These concepts can clearly be extended beyond the traditional school walls. As Martha Nussbaum (2003, 405) explained, "the relationship between compassion and social institutions is and should be a two-way street: compassionate individuals construct institutions that embody what they imagine; and institutions, in turn, influence the development of compassion in individuals."

My vision of college education always involves fun. I figure, if it seems fun to me, it is at least more likely that my students will also find it fun. If what spews out of my mouth bores me, chances are decent that it will bore them, too. That might sound simplistic, but I do not believe it is. Rather, I think putting "fun first" is essential to teaching about peace because it helps avoid that "bummer" factor described earlier in this chapter. Further, and even more critically, a fun classroom inspires students to get involved.

I believe that it is creativity that will allow us to create partnership-based systems of education that teach both about and for peace. Such classrooms would be based on caring and commitment to change. Although creativity is often considered the sole domain of the arts or of artists, as scholars like Galtung (1996), Martin Seligman and Mihaly Csikszentmihalyi (2007), and Glenn Paige (2009) have noted, creativity is far more inclusive. Creativity allows us to see how we have contributed and continue to contribute to social problems in the world, why it is our responsibility to do something about them, and the difference we can make. Creativity can help us envision a better world—the first step in making changes toward creating that better world (Jones, Johnson, and Haenfler 2007; Paige 2009; Urbain 2009). "Dreaming and creating visions are part of everyday life. When people imagine, they express a cherished wish for how they would like to live and how they would like the world to be" (Harris and Morrison 2003, 38).

When we use our creativity to reach people, we are viewed as more authentic (Seligman and Csikszentmihalyi 2007). This authenticity helps people shift their value systems toward peace and justice (Van Slyck and Stern 1999). When we use our creativity, we realize that one person can indeed make a difference, and that one person can inspire others to do so, as well (Jones, Johnson, and Haenfler 2007). We begin to see that every one of our actions, even our inactions, is a form of activism towards something. We can "teach to transgress," as bell hooks (1994) called it, or challenge the status quo when we step out of our normal, mundane, and repressive boxes and engage in creative peace education. When we are creative, we see that we can be more intentional about creating a more peaceful planet, a global nonkilling society, and that even the little things we do make a difference (Paige 2009; Urbain 2009).

Creativity and Education

David Feldman and Ann Benjamin (2006) explained that there has been little focus on creativity at educational levels beyond early childhood. I think this is because people equate creativity with play, and in a dominator system, play is solely the domain of kids. Fun and academic rigor are viewed as mutually exclusive. Friedrich Froebel (1887) was one of the first to recognize the importance of creativity and play in education. John Dewey (1902) likewise called for less restrictive and more creative schooling; he criticized the commonly used recitation methods, arguing instead for more direct experience and more play. Additionally, US educators at the elementary school level have been influenced by the cognitive development work of Jean Piaget since the later 1950s. Many Piagetian programs emphasized ways to encourage children to generate new ideas or to think of things in new, creative ways. Creative, open education was, according to Feldman and Benjamin (2006), "the order of the day" in US classrooms in the later 1960s, with hands-on and inquiry-based methods supplementing, if not replacing workbooks and textbooks in many schools.

Most scholars mark the beginning of contemporary creativity research with J. P. Guilford's Presidential Address before the American Psychological Association on September 5, 1950. Aside from Guilford's (1950) call, in the United States, the drive to study creativity arose from concerns about national defense and focused on technological inventiveness, thus creativity in this sense was popular, yet still dominator-focused. As the focus shifted toward defining creativity as rebelliousness or as having the capacity to break with tradition, the research community quickly found itself without government support. Differing ideas about creativity, embedded in conflicting cultural values, proved catastrophic for creativity research in America (Craft 2005).

Brazilian educator and Sao Paulo Minister of Education Paulo Freire created a progressive model of education and creativity, and used the name of his educational theory as the title for his book *The Pedagogy of the Oppressed* (1974). The concept developed as part of a literacy program for people living in the slum areas of Sao Paulo. Freire's pedagogy is "intended to make the oppressed people creative and throw away their chains of poverty and oppression" (1974, 367–68). Thus, Freire linked creativity in process to creativity in outcome. Along similar lines, a Catholic priest, Ivan Illich, wrote *Deschooling Society* (1970)—a best seller about education and creativity seen from the radical humanist paradigm. His central theme is that schooling in general is dysfunctional for creative individual development; schooling tends to make people more stupid than if they had not been in school. The best learning goes on outside school, in real environments (ibid.). In a Norwegian context, the same radical humanist ideas of schooling were elaborated by Nils Christie in *If School Did Not Exist* (1971).

Personality studies have demonstrated that creative people of all ages tend to be nonconforming, independent, intrinsically motivated, open to new experiences, and risk seeking. They are tolerant of ambiguity, have self-confidence and tend to pursue tasks for intrinsic rewards (Amabile 1985, 1996; Amabile, Hennessey, and Grossman 1986; Eisenberger and Cameron 1996; Hennessey and Amabile 1998; Feist 1998; MacKinnon 1978; Simonton 2000, 2003). A distant future focus, compared to a near future focus, has been shown to lead to more creative negotiation outcomes (Okhuysen, Galinsky, and Uptigrove 2003) and to enhanced creative insight (Förster, Friedman, and Liberman 2004). Creative people focus on potential gains rather than losses (Friedman and Förster 2004; Lam and Chiu 2002). Finally, creativity seems to flourish when people are in positive or neutral affective states, rather than negative affective states (Amabile et al. 2005; Fredrickson 2001; Fong 2006).

As noted, there has been little focus to date on creativity and higher education. Yet, some evidence suggests it is indeed valued. Jackson and Shaw (2005) compiled a list of the most common ideas academics associate with creativity, and they were: originality; being imaginative; exploring for the purpose of discovery, or doing/producing new things (invention); doing/producing things no one has ever done before (innovation); doing/producing things that have been done before but differently (adaptation, transference); and communication. When Robert Sternberg and Tamara

Gordeeva (1996) asked 252 research psychologists what made a psychology article influential, the items that were rated as most important centered around creativity and novelty: making an obvious contribution to psychological knowledge, adding something new and substantial; presenting a useful new theory; generating new research; and providing new and exciting ideas.

One concern is that most definitions and descriptions of creativity come from the Western world and thus reflect western values, i.e., radical innovation may be seen as creative in the United States, but could lead to social sanctions in Japan (Westwood and Low 2003). Eastern cultures have been less concerned with outcome or product, and more with the role of creativity in providing personal fulfillment and enlightenment, or connection to an inner realm of reality (Chu 1970; Kuo 1996; Lubart 1999; Mathur 1982). As always, there is much to be learned by understanding other cultures.

How Creativity Helps

Creative institutions, as well as creative individuals, are more productive. In fact, Robert Fritz (1994) explained that the most important developments in the world have come from the creative process. Anna Craft (2003, 114) explained that "the economy demands creativity, and a healthy economy is necessary to a wealthy society[,] which then produces assets for general consumption, better public amenities and services." Economists are now seeing creativity as a form of capital, and thus as an engine of economic growth and social dynamism. Florida (2004) emphasized that a company's most important asset is not raw materials, transportation systems, or political influence. Rather, it is creative capital—creative thinkers whose ideas can be turned into valuable products and services.

Abraham Maslow (1970) was perhaps the first to recognize that the creative individual is a fulfilled person and one who has personal agency. Additionally, Maslow and others have recognized that creativity is not the sole domain of unique capabilities like those of Albert Einstein, but instead is open to everyday life and problem-solving (Craft 2003; Amabile 1996; Feldman, Csikszentmihalyi, and Gardner 1994; Runco and

Richards 1997). Craft (2003) described "lifewide" creativity, meaning creativity that is useful for a breadth of tasks. This is distinct from "extraordinary creativity," which involves the production of new knowledge in an area of interest, as established by experts in that field (ibid.).

It is through creativity that we can reach learners of all sorts. By "all sorts," I mean all age ranges, in all settings, and of all learning types. Howard Gardner's (1983) work on multiple intelligences created the framework for understanding that not all people learn in the same way. He argued that humans do not just have one form of intelligence, but rather seven: linguistic intelligence, or a strong ability to understand and use spoken and written language; logical-mathematical intelligence, or the ability to analyze problems logically; musical intelligence; bodily-kinesthetic intelligence; spatial intelligence; interpersonal intelligence; and intrapersonal intelligence. More recently, Gardner and others have argued that there are more than seven intelligences. In 1999, Gardner concluded that there is also a naturalist intelligence, i.e., an ability to understand and appreciate nature. Lin (2006, 155) referred to this as ecological intelligence, or the "innate ability of all species to live in harmony with their environment and to adjust to changes and be sustained and survive . . . [, and] the ability to see life as an interconnected web." Others have argued for a spiritual intelligence, an existential intelligence, and a moral intelligence, although Gardner has not concluded they meet enough of the criteria he used to determine his designated intelligences.

In *Intelligence Reframed: Multiple Intelligences for the 21st Century,* Gardner explained, "I want my children to understand the world, but not just because the world is fascinating and the human mind is curious. I want them to understand it so that they will be positioned to make it a better place" (1999, 181). Thus, not only are programs that are devised around Gardner's multiple intelligences concept more creative and more appropriately suited to diverse learners, they are also well suited to teach peace. Creativity allows us to create wonderful interactive games and simulations, which are a great way to handle controversial topics in a way that encourages broad participation. I begin my visioning for a new semester with the multiple intelligences in mind. I then consider how to utilize as many as possible in crafting assignments.

Helen Timperley and Viviane Robinson (2000) suggest that teachers may need to be helped to take a more creative approach in tackling the variety of demands placed on them if they are to avoid becoming overwhelmed by the job. The reasoning behind this claim is that creativity mitigates and counteracts the deadening effects of repetition and overload, including the impact of so-called "innovation fatigue." Creativity is, according to Galtung (1996), the most effective way to deal with contradictions.

Creativity helps us see unique ways to incorporate peace education into existing courses or programs, or to move forward with proposals for new programs. "Peace education enhances the purpose of education, which is to reveal and tap into those energies that make possible the full human enjoyment of a meaningful and productive existence" (Harris and Morrison 2003, 5). I humbly present here some of the activities and ideas I have used that I believe tap those creative energies.

Recommendations for Creative Peace Education

At the structural level, universities should allow faculty regular opportunities to brainstorm and to collaborate in the creation of new courses and programs. Faculty should be provided the chance to share innovative teaching methods, and must be rewarded for introducing new methods that engage students and help them become actively involved in creating peace (Burke 2001) Further, it is very easy for universities to offer professional development for faculty that help enhance their knowledge and skills related to peace education and to provide useful new tools to stimulate creativity.

Although creativity is not the sole domain of artists, there is much that can be accomplished when peace education is integrated with the arts— music, theatre, visual arts, and more. Paige (2009) explained that an investigation of works of art that "uplift the human spirit" can open the door for a more peaceful, nonkilling world. Universities can showcase student and faculty work that condemns violence and advances peace. Further, universities can ensure that their arts programs serve as centers for common creativity around the pursuit of peace (Paige 2009; Urbain 2009).

Community colleges have created some innovative peace education programs. For instance, Daryl Smith (2007) cited Truman College, part of the City Colleges of Chicago, which sponsored forty-five Sudanese boys who lost their families in recent atrocities in Sudan, housing them and allowing them to take classes free of charge. He commented, "Sponsoring students in the United States is something that nearly every community college can do. Unfortunately, many of the foreign students whom community colleges sponsor now are not the neediest, but come from stable communities and, like more traditional exchange students, can afford American college educations. Community colleges could do more to reach out to youths who have been scarred by violence" (30).

The study of human rights is a form of peace education and can easily be integrated into a number of college and university courses, including history, sociology, political science, literature, and more. Since the various ways in which human rights can be *violated* are in themselves controversial, as are many recent issues related to human rights—such as the use of torture in the fight against terrorism—current affairs content can easily be included in the form of debates, discussions, group activities, and other methods that teach for peace. Susan Opotow, Janet Gerson, and Sarah Woodside (2005, 306) have asserted that the study of human rights can encourage students to be morally inclusive, an attitude characterized by a willingness to "extend fairness to others, allocate resources to them and make sacrifices that would foster their well-being."

Multicultural experience seems to enhance creativity, as observed by Westwood and Low (2003, 173): "In short, multicultural experience may foster creativity by (a) providing direct access to novel ideas and concepts from other cultures, (b) creating the ability to see multiple underlying functions behind the same form, (c) destabilizing routinized knowledge structures, thereby increasing the accessibility of normally inaccessible knowledge, (d) creating a psychological readiness to recruit ideas from unfamiliar sources and places, and (e) fostering synthesis of seemingly incompatible ideas from diverse cultures."

An individual who has been exposed to different cultures may be able to spontaneously retrieve seemingly disparate ideas from each culture, and then juxtapose and integrate those ideas in novel ways (Chiu and Hong 2005; Chiu and Leung 2007). Expanding access to study-abroad programs for both students and faculty is highly recommended.

Service learning is another useful method in teaching about and for peace. Different from volunteering, service learning is as "the integration of community service activities (as defined by the community) into the curriculum through intentional analytical processes such as journals, papers, and other expositional forms to enhance students' learning of course content" (Marullo and Edwards 2000, 747). Service learning has long been utilized as a way to both engage students and for praxis objectives (Jacoby 1996). Through service learning, students connect to one another and to their community, develop a sense of empathy and pride (Koliba 2000), acquire more finely tuned critical analysis and writing skills and can better see connections between theory and practice (Alberle-Grasse 2000; Kuh 1995; Parker-Gwin 1996; Roschelle, Turpin, and Elias 2000). Service learning may have a long-term impact on students. Melissa Alberle-Grasse (2000) found that students who engaged in service learning were more likely to enter careers in the nonprofit sector, or in service and advocacy organizations. Robin Crews and Kathleen Weigert (1999) have shown how service learning enhances peace education.

In the classroom, peace education should take place through discussion, with learners guiding their own education, as Freire (1974) argued. Teachers and students should both be active participants in teaching and learning. It is essential to create an educational environment in which young people feel comfortable when learning through inquiry and cooperation, both in the actual and the virtual classroom, and in working with people whose backgrounds may be very different from their own. Hal Pepinsky (2006, 434) highlighted the importance of allowing room for the voices that are often left out or marginalized. He explained, "Within each of us, as I see it, peacemaking potential is enhanced by balancing our attention among three categories of action: talking to others, listening to others, and listening to oneself" (ibid.).

Some Creative Ideas

There are a number of ways to set the tone in a classroom so that students feel comfortable getting involved. I like to begin with an easy icebreaker that asks students to speak with others, speed-dating style, about a variety of prompts related to peace. Not only does this get students thinking about peace, but it demonstrates that not everything that happens in the classroom must originate with me. I like that it gets students moving around, rather than sitting passively. Further, this activity shows that students will be expected to talk with one another and to share things about themselves, and that I, as their professor, will do the same. At the beginning of the semester, I often use another idea that I call "the blob." Students begin with a partner and must find one thing they have in common (they are instructed to look past the obvious and delve into deeper similarities or connections). After a short time, pairs of students connect to other pairs, so now a group of four must find some common ground. This can be repeated until the entire group is one big cluster—a beautiful symbol of shared humanity.

As a criminologist, like Hal Pepinsky (2006), a forebear of peacemaking criminology, I also must go on to actively confront the indoctrination my students have likely experienced from a form of "war-making." There is a war-making, dominator paradigm that is prevalent in lower education, in general, and specifically in students' understanding of criminal justice, where the prevailing response to crime for decades has been to make "war" on it. I must show my students that there is another way, both through what I teach and how I structure my course. One way that I try to do this is to start each course with a new syllabus each semester. I find this helps keep me engaged in the topic, as I search out new material and then inevitably find new ways to utilize it. I think students pick up on this "freshness" and I feel it helps them see that I am not just paying lip service to the idea that education is a process.

Pepinsky (2006) recommends "grading through non-grading," a technique of assessing student journals that emphasizes reflection over quantity. I typically allow students to revise and resubmit their work for full credit. While this inevitably makes more work for me, it is consistent with my philosophy that learning is a process, not a product. I usually allow students to take "exams" home and to even work in small groups to complete them, using their textbooks, notes, and other resources. Thus the exam becomes more an extension activity in which students synthesize the material, and less a solitary formulaic trial. They usually report feeling less stress, enjoying working with others who may have a more complete understanding of some subjects, and valuing the fact that I trusted them to show me what they knew in a different manner than is typically expected.

Pepinsky (2006) also suggests a peacemaking classroom is one in which uncertainty is acceptable. Instructors can establish a careful balance between creating an agenda and allowing for change to happen organically. I love that idea. Rather than a static document, syllabi can be fluid, reflecting what is happening in the world and what emerges out of classroom activity. Assignments that ask students to take the lead in class discussions or to arrange for guest speakers relevant to a specific topic can help make this happen.

I believe students need the opportunity to work in many different arrangements, so class activities will vary between partners, small groups, and larger ones. Using the multiple intelligences as a framework, I regularly ask students to share what they have learned by writing a haiku, a song, or a mock news story (modeling from the satiric *The Onion*). When I was volunteering in my daughter's kindergarten class, I saw how wonderfully her teacher used different groupings and activities through "centers." Why not in college, I thought? I often set up centers around the room and ask students to move through them in groups to engage in a variety of exercises. Some will involve arts, some discussion, some written work, and some manipulation. In one of our most fun classes, students used Play-Doh to show their classmates a concept. Students can make short videos using simple and widely available computer applications.

I often include some type of service-learning in my courses, and then require students to reflect verbally and in writing on how that experience connected to our course material and, specifically, to creating a more just world. When I don't require service learning, I will ask students to attend three or four relevant events outside of class, like seminars, film screenings, or conferences. Sometimes we attend as a class, taking an "on-campus field trip." Not only does this allow them to learn from other people and methods, but it generally connects them to new groups and opportunities. As Neil Postman (1996) wrote, there is no reason schooling must take place in a dingy classroom with your behind parked in an uncomfortable desk.

In addition, I like to have students help me organize events on campus. Depending on the class, we might organize a hunger banquet, a "sweatshop fashion show," a film festival, a human rights fair, or some other event in which my students help arrange speakers, agendas, food, and other details. We then open these events up to the campus and the broader community so we can share what we have learned, and learn even more from attendees. This embodies the teachers-as-learners and learners-as-teachers notion that Freire (1974) emphasized.

In sum, educators at all levels must be conscious that simply teaching about peace is not enough to transform our culture. Rather, it is imperative that we teach *for* peace, as well, which requires addressing the methods we use and structures we create. It is my hope that this chapter highlights how creativity can help, and provides the beginning of a conversation on creativity and peace education in colleges and universities.

11

Fostering a Culture of Nonviolence through Multicultural Education

Elavie Ndura

Introduction

What do a casual conversation at a diner, an impromptu discussion with a US Census worker, and Arizona Senate Bill 1070 have in common? They are all framed by damaging assumptions about what makes us American and what makes us human.

I was busy reviewing applications for the Shinnyo Fellowship for Peacebuilding through Intercultural Dialogue—a partnership between the Shinnyo-en Foundation and George Mason University—while waiting for my tuna-melt sandwich at a diner in Denver, Colorado, where I was to present two papers at the 2010 annual meeting of the American Educational Research Association. A tall man in his sixties and of seemingly Caucasian background interrupted me by inquiring, "Where in Africa are you from?" Startled by his obvious assumption, I inquired back with a smile, "How do you know I'm from Africa?" Unconfused by my beautiful blue George Mason University sweatshirt and the stack of papers I was reviewing, he questioned further, "Are you a diplomat?" I smiled again and questioned back, "What makes you think I'm a Diplomat?" He persisted, "How long are you staying in America?" and "What do you think about us Americans?" I could barely hold my amazement at how far his assumptions were leading him. I smiled some more and denied him direct answers. Undiscouraged, he asked, "Have you found Jesus?" and proceeded to hand me a paper that he claimed contained the information I needed in order to find Jesus and "be born again."

I refused to accept it. I finished my sandwich and as I headed out, I handed him my business card and said, "Google my name, and read my books." I think I was hoping that my business card would help to establish my identity as an American—in fact, a professor at one of the best universities in the United States—or at least my right to reside in the United States for as long as I would like. A few days later, a letter was delivered to my GMU office. It contained the paper that I had rejected at the diner, with lots of illegible scribbles all over. It was from Alan, the overzealous and all-assuming missionary. I guess he had chosen not to read my books, and persisted in his quest to change me into what he perceived as a worthy American. I tore the correspondence into pieces and threw it away in the recycling bin down the hall by my office.

A few weeks later, a knock on my front door broke through my kitchen duties. As I opened the door I was greeted by a man most likely in his fifties and seemingly of Caucasian ancestry. "I am with the US Census Bureau and I need to ask you a few questions," he said hurriedly. I let him in, stressing that I could only spare a few minutes. Somehow the census conversation turned into a passionate discussion about the current economic crisis. He insisted that President Barack Obama was responsible for the crisis because he did not know what he was doing. Unable to contain my shock, I asked him to reflect upon the policies and actions of former President George W. Bush and their impact on our daily life. To my argument that President Barack Obama is a thoughtful, intelligent, and articulate leader, he responded that he had inherited those skills from his mother. When I reminded him that Obama Senior was also a brilliant African man, he blurted, "That's why even at work I prefer to work with Africans rather than Black Americans!" as he walked out of my modest Virginia townhouse—clearly in a deliberate state of unconsciousness not unlike that of the born-again missionary at the Denver diner.

During the same time frame, and up to the writing of this chapter, the media and professional circles have been confounded by the immigration debate generated by Arizona Senate Bill 1070 (S.B. 1070) that Governor Jan Brewer signed into law on April 23, 2010. The bill makes it a state crime to be in Arizona without federal authorization, and a punishable offense to support someone without the appropriate documents. Although denied by its proponents, S.B. 1070 will clearly magnify differences of race and ethnicity, deepen the gulf between culturally diverse communities, and cause people of color to live in constant fear regardless of their immigration status.

It is against this backdrop that I inquire: What makes us American? What makes us human? How do our assumptions about and responses to these questions shape our interpretation and implementation of the United Nations' (UN) Universal Declaration of Human Rights? How do they impact our quest for a culture of nonviolence?

Navanethem Pillay (2008), UN high commissioner for human rights, summarizes the vision of the Universal Declaration of Human Rights in distinctive terms that make human rights an integral component of and a prerequisite for the quest for nonviolence and peace:

> The comprehensive vision of human rights set forth in the Universal Declaration . . . contemplates a world with the full realization of civil, political, economic, social and cultural rights without distinction . . . a world in which every man, woman and child lives in dignity, free from hunger and protected from violence and discrimination, with the benefits of housing, health care, education and opportunity. . . . Development, security, peace and justice cannot be fully realized without human rights. . . . Each of these pillars are undermined when discrimination and inequality—both blatant and in subtle ways—are allowed to fester and poison harmonious coexistence.

The central purpose of this chapter is to outline ways that multicultural education can help create safe spaces and engage individuals, groups, and communities in critical conversations around cultural identity and the urgent quest for a culture of nonviolence. Following a brief discussion of forms of violence and approaches to nonviolence, an overview of the principles and practices of multicultural education is presented. Then, the paper outlines ways that multicultural education can be implemented to foster a culture of nonviolence in schools and communities.

The conclusion highlights recommendations for building collaborative structures to further human rights, nonviolence, and peace.

Forms of Violence and Approaches to Nonviolence

From the stories that flood the media, the reported and unreported instances of bullying in schools, deadly encounters with gender violence, to incalculable cases of child abuse, families and communities around the world lead lives of struggle, leaving nonviolent livelihood to subsist primarily in hopes and dreams. Still, it is because there is hope for creating cultures of nonviolence that contributions to this book, like the current chapter, have been developed. How is violence conceptualized? Johan Galtung (1965) conceptualizes violence in four ways: First, he defines violence as "biological incapacitation." Noting that this form of violence is often described as "direct" and "intended," he argues that "violence is deliberate health-reduction." Second, he conceptualizes violence as "reduction of action-space," including the use of physical constraint and brainwashing. Third, Galtung defines violence as "negative influence approach." Fourth, he conceptualizes violence even more broadly as "influence," indicating that this concept includes all attempts to influence *alter* (or the other), positing that any influence interferes with others' free will.

David Francis (2006) conceptualizes violence in three categories: "direct violence," "structural violence," and "cultural violence." He indicates that direct violence is physical, emotional, and psychological. The current wars in Iraq and Afghanistan, the terrorist attacks of September 11, 2001, and family domestic violence are examples of direct violence. "Structural violence" refers to deliberate policies and structures that cause human suffering, death and harm. The apartheid system in South Africa and Jim Crow laws in the United States exemplify structural violence. "Cultural violence" denotes cultural norms and practices that cause discrimination, injustice, and human suffering. The forced removal of Native American children from their families and confinement in boarding schools in the mid-nineteenth century is an example of cultural violence.

Clearly, all forms of violence are linked by their unavoidably negative impact on human life. Also, while direct violence is the form of violence that is most often recognized and discussed, structural and cultural violence are quite often its underlying causes. For instance, religious intolerance caused the bloody ethnic crusades in the Middle Ages, and continues to pit Catholics against Protestants in Ireland today. Racial and ethnic intolerance resulted in the Jewish holocaust during World War II, as well as the Burundian genocide against Hutus in 1972 and the Rwandan genocide of 1994. Matthew Shepard of Laramie, Wyoming was murdered in 1998 because of intolerance against his sexual orientation as a gay man. And who will ever forget slavery, often characterized as the greatest crime against humanity, and its ensuing devastating oppression of Blacks and other people of color for centuries in the United States.

While the human tendency is often to respond to violence with violence, literature reveals a rich array of nonviolent alternatives to conflict. These alternatives are also linked and they overlap. In chapter 1 of this book, Anthony Adolf describes four types of nonviolence: spiritual nonviolence, physical nonviolence, structural nonviolence, and intellectual nonviolence.

Gene Sharp (1959) groups all behaviors and beliefs characterized by an abstention from physical violence under the term "generic nonviolence." He distinguishes "generic nonviolence" from "pacifism," which he defines as including "the belief systems of those persons and groups who, at a minimum, refuse participation in all international or civil wars or violent revolutions and base this refusal on moral, ethical, or religious principle" (44). He then describes nine types of generic nonviolence:

(1) *Non-resistance* is based on the principle that all physical violence must be rejected. He lists the Mennonites and the Amish as Christian sects who espouse non-resistance as their form of nonviolence.

(2) *Active reconciliation* is also based upon principle, and refers to both outward actions and improvement of one's own life before trying to change others. He cites the Society of Friends (Quakers) as an example.

(3) *Moral resistance* is based on the principle that individual moral responsibility is crucial to the call to resist evil (such as war, slavery, etc.), and that such resistance must be carried out by only peaceful and moral means. He posits that a significant number of Western pacifists practice this type of generic nonviolence.

(4) *Selective nonviolence* is characterized by the refusal to take part in particular violent conflicts, like international wars, while sometimes remaining willing to use violence to achieve desired goals. Jehovah's Witnesses are listed as an example.

(5) *Passive resistance* refers to actions meant to achieve or thwart social, economic, or political changes. This category is not inspired by a principle, but by the realization that the resisters do not possess the means of violence necessary to win or that they are unlikely to win by violence. He includes strikes and boycotts among examples of this type of generic nonviolence.

(6) *Peaceful resistance* is more active than passive resistance and seeks to achieve or thwart social, political, or economic changes, and is often grounded in a belief in the relative moral superiority of nonviolent over violent methods of conflict resolution. Sharp cites as examples the 1955–57 bus boycott in Montgomery, Alabama in the United States.

(7) *Nonviolent direct action* aims at establishing new patterns or policies, or disputing the institution of new patterns or policies seen as undesirable or evil, through the use of direct nonviolent intervention. He cites the example of the work done by the Congress of Racial Equality against racial segregation and discrimination in the United States.

(8) *Satyagraha* was developed by Mohandas Gandhi. It's based on a principle that seeks to attain truth through love and right actions. Its main goal is social improvement through education, decentralized economic production and consumption, and improvement in the lot of oppressed people.

(9) *Nonviolent revolution* seeks to encourage individuals to improve their own lives; gain the acceptance of nonviolence, equality,

cooperation, justice, and freedom as the values around which society should be framed; build a more equalitarian decentralized, and libertarian social order; and combat social evils by nonviolent resistance and direct action. Sharp summarizes the main goal of nonviolent revolution as the substitution of nonviolent, cooperative, equalitarian relationships for such aspects of violence as exploitation, oppression, and war.

Several questions emerge at this point: How can the quest for nonviolent livelihood be sustained in our inherently violent world? It is commonly believed that there is power in numbers. So, how can we create a united movement of nonviolence across our socio-cultural differences of race, ethnicity, religion, social class, ability levels, and sexual orientation? What kind of education do we need to create to prepare citizens who are knowledgeable, active, and committed agents of peace and nonviolence? The following sections discuss the main principles of multicultural education and how its practice can help foster a culture of nonviolence.

What Is Multicultural Education?

The most practical definition of multicultural education is found in the stated mission of the international organization that bears its name, the National Association for Multicultural Education (NAME). The mission statement describes multicultural education as a philosophy, a pedagogy, and an academic discipline that cultivates citizens who respect and appreciate cultural diversity; promotes the understanding of unique cultural and ethnic heritage; promotes the development of culturally responsible and responsive curricula; facilitates the acquisition of the attitudes, skills, and knowledge necessary to function in various cultures; seeks to eliminate racism and discrimination in society; and facilitates the development of knowledge, dispositions, skills, and commitments necessary to achieve social, political, economic, and educational equity.

Thus, multicultural education prepares citizens to become agents of social transformation who labor to achieve equity and social justice by challenging all forms of discrimination (Nieto 2000, 2004) and resisting all forms of oppressive social relationships (Sleeter 1996). Such citizens "support and defend social justice, reject politically correct discourses that promote individual and structural hypocrisy, and courageously dedicate their talents, time and resources to the development and implementation of programs aimed at the eradication of racism, classism, sexism, and other forms of oppressive injustice" (Ndura 2007). In essence, effective multicultural education helps citizens become agents of peaceful coexistence who validate others' narratives of suffering, take ownership of their group's actions towards other groups, are empathetic and trusting towards others, and develop nonviolent dispositions (Salomon 2002).

Sustaining the Quest for Nonviolence through Multicultural Education

The root of all forms of violence is the human tendency to dominate, oppress, and dehumanize, even exploit those whose cultural identities, orientations, and dispositions diverge from the society's expected norms, and thus challenge the worldview and social position of the dominant group by their mere existence. Existing literature often highlights cross-cultural communication as the quintessential strategy to build intergroup understanding and peaceful coexistence. I argue that building bridges of caring consciousness is a prerequisite to foster peace and nonviolence in our families, schools, and communities.

Bridges of caring consciousness are characterized by (1) deep understanding of one's own cultural identity, orientations, and dispositions, which can only be achieved through sustained, honest, critical self-reflection; (2) a genuine interest in understanding others' narratives resulting from their identities, orientations, and dispositions; (3) unshakable conviction that human interdependence is a constant reality that shapes the journey of self and others (Dalai Lama 2002; Martin Luther King Jr. 2002; Thich Nhat Hanh 2002); and (4) commitment to and active engagement in the individual and collective task to transform structures, institutions, and social relations to maximize opportunities for the self-actualization of self and others in diverse contexts devoid of fear, tension, suspicion, discrimination, and prejudice.

Such bridges of caring consciousness, which are grounded in the inalienable pursuit of the common good, are engineered through critical multicultural education. Critical multicultural education is transformative and transforming, and denotes the transformation of the policies, practices, instruction materials, and strategies with the purpose of building educational systems that empower educators and learners to become transformative intellectuals, cultural border-crossers, social activists, and critical engineers of a new social order (Giroux 1988; McLaren 1998; Ndura 2006a). Critical multicultural education empowers individuals and communities to reclaim their humanity, a concept that echoes the Freirian view that "to be human means to make and remake one's self through making history and culture, to struggle against the limiting conditions that prevent such creative action, and to dream into existence a world where every person has this opportunity and responsibility" (Glass 2001, 19).

Multicultural education sustains the quest for nonviolence by preparing citizens to become peacemakers. Cavanagh (2009) explains that the role of the peacemaker is to build trust, heal harm to relationships, restore dignity of persons affected, respect biculturalism/multiculturalism, be aware of power differences, and create safety.

Critical multicultural education sustains the quest for nonviolence by developing cultural competence, an essential cornerstone of the bridges of caring consciousness. Cultural competence denotes the informed dispositions, behaviors, and practices that validate the individual and collective identities and narratives of culturally different people and communities (Ndura 2006b). Cultural competence empowers individuals to challenge taken-for-granted policies, attitudes, and practices. It enhances individuals' understanding of their cultural identities and life experiences, and the cultural identities and life experiences of other people and groups. It fosters cross-cultural communication and appreciation for self and others. Through the process of self-discovery and self-exposure that effective critical multicultural education facilitates, cultural competence empowers individuals to validate other people's cultural frames of reference and the ways in which these shape their perceptions of self and others, as well as their worldview (Ndura 2006b, 44). By empowering individuals to uncover and expose the incalculable losses and infinite human suffering caused by manmade divisions and conflicts across generations, cultural competence enhances individuals' and communities' commitment to work together to restore humanity within and among all people.

How is critical multicultural education to be implemented? To maximize its contribution to the quest for peace and nonviolence, multicultural education should permeate all aspects of school curriculum and extracurricular activities at all educational levels. Significant attention should thus be devoted to the critical examination of relationships, instructional materials, and pedagogy with the intentional purpose of creating educational contexts and experiences that enhance cultural competence and build bridges of caring consciousness. The following illustrative questions should be considered to clarify and inform the transformative process: To what extent are educators and learners actively engaged in intentional and planned explorations of issues of power, representation, voice, and agency? To what extent are trusting and safe spaces established to facilitate engagement in courageous conversations about human diversity, discrimination, homophobia, racism, and oppression? To what extent does the educational context foster the development of crucial listening skills to allow participants to actually hear themselves and others when their mutual life-shaping narratives are shared? To what extent are educators and students actively engaged in the imagination of cultures of peace and nonviolence and a society defined by the common good? To what extent are they actively engaged in transformative social actions that actualize individual and collective commitments to peace and nonviolence?

Conclusion

Galtung (1965) posits that "the best service peace research could offer to the world today probably consists, not so much in understanding conflicts better, . . . [but] in providing politicians with an enormous repertoire of actions short of violence that can be applied in conflict situation; in other words, in extending the region of positive, or at least neutral action [and] possibilities in conflict situations" (251). I propose that anchoring education, research, and service endeavors at the intersection between peace education and critical multicultural education would be the greatest contribution to the world. This intersection provides numerous models of the kinds of attitudes, dispositions, and behaviors that reflect a peace-filled life, and that provide inspiration for the work carried out in schools and communities to establish peace-filled environments of caring and success—all of which can help reduce the threat of violence (Johns 2000).

The point of describing various forms of violence is not to imply that some forms of violence are more or less tolerable than others. Violence of any kind destroys the world's social fiber, weakens the soul, and undermines the human potential to care, love, and self-actualize.

Rosemary Henze (2000) argues rightly that "all forms of harassment— and violence constitute[s] ultimate harassment—have in common intolerance and oppression, whether people are victimized because of their race or ethnicity, gender, sexual orientation, physical disability, religion, or any other characteristic" (19). Therefore, this chapter positions critical multicultural education as the source of guiding principles and transformative practices that can foster cultures of nonviolence by developing cultural competence and engineering bridges of caring consciousness.

Multicultural education is critical to the quest for peace and nonviolence because it nurtures a vision that focuses citizens of the world on the common good, both locally and globally. This vision is achieved through the nurturing of empathy and respect for individual differences and cultures, which lead to constructive engagement in thoughtful conversations and courageous social actions designed to dismantle systems of dominance and help build communities characterized by equity, understanding, peace, and nonviolence (DeMulder, Ndura-Ouédraogo, and Stribling 2009; Ndura-Ouédraogo 2009).

Ultimately, the quest for cultures of nonviolence is a quest for social responsibility. Steven Wolk (2009, 665) explains that social responsibility is about "shaping human beings with intellectual curiosity, a caring heart, and a belief in the common good." He adds that "the very heart of teaching for social responsibility" is teaching for caring, and that this means being honest about our problems and injustices. Living a socially responsible life, he contends, means understanding and acting to improve the many problems confronting our communities, especially involving culture, gender, economic class, and sexual orientation. He concludes that "social responsibility not only requires an understanding of the abuse of power[,] but also commands the consciousness to see it and [to make] the ethical commitment to stop it" (668).

Therefore, rather than constructing an argument around which of the conceptualizations of nonviolence described in this chapter is preferable, I propose that proponents and practitioners of nonviolence critically assess ways to make their much-needed work emulate even higher and more consistent levels of social responsibility. This effort should be inspired by and grounded in the realization that the pillars of nonviolence—as taught by prominent historical and contemporary voices of nonviolence such as Henry David Thoreau, Mohandas Gandhi, Martin Luther King Jr., the Dalai Lama, Thich Nhat Hanh, and Nelson Mandela—are truth, harmony, brotherhood, justice, fearlessness, and the capacity to sacrifice (Ndura 2006b).

Creating cultures of nonviolence requires not only the development of cultural competence and the building of bridges of caring consciousness, but also the creation of collaborative structures to further human rights and peace. Collaboration across the disciplines of multicultural education, conflict resolution, peace studies, and social justice education is long overdue. Partnerships between educational institutions and nongovernmental organizations would greatly expand and strengthen the nonviolence movement. A consortium for the culture of nonviolence should be created to encourage the sharing of ideas among the groups that identify with the various conceptualizations of nonviolence, with the purpose of mounting even stronger resistance against all forms of violence and threats of violence.

In the final analysis, the overzealous missionary whose unchecked assumptions threatened to rob me of my American identity, the oblivious US Census worker who failed to grasp my pride in what Barack Obama's presidency represents in the United States and the world, and the proponents of a racially divisive immigration law in Arizona are all missing the essence of what makes each of us human. We are human because, whether we recognize it or not, we share the suffering brought by our failure to love and care for one another, and by our silence in response to social injustice and violence. We are human because, when given the opportunity, critical multicultural education can enhance our capacity to love and care about ourselves and others, thus empowering us with the knowledge and commitments necessary to live and work for peace and nonviolence.

Part Four

Ethics and Practices of Nonviolence

Beyond its application to large-scale phenomena such as social movements and educational methods, nonviolence is equally powerful as a moral and pragmatic compass for our individual lives, as well. Indeed, it is the practice of nonviolence at the intensely personal level—in our relationships, ethics, spirituality, and psychology—that can be the most impactful (and elusive) aspect of the paradigm. The chapters in this section quite literally bring nonviolence home, in the stories we tell and the emotional lives we lead. These narratives and analyses draw out the psycho-social nature of nonviolence, its intimate connections with worldviews and cosmologies, and its devolution upon practices of forgiveness and compassion. These engaged, situated, and essentially relational attributes are transformative of not only individual consciousness, but of sociopolitical reality, as well. While it may well be easier on some level to move a mountain than to move ourselves, the cogent reminders offered here argue that both will occur simultaneously or not at all.

Wayne Regina connects nonviolence and peacemaking to Bowen theory, which is rooted in the notion that "the fundamental forces that shaped the formation of the cosmos and life on Earth are the same fundamental forces that continue to shape and influence humans and their relationships today." This emerging psychology of nature asks us to work toward becoming self-aware peacemakers who manifest a "'power in presence' that positively influences others." As Regina observes, "a calmer, looser, more humorous, clearer, more well-defined, flexible, and socially-connected person . . . makes a difference not only for her but for others in her world." In the end, the application of Bowen theory to the nonviolence perspective "offers us immediate opportunities to make conscious choices every day," and likewise offers us guidance toward "leading a life with integrity, intentionality, and mindfulness" throughout the various challenges and opportunities presented before us.

One challenge of particular salience is the capacity for forgiveness in even the worst of situations. As Tülin Levitas reminds us, "the task of forgiveness begins with truth, that is, the acknowledgement of the events that have taken place." This honest dialogue and impetus toward accountability "has to do with letting go of the pain and beginning to create the possibility of a relationship with the perpetrator," and most critically it "requires the ability to empathize with the offender." How are we to maintain compassion and foster relationships with those who have caused us injury or despair? For Levitas, the answer lies in establishing and reaffirming a sense of common humanity that pervades all aspects of our lives, and in this manner we may come to discover "the restoration of the relationship that has been ruptured." Forgiveness, and the potential for reconciliation that it offers, "allows one to look into the heart of the other and acknowledge his or her full humanity," kindling a transformative nonviolence that can serve equally to undo apartheid abroad and our interpersonal barriers at home.

Perhaps the foremost figure who connected these personal practices with the social dimensions of nonviolence was Mohandas K. Gandhi. No meaningful discussion of the field could be possible without reference to this seminal figure, and thus, Nancy Snow vividly conveys to us the "deeply spiritual, pantheistic worldview" held by Gandhi. Contending that his "approach to the moral psychology of nonviolence should be considered a paradigm or a blueprint for others," Snow traces the roots of Gandhi's vision to nearly all of the great faiths, and yet also reminds us that in his life's arc the whole exceeded the sum of its parts. For Gandhi, nonviolence "is more than just a method. It is, instead, a moral discipline, a way of life and a form of therapy and recovery from the devastating psychological effects of oppression." Concomitantly, nonviolence requires that we go beyond simply refraining from harming others to actively loving them, "including oppressors, [which] imbues its use as a political tool with moral authority."

The extension of these grounded practices of nonviolence to the thoughts, words, and deeds of our lives brings us full circle to the inherently revolutionary potential of the nonviolence paradigm. As Snow aptly concludes, "Gandhi's insights into the value of making common spiritual cause in the quest for justice are instructive for our own day and well worth emulating." Understanding, updating, and applying the legacy of these teachings is the central task at hand, as we seek to turn crisis into opportunity, hate into love, conflict into peace, and violence into nonviolence.

12

Bowen Theory and Peacemaking

Human Evolution through
Nonviolent Conflict Resolution

Wayne F. Regina

One of the most iconic photographs of a divided America during the Vietnam War was that of an antiwar protester surrounded by armed National Guard soldiers. A young American man can be seen placing a flower in the rifle barrel of a guardsman. Upon further investigating the picture, it becomes apparent that another soldier has two flowers protruding from his gun barrel, as well. The year was 1967 and this picture, viewed worldwide, was indicative of a nation torn between war and peace. The competing narratives of the photograph reached deeply into the nation. For some, it represented a powerful statement of nonviolent resistance against an overpowering military force. For others, it demonstrated the need to act decisively against a youthful population willing to sacrifice the good of the country for their own idealistic and self-serving ends.

Most people in human rights and peace movements would agree that this photograph tells a story of brave protesters willing to risk their lives for their principles, using nonviolent responses against overwhelming odds. A closer investigation of this photograph from the Vietnam War protest suggests something more nuanced and perhaps more important. On one level, the protester's gesture can be interpreted from the perspective of bravery standing against overwhelming and oppressive forces. In fact, from an antiwar or pro-peace perspective, it is easy to invoke a narrative about heroes and villains from this photograph: the anonymous military policemen threatening the protesters and blocking their right to constitutionally protected free speech and assembly, and a young man's ironic gesture of placing flowers, symbolizing peace, in a gun barrel, symbolizing violence. Conversely, those who supported the National Guard embraced a "law and order" narrative, one in which the stability and security of the state was best assured through a strong, disciplinary presence.

There is, however, a third competing and compelling narrative that bears investigating. This narrative essentially suggests that our thinking and our actions either promote nonviolence through encouraging our own emotional maturity, and thus the emotional maturity and more healthy functioning of others, or they undercut peace through thinking and acting in ways that undermine our emotional maturity and the emotional functioning of others. In this alternative narrative, then, placing a flower in a gun barrel can be interpreted as an aggressive act, ironic or otherwise, that escalated the conflict in this tense situation, disrespected the soldiers who were simply following orders, and increased the potential for a more violent outcome.

This chapter investigates the nature and power of nonviolence and peacemaking in ways that are both profoundly personal and socially responsible. It looks at the nature of attachment and conflict, our ability and willingness to assume increased levels of self-responsibility and accountability for our actions and our thinking, and a recognition that our actions and behaviors either promote peacemaking or undercut it.

Throughout this chapter, I will use Murray Bowen's family systems theory, also known as Bowen theory, to provide a framework for what peacemaking means and how one's level of basic differentiation, or emotional maturity, is intimately bound up in one's capacity to promote peace within the self, and therefore interpersonally with others. I will discuss the contributions of evolutionary biology in understanding human behavior, how the limbic brain is wired for detecting and reacting to threats, and how cortical management of limbic hyperarousal can set the stage for nonviolent conflict resolution and peacemaking strategies. The essence of this chapter centers on the idea that higher levels of emotional maturity create personal and interpersonal fields of influence that promote peacemaking, and as emotional maturity or differentiation levels decline, so too does our capacity for personal peace and our ability to positively influence others to engage in effective, nonviolent resolution of conflicts.

An Alternative Paradigm for Peacemaking

Peacemaking is often investigated from the perspective of techniques, methods, outcomes, and points of view that examine end results, process results, or both, as determinants of success or failure. For example, during a peaceful demonstration, participants might focus on their degree of media coverage, the effectiveness of their message in reaching a target audience, and whether or not the results of their actions met their hopes and expectations. Alternatively, other groups may intensely focus on interpersonal process, such as creating consensus, as a means of advancing the group's agenda. From this perspective, process is outcome. For some, achieving consensus is peacemaking. From these various perspectives, then, results, process, or both can be the standard for determining success.

A Bowen theory perspective offers a different framework for understanding the nature of peace and peacemaking. It suggests that we must learn from what nature has to teach us, and that the power of personal presence is what creates opportunities for peace (Friedman 1985, 221; Kerr and Bowen 1988, 24). From a Bowen theory viewpoint, peacemaking is about seeing systems (i.e., the "whole picture") clearly, understanding the nature of personal power through acceptance of personal responsibility, and promoting "right action" in others as an outgrowth of self-management, especially in intense emotional environments. What Daniel Goleman (2006, 43) refers to as "empathic resonance" or fields of influence is best achieved when individuals take charge of their own lives, avoid "will conflicts" with others, minimize displacing blame, clearly define a self, and remain flexibly and reasonably engaged in their interpersonal world (Friedman 1987, 29; Kerr and Bowen 1988, 107).

Bowen theory is a natural outgrowth of evolutionary biology (Kerr and Bowen 1988, 45), which teaches us about the power of in-groups and out-groups. Humans naturally sort people into in-groups and out-groups, and this process begins early in childhood (Bigler, Brown, and Markell 2001, 1151; Tajfel and Billic 1974, 159–61). In order to make sense of the world, humans naturally categorize. From an evolutionary perspective, kinship systems are one such in-group, and these are the most powerful and important relationships for humans. Kinship connection, including the concept of inclusive fitness, suggests that humans and nonhumans take greater care of and protection for close relatives, who are, of course, those who also share the most genes (Kerr and Bowen 1988, 46–47). Clearly, in-group designations are functional from an evolutionary perspective.

Humans distinguish between in-group and out-group membership for other reasons, as well, including for such important evolutionary outcomes as social cohesiveness. In social cohesiveness, humans form in-groups to more efficiently gather and utilize resources, as well as for protection, social engagement, and mate selection (Mendoza 1984, 6). Activists demonstrate social cohesion to find common purpose in determining policy and promoting social action. Meetings are effective places to discover like-minded men and women, as well. Unfortunately, as emotional intensity increases, in-group and out-group processes can accentuate togetherness pressures, resulting in greater "herding" tendencies in thinking, feeling, and behaving (Friedman 1991, 18–19).

These automatic reactions are more "mindless" and, as such, can actually prevent individuals and groups from clearly and objectively assessing the progress of their movement or the effectiveness of a particular campaign (Miller 2002, 67). In more extreme cases of herding or "stuck togetherness," attachments to outcomes are high, and the group mindset automatically encourages in-group members to think, feel, and act similarly (Kerr and Bowen 1988, 77). Out-group members are often denigrated to a fused, depersonalized "sameness," as characterized, for example, by references such as "corporate America," the "military-industrial complex," or even "politics and politicians as usual." Certainly, there is comfort and security in "us versus them" designations, though sweeping generalizations in this kind of reductive polarization can actually generate a more conflictual, less emotionally mature, and, ultimately, less effective model of peacemaking. Bowen theory offers a different way forward. It is a systems theory that eschews polarizations that create false dichotomies, since extreme separateness and attempts to develop a solid sense of self and relationships at the expense of others is ultimately less effective (Friedman 1996, 15).

Murray Bowen was a radical psychiatrist who worked professionally from the 1950s until his death in 1990. His extensive investigations
regarding individuals and families helped him formulate his eponymous
theory. Bowen was an astute observer of human and nonhuman nature.
He observed that the same basic processes existed in both the nonhuman world and the human world, as well as within the wide spectrum
of human functioning. In fact, Bowen and his followers postulated that
the fundamental forces that formed the cosmos and life on Earth are the
same fundamental forces that continue to shape and influence humans
and their relationships today (Friedman 1991, 146–47; Kerr 1981, 263–64;
Kerr and Bowen 1988, 26). As a result, Bowen theory can be conceptualized as a kind of universal theory, akin to Darwin's theory of evolution; it
is a theory that applies across species, as well as within human relationships irrespective of gender, race, socioeconomic status, religion, tribe,
ethnicity, or family structure (Friedman 1991, 167–68). To understand the
power and scope of Bowen theory, we must review its five central concepts
relevant to our work as peacemakers in the world. These central concepts
are (1) the individuality and togetherness life forces, (2) the emotional
system, (3) differentiation, (4) chronic anxiety, and (5) emotional triangles
and de-triangulation.

Bowen Theory Concepts Relevant to Peacemaking

Bowen's innate curiosity about the natural world led him to look at the
connections between people and nature. As a scientist, Bowen believed
that conjecture about the workings of the human mind was speculative,
whereas observations of human behavior were more "objective." As a
result, Bowen began formulating a theory of human and family functioning that was based in evolutionary theory, as well as observations of human
interactions. Supposition about the human psyche was unnecessary (Kerr
and Bowen 1988, 223). In this way, Bowen theory was significantly different from the psychoanalytical model postulated by Freud, which was the
dominant paradigm at the time.

Individuality and Togetherness Life Forces. Bowen's promising theory was essentially different from Freud's theory in another way. Bowen

228 • Ethics and Practices of Nonviolence

noticed that the human and nonhuman worlds were profoundly connected, and that the same essential forces that regulated all life regulated
humans, as well. He labeled these processes the individuality and togetherness life forces (Kerr and Bowen 1988, 59). Bowen defined individuality as a general life force, biological in nature, that pushes life forms
toward uniqueness and distinctiveness (Kerr 1981, 236). Bowen described
togetherness as the balancing, general life force, biological in nature, that
drives life forms toward connection and relationships (Kerr 1981, 236).
The interrelationship between individuality and togetherness, then, deter-
mines the life form's level of emotional maturity. Bowen's work concentrated on how these essential life forces express themselves in humans. As
a natural extension of evolutionary, biological processes, Bowen theory
is an ecological model of humans and their emotional relationships with
one another and the natural world.

The Emotional System. To distinguish his theory from psychology's
established, internally based models of human development, Bowen highlighted universal processes that link humans to evolution (Bowen and Kerr
1988, 28). In fact, this viewpoint led Bowen to theorize that most human
behavior is actually automatic behavior that is embedded in billions of
years of evolutionary history. In effect, Bowen theorized that most human
behavior is a function of involuntary processes that are outside of conscious selection, rather than expressions of cognitive or feeling processes,
as is commonly assumed. He defined this automatic functioning and reactivity the emotional system, which he differentiated from both the thinking or intellectual system and the feeling system (Kerr and Bowen 1988,
30–31). The feeling system refers to a more conscious, deliberate form of
responsiveness to stimuli than, say, the reptilian emotional system. A bird
fleeing a hawk, a sunflower following the path of the sun, or a mother
protecting her baby—these are all examples of automatic, "instinctual"
behaviors operating through the emotional system.

Like all life forms, Bowen theorized that most human behavior is
a function of all that was "written" before in evolutionary history. The
emotional system is based, in part, on the oldest evolutionary portion
of our brain, the "reptilian" brain, but it is more correctly understood as
functioning at a cellular level, with behaviors that are essentially reflexive

in nature (Friedman 1991, 140). While humans may attribute many of these behaviors to differing motivations, Bowen theory postulates that this automatic reactivity is something humans have in common with all living creatures. Bowen believed that human reasoning and self-described motivations for most behaviors are really surface justifications of deeper, evolutionary, i.e., emotional, processes (Kerr and Bowen 1988, 28). As a result, Bowen theory suggests that much human behavior, including how we interact with other humans and the natural world, goes beyond the human, connecting us with life itself (Bowen 2002, 417).

For example, as stated previously, "herding" behaviors that cluster humans into in-groups and out-groups are automatic and based on evolutionary biology. Togetherness in humans, as well as other animals, is associated with lower levels of stress, increased group functioning through an established hierarchy, and greater calm as members within a group feel connected to one another (Ferrera 1996, 200–201). As togetherness pressures increase to the point of "stuck togetherness," however, self-integrity decreases. As a result, self-identity, self-definition, and self-management become more impaired, and out-group individuals are more likely to be perceived as in-group enemies. In-group functioning becomes dependent on the out-group's vilification, stripping out-group members of their individualities and even their important contributions to the functioning of the larger social, national, or international systems. In essence, a significant price is paid for this kind of fused togetherness: more conflict, less resilience, and a greater willingness to seek out heroes and villains in a narrative based on a right/wrong, us/them exclusivity. Temporary benefits that are derived from intense herding quickly evaporate as self-integrity is sacrificed for "stuck togetherness," resulting in increased discord, tension, emotional reactivity, and loss of peace and peacemaking opportunities (Friedman 1996, 18–19).

Bowen theorized the emotional system as a sophisticated incorporation of nature and nurture, with influences that include genetics, environmental circumstances, family patterns and emotional "inheritances," and a variety of additional, noteworthy attributes (Kerr and Bowen 1988, 48). Emotional reactivity expresses itself through the emotional system, and so has its origins in evolutionary survival mechanisms. In addition to highlighting humans' link with all other life forms and to evolutionary processes, Bowen also discussed what makes humans distinctive. With the assumption that humans may represent the pinnacle of current evolutionary processes, Bowen believed that humans have a relatively or exclusively unique capability to think, feel, and act in more autonomous ways than other life forms. As such, we, as humans, can increase our capacity for more mindfulness and intentionality (Kerr and Bowen 1988, 106–7). As a part of our evolutionary uniqueness as a species, Bowen underscored the advancement of our decidedly developed feeling system (as distinguished from the older emotional system), as well as our remarkably sophisticated intellectual system. Bowen suggested that the intellectual system—as epitomized in its most recently evolved component, the prefrontal lobe where higher order thinking takes place (planning, foresight, and so forth)—permits us more emotional autonomy than "lower" life forms (Kerr and Bowen 1988, 36–37).

Specifically, Bowen understood that the human brain is a remarkable organ that provides us the opportunity to reflect on our actions, anticipate the consequences of our behavior, and respond more thoughtfully in times of stress and conflict. Furthermore, with a concerted effort over time, Bowen theory demonstrates that we are capable of modifying some of our automatic expressions, replacing them with thoughts and actions that are more conscious and intentional (Friedman 1991, 163). With improved calmness and clarity of thought comes the possibility of more peaceful, nonviolent responses.

One of the characteristic features of Bowen theory, then, is the idea that, as social animals, we can cultivate the ability to progress beyond our evolutionary "programming" and respond more mindfully, rather than simply reacting automatically. During demanding times and stressful situations, however, "instinctual" impulses will predominate unless we consciously cultivate more mindful thinking and acting. In the language of Bowen theory, this greater capability for increased independence and emotional autonomy is called differentiation. In peacemaking, an individual's differentiation level—that is, her capability to think clearly, act intentionally, self-soothe, and self-manage in emotionally intense situations—is the most significant variable enabling successful conflict resolution.

Basic and Functional Differentiation. Bowen theory's third and perhaps most important central concept is differentiation. A synonym for differentiation is emotional maturity. Differentiation is a multifaceted theoretical concept, and different authors and practitioners of Bowen theory concentrate on different components (Bowen 2002, 473; Friedman 1991; Kerr and Bowen 1988, 98, 140; Regina 2000, 114; Regina and Pace 2008, 499). With regard to peacemaking and conflict resolution, I define differentiation as the relationship between and expression of the individuality and togetherness life forces (Regina 2000, 114). In this regard, differentiation is conceptualized as a person's ability to clearly and effectively define a self; contemplate her thinking, feelings, and behaviors; manage herself in challenging situations, and stay reasonably connected to others. In effect, differentiation is the aptitude for responsibly developing personhood, while simultaneously nurturing the capacity for meaningful relationships with others. Basic differentiation tends to remain stable throughout life unless a person works consciously and intentionally to raise it, or encounters challenging life circumstances that provide opportunities to emotionally mature. There are many factors that affect differentiation, the most important being the basic differentiation of one's parents and the accumulation of one's life experiences. Interestingly, research in the field of epigenetics suggests that significant and powerful experiences may affect individuals at the level of the expression of their genes, and that these genetic expressions can be passed on directly to offspring in one generation (Kaati, Bygren, and Edvinsson 2002, 687). This research is not only provocative regarding the potential impact of intentional, powerful changes in thinking and acting in a single generation, but it is also consistent with Bowen's theory, which postulates that changes in a single generation can have powerful effects on individuals, as well as on intimate relationships and non-intimate groups.

In contrast to basic differentiation, an individual's functional differentiation can increase or decrease based on his current and accumulated life circumstances and stressors (Kerr and Bowen 1988, 98–99). As a person's "core," basic differentiation increases, emotional swings in functional differentiation lessen, and the person demonstrates an increased capacity for adapting to life events and circumstances. Higher levels of differentiation provide a type of "inoculation" from life's trials and tribulations. In contrast, as basic differentiation decreases, so too does functional differentiation. In fact, the lower one's level of basic differentiation, the less one is capable of adjusting to changing life events and the more vulnerable one is to stress. When life circumstances become extremely challenging, one's functional differentiation may decrease, and this lower level of basic differentiation can become more manifest as one struggles to adapt to challenging conditions.

Differentiation is broadly synonymous with emotional maturity, personal integrity, adaptability, and personal responsibility for one's being and destiny (Friedman 1996, 36–38). In Bowen theory terms, successful life functioning relies on the manifestation of a "solid" sense of self, and the ability to effectively interact and participate with others. In this way, a stronger "self" is developed and maintained, as are lasting and meaningful personal and intimate relationships with important others (Kerr and Bowen 1988, 107; Regina 2000, 114).

To summarize, as a person's differentiation level increases, so too does her personal integrity and adaptability. She is more responsive to her environment and her thinking, feelings, and her actions are more reliable, mindful, and self-directed across life circumstances. She is more emotionally liberated from the shackles of automatic reactivity and can separate her responses based on the uniqueness of each situation. She can express her feelings and thoughts more spontaneously and appropriately, and has more capability to manage her life independently; she is an individual willing "to take responsibility for one's own emotional being and destiny" (Friedman 1996, 16).

In comparison, a person with a lower level of basic differentiation is less emotionally free, as he has less ability to manage his life, fewer resources upon which to draw, less resiliency, and is more dependent on others in his life and life circumstances. He is less able to accept personal responsibility, is more focused on getting others to change, and is more willing to blame others for his lot in life. In effect, he also has a higher level of chronic anxiety.

Chronic Anxiety. Bowen theory's fourth central concept is chronic anxiety, and it is highly relevant to peacemaking. In many ways, chronic anxiety can be conceptualized as the opposite of differentiation. Chronic anxiety is a person's reaction to a perceived threat (Kerr and Bowen 1988, 113). Acute anxiety, on the other hand, is a reaction to an actual threat and, as such, is a "surface" anxiety, whereas chronic anxiety is a "deeper" anxiety that is a part of the older emotional system. All living organisms react emotionally to threats and changes in their environments, and humans are no different. The extent of these reactions is a function of chronic anxiety. Bowen theory suggests that chronic anxiety and differentiation exist in an inversely proportional relationship such that as differentiation increases, chronic anxiety decreases, and vice versa (Kerr and Bowen 1988, 226). And, like differentiation, multigenerational and nuclear family influences are highly related to levels of chronic anxiety, such that the greater the chronic anxiety in the family system, the more chronic anxiety is "inherited" by the offspring. As chronic anxiety increases, a person becomes more vulnerable to symptom expression. These symptoms can manifest physically, emotionally, and socially. Patterns from current and previous generations, which are related to genetic and environmental factors, will affect how chronic anxiety is manifested and expressed.

How chronic anxiety is revealed through emotional reactivity is critical to understanding peacemaking and conflict resolution. The higher the level of chronic anxiety, the greater the emotional intensity in a person's life and the more threats to existence are perceived. The higher a person's level of chronic anxiety, then, the greater the likelihood that a person will generate conflict, aggression, and even violence.

Peacemakers often find themselves in emotionally intense situations in which their anxiety may be aroused, thus exposing their predisposed ways of managing anxiety. These predisposed ways of managing anxiety are a function of chronic anxiety. That is, a person with a lower level of chronic anxiety will be predisposed to handling intensity with greater personal responsibility and effectiveness, whereas a person with a higher level of chronic anxiety will more likely react to perceived threats with increased emotional intensity, blaming others, and pressing others to change. As such, in addition to the importance of differentiation levels, chronic anxiety levels are crucial variables in the success or failure of peacemaking efforts. Chronic anxiety is often expressed and bound in emotional triangles.

Emotional Triangles. Bowen theory's fifth and final central concept that is pertinent to peacemakers and peacemaking is the emotional triangle. Bowen (2002, 469) said that for humans, the basic, stable relational system is the emotional triangle. Bowen noticed that two people, under stress, will routinely and unconsciously bring in a third "other" in order to convey a sense of calm and order. This is called triangulation or "triangling." While the third "point" on the triangle can be another person, such as an in-law or an affair within a marriage, the third "other" may be anything that tends to stabilize the relationship by distracting it from the conflict. This third other can take many forms, including a physical object—for example, an attachment to possessions such as a car or a house; substances such as food, drugs, or alcohol; belief systems, including religion, political convictions, or a "cause"; and any other attachments. In Bowen theory, the triangle's sides are channels through which chronic anxiety moves. The proximity between two people and a third "other" in an emotional triangle delineates who occupies the "inside positions" of the emotional triangle and who inhabits the "outside positions" of the emotional triangle (Kerr and Bowen 1988, 136). In general, people on the inside position will often maintain their relative proximity by keeping the third person on the outside as much as possible.

By its very nature, triangulation promotes emotional reactivity, which, in turn, decreases people's ability to successfully manage conflict. Inside and outside positions of an emotional triangle can shift depending on the degree of anxiety or conflict between the participants. While triangulation generates transitory stability through changing coalitions, it does not provide the opportunity to peaceably improve the relationship between people. In fact, the quality of interpersonal relationships declines. Increased conflict usually results from emotional triangling.

Chronic anxiety provides the fuel and the glue for emotional triangles. As such, chronic anxiety can become "bound" or calcified within a third person, object, substance, symptom, or cause. When this happens, a person can get attached to the rightness of his position, become positively or negatively reactive towards another person, or develop "addictions" to substances or even a cause. These are all attachments, which Bowen theory refers to as anxiety binders. All attachments, then, undercut people's ability to function with greater levels of personal autonomy and independence, as "self" is siphoned off to maintain attachments. That is, emotional triangulation, and its resultant attachments, undercuts differentiation. Chronic anxiety then drives the emotional process and further increases emotional reactivity. Anxiety binders create avenues for people who are reactive with one another to remain joined through the conflict (Regina 2000, 120).

In summary, triangulation arises when emotional intensity between two people is not worked out in peaceful, more differentiated ways, i.e., through mindful, direct discourse that produces satisfactory outcomes, reduces tension, and promotes cooperation. When the tension between two people or groups grows and the conflict is not properly handled, triangulating in someone or something else temporarily stabilizes the situation, but the price of that temporary stability is usually high and the conflict remains unresolved.

The person, object, or belief that binds the anxiety undercuts a person's "self," resulting in greater emotional intensity and decreased clear thinking. Behaviors become more "mindless" and automatic, as survival reactions replace more conscious reflection and engagement. This, in turn, hampers attempts at reaching peaceful solutions as positions harden, resulting in gridlock. The same processes operate at the level of groups, in which entire groups can occupy inside and outside positions, such as with pro-choice and pro-life proponents, with the issue of abortion occupying the third point on the emotional triangle. In this example, both sides passionately adhere to the rightness of their positions, with the other side often vilified as radical, rigid, and extreme. As a result, constructive dialogue between the groups around common interests such as reducing the need for and number of abortions is all but absent. In-group and out-group thinking can help bond and bind the in-group against a common enemy of the out-group, but rarely do the two groups engage in working together. Emotional regression and further polarization ensues.

De-triangulation provides the opportunity to stem this emotional regression by individuals and groups (Kerr and Bowen 1988, 150). De-triangulation transpires when a person refuses to continue the conflict by blaming others and failing to address the source of the dispute directly. In fact, de-triangling is differentiating, as a person accepts personal responsibility for her part in the conflict and seeks to connect directly with the person or group with whom she is experiencing disagreement. De-triangling allows a person to begin releasing attachments—attachments to being right, vilifying others, or anxiously focusing on being victimized. It provides a mechanism for calming down and approaching the conflict more intentionally. Of course, the anxiety generated and "absorbed" through these attachments makes thinking clearly and acting responsibly difficult, but not impossible. A long-term commitment to increasing one's level of basic differentiation is the key to success. Without such an enduring dedication, most efforts at de-triangulating are not especially successful. With an effort to assume greater personal authority and personal responsibility, reaching out to others in order to resolve differences becomes more possible and probable. De-triangulation provides a roadmap for resolving disagreements through clarity of thinking and responsible action. De-triangulation requires a person to view the situation more objectively and to understand how systems operate.

In order to de-triangulate from a difficult and painfully intense situation, the person must physically and emotionally step back from the event in order to see it more clearly and objectively. This provides an opportunity to consciously manage emotional reactivity by engaging in self-soothing activities including steady breathing, thought stopping and other self-talk to calm one's ruminations, meditating to reduce heart rate and blood pressure, accepting personal responsibility for one's part in perpetuating the conflict, and interacting respectfully with the other party in an effort to find common ground through common interests (Regina 2000, 122). Peacemakers must also focus on de-triangulating disputants from their attachment to the conflict. This means approaching the other party with high regard, and maintaining an attitude of compassion and good humor to avoid regression into inflexible, immovable seriousness and attachment to positions.

In all human interactions, managing conflict directly will initially raise anxiety and thus tension between disputants. For many people, it is easier to avoid conflict. As such, de-triangling means tolerating immediate anxiety increases for the sake of lasting anxiety reduction and relief (Kerr and Bowen 1988, 151; Regina 2000, 121). In peacemaking, this means the peacemaker must accept personal responsibility for his part of the conflict, be minimally reactive and moderately to highly differentiated, and maintain composure in intense situations. When de-triangulation happens, individuals in the discordant system can seek enduring alternatives to a conflict based on common interests, and thus avoid reactive patterns of blaming and attacking.

Applying Bowen Theory to Peacemaking

Bowen theory provides us with a model of thinking that translates into action. Focused thinking, however, is not always necessary, of course. When people are living in the moment, occupied with work and play, and involved with friendships, acquaintances, and intimate relationships, more highly differentiated people simply exist—they do what they do when they need to do it. As emotional intensity increases in personal, interpersonal, and social environments, however, humans are tested to live with greater intentionality and mindfulness, rather than reacting emotionally and instinctually. Our capacity to manage ourselves is thus more challenged, as is our ability to think more clearly and act in ways that are consistent with our values, beliefs, and lifestyles.

If our work takes us to places of conflict, if we are called to action to right injustice, or if we simply get into an argument with a stranger in a grocery store, evolutionary biology can work against us. When threatened, we automatically react accordingly, and we can quickly escalate into a flight/fight stance. We are at the mercy of our evolutionary history. If we are working with a political group or nongovernmental organization, or if we have simply come together to address a common cause, we may be pulled from a state of calmness and risk entering into more reactive engagement that may initially feel right but can ultimately be counterproductive to our long-term goals as peacemakers. In these instances, how do we maintain our integrity in the face of these counter-differentiation pressures?

The goal for peacemakers is a long-term commitment, over years and decades, toward increasing levels of differentiation. It necessitates us to manage the emotional intensity of the moment, to self-soothe our reactive impulses, and to not triangulate as a way of temporarily feeling better. This is not a quick fix and it requires an ability to understand how human systems function. Differentiating also entails a type of persistence and motivation that often runs counter to our cultural conditioning. Nonetheless, a commitment to increasing one's level of differentiation acts as a kind of "inoculation" against capricious and emotionally reactive thinking, feeling, and acting. Knowing our personal signs of emotional reactivity and subjective thinking can provide guideposts when we stumble. When experiencing emotional reactivity, we can choose to self-soothe our agitated beings and calm our racing hearts. We can decide to override our initial impulses and seek more intentional responses. Committing to increasing emotional maturity strengthens the self, and the stronger the self, the more durable and effective all of our relationships become. Being more calm, nonattached, present, and engaged allows us to create resonance fields of influence that can positively affect others. Just as reactivity breeds more reactivity, calm breeds greater calm. More differentiated togetherness influences others to self-reflect, responsibly engage, and work toward common interests.

More differentiated peacemakers provide clarity, consistency, and connection in social encounters. They demonstrate more capability in family and work relationships. They can clarify an "I" in intense environments that instinctually pull towards stuck togetherness. More differentiated peacemakers, in effect, create a "power in presence" that positively influences others. Brain research supports this alignment of brain patterns (Goleman 2006, 39–40). Mirror neurons mimic the brain states and thus the experiences of others, reinforcing the notion that we influence others for good or for ill (41–43). Limbic systems can align with resonance, and laughter and humor are powerful tools for reaching others and promoting peace. In fact, laughter and humor are powerful antidotes for "reptilian" regressions into attachment and seriousness. In essence, a calmer, looser, more humorous, clearer, more well-defined, flexible, and socially connected person displays an emotional maturity that makes a difference not only for her, but for others in her world. In fact, more differentiated peacemakers are more naturally differentiated leaders. They avoid the polarizing that leads to vilifying out-groups. A sense of group unity is achieved through common cause, not through common animosity.

In truth, these notions of applying principles from evolutionary biology through Bowen theory may sound quite radical. It is easier to become reactors in the evolutionary game of "us versus them." It is easier to resist change than to assist in shaping it. It is simpler to say "no" than to find ways to say "yes." It is less complicated to put a flower in a gun barrel than to speak to and humanize the soldier holding the gun. Making a long-term commitment to increasing one's emotional maturity requires self-honesty, patience, persistence, nonattachment, engagement, and a willingness to live by the power of one's convictions. It means apologizing for mistakes and developing compassion not only for friends, but also for adversaries, which can be painful and difficult. What might have been different, for example, if the Vietnam War protester would have reached out to the National Guard soldiers instead of dishonoring them by putting flowers in their gun barrels? How might the protester and the guardsmen have responded differently if the protester had established a personal dialogue with the guardsmen, rather than escalating the standoff? Perhaps, a different kind of peace may have prevailed. An approach to peacemaking through Bowen theory affords people the opportunity to develop long-term solutions to seemingly intransigent problems.

In the final analysis, peacemaking through Bowen theory is about contributing to the evolution of the species (Friedman 1986, 233). It offers us immediate opportunities to make conscious choices every day about who we are and what we do. It is about leading a nonviolent life with integrity, intentionality, and mindfulness under all kinds of situations and circumstances. While none of us will fully develop this capacity in our lifetimes, we can make the commitment to peacefully resolving conflict through increasing our emotional maturity, and thus come to enjoy the journey along the way.

13

Forgiveness, Reconciliation, and Conflict Transformation

Tülin Levitas

In July 2004, a Fulbright-Hayes grant took me to South Africa for a month. The very first day that I was in South Africa, I was taken to a place at the outskirts of Johannesburg called the "Cradle of Humankind." This was a place where the fossil remains of one of our common ancestors was discovered. Professor Lee Berger, the paleontologist who was excavating the site, welcomed us home, since Africa was the place from which all humanity originated. That same day, in the afternoon, we were taken to the Apartheid Museum. The contrast between these two sites in a sense symbolized South Africa and the conceptual underpinning that is in its history: while in the cradle of humanity, we experienced connectedness to all humanity; at the Apartheid Museum, we witnessed the suffering that is caused by dehumanizing human beings and treating them as the "other." Thus, South Africa appeared before me as a land of great contrasts, a land of great beauty, yet ravaged by foreign powers, resulting in a land of great poverty.

The year that I visited South Africa, the country was celebrating the tenth anniversary of its democracy. As South Africa ended the evil system of apartheid and established its democracy on April 27, 1994, it had a number of choices as to how to deal with its violent and oppressive past. Black South Africans could have held Nuremberg-style trials of their oppressors, or they could have thrown their oppressors out of their country, or they could have incarcerated or killed all of their oppressors. Yet, South Africa chose a path of forgiveness and reconciliation to end the conflicts that resulted from apartheid, and to move on as a unified country. This very process is referred to as a "miracle in progress" by many South Africans, and constituted an epiphany for me. After observing South Africa's experiment in reconciliation, I came to understand how powerful compassion, forgiveness, and reconciliation can be in transforming conflict and moving ahead peacefully.

In this chapter I focus mainly on the example that South Africa provides through the workings of its Truth and Reconciliation Commission as a form of nonviolent conflict resolution. I argue that the work of the Commission was based on a conceptual framework of interconnectedness that enables human beings to have compassion toward each other, which in turn enables them to forgive each other and allow reconciliation to take place in order to resolve previous conflicts. I also show that this conceptual framework can be seen as a thread that connects different cultures, traditions, and philosophies across time and space. In both Eastern and Western traditions, in the philosophies of both contemporary and ancient thinkers, and in the worldviews of both male and female philosophers and scholars of religion, we can see that interconnectedness and compassion make it possible for human beings to resolve conflicts and live peacefully with each other. Archbishop Desmond Tutu states that for him, the source of forgiveness is based both on his Christian beliefs and on the South African notion of *ubuntu*. Buddhist metaphysics states that everything in the universe is interconnected and therefore requires nonviolence towards all sentient beings, while Confucius defines the self in terms of interpersonal relationships, and Taoism defines it in terms of one's relationship to the world of nature. Aesara, a fourth century BCE philosopher, focuses on compassion as a necessary condition for justice, as do Karen Armstrong and Pumla Gobodo-Madikizela today.

Focusing on South Africa, we need to look at what the system of "apartheid" amounted to in practice. "Apartheid" literally means apartness, separateness. It was adopted by the National Party in the early 1940s as a system of segregation between different racial groups. It was a form of ethnic mobilization implemented to secure economic, cultural, and political advantage for the dominant white population by legislating and enforcing territorial separation between different racial groups. Through the Natives Land Act of 1913, 75 percent of the population that was not white retained rights to only 7 percent of the land. Further, South Africans of color were subject to taxation, and therefore they employed nontaxable alternatives such as a cash economy in order to avoid supporting the advancement of oppressive state structures. No person of color could vote in South Africa; their political voices could only be heard indirectly through tribal institutions or councils. The apartheid system established a clear separation between different racial groups: whites, Indians, coloreds (people of mixed races), and black Africans. These groups were separated with regard to transportation, education, amenities of all kinds, and politics. The Group Areas Act of 1950 forced the relocation of three and a half million people, and the Prohibition of Mixed Marriages Act of 1949 prohibited people of different racial groups to marry each other. Apartheid denied South African citizenship to black Africans and it diffused nationalism by promoting tribal ethnicities. Apartheid was followed by the Bantu Self-Government Act in 1959 and by the Bantu Homeland Citizenship Act in 1970. Thus, native Africans became aliens in their own land. Two separate worlds lived side by side: the world of dominant white Afrikaners, and that of marginalized and oppressed native black Africans. The "house of apartheid" was built on these foundations. As a reaction to this system of legal segregation and oppression, a resistance movement started to take root in South Africa.

Various movements within South Africa, such as the African National Congress (ANC) or the Pan Africanist Congress (PAC) were formed in order to oppose and end the apartheid system. The ANC emphasized non-racialism and advocated a unified South Africa, and started out as a nonviolent resistance movement influenced by Mohandas Gandhi's *satyagraha* movement; however, due to the group's lack of success in ending apartheid, it eventually resorted to armed struggle, as did the PAC, which had an agenda by and for blacks only. The leaders of the ANC were Nelson Mandela, Walter Susulu, and Thabo Mbeki. The ANC's freedom charter stated that the land belonged to all people. Different groups, such as trade unions; student groups; religious institutions; and sporting, educational, civic, and women's organizations constituted internal opposition to apartheid. They wanted to overthrow the Bantustan (segregated home-lands) system and the leaders of South Africa and establish a unified, fully democratic South Africa. The international community also called for reforms in South Africa. Finally, the South African government withdrew troops from townships and lifted restrictions on the ANC and PAC, thus allowing people to lead relatively normal lives. In 1985, F. W. de Klerk became prime minister and repealed some apartheid legislation.

On April 27, 1994, general elections took place for the first time in South Africa. These were the first free, democratic elections in South Africa without discrimination on the basis of race or sex. People feared that the election day would be a disaster, but fortunately that did not happen. As Archbishop Desmond Tutu (1999, 7–8) says, these elections constituted in a sense a spiritual experience. The black person apparently entered the booth as one person, and exited as a transformed person. White South Africans were also transformed by the experience since, according to Tutu, they could not truly be free until blacks were also free. South Africa had made a peaceful transition from oppression and injustice to democracy and freedom. On May 10, 1994, when Nelson Mandela was inaugurated as South Africa's first democratically elected president, he invited his white jailer of twenty-seven years to attend as his honored guest in order to show his willingness to forgive. The world in a sense witnessed a miracle: instead of a blood bath, there was a peaceful transition of power.

Nevertheless, the past had to be dealt with. South Africa could have chosen to exercise retributive justice and its nascent democracy might have ended up in ashes; indeed, there was no clear victor in South Africa who could claim victor's justice, since both sides had performed atrocities. Following the Nuremburg Trials at the end of World War II, the victorious Allies left Germany to begin rebuilding, but in South Africa following apartheid, it was well understood that white, black, colored, and Indian populations would still need to continue living together in a unified country. Therefore, Nuremberg-style trials were rejected. Members of the previous government recommended letting bygones be bygones, but that idea was also rejected because national amnesia would have victimized native South Africans yet again, since forgetting about the past ensures repeating it. South Africans wanted to balance justice, accountability, peace, and reconciliation, and it appeared that a commission might work better than court cases in getting to the truth. Therefore, South Africa established its Truth and Reconciliation Commission (TRC), chaired by Archbishop Desmond Tutu, which allowed people to tell their stories in their own words. Amnesty applicants had to make a full disclosure in order to apply for amnesty.

As Tutu says, the concepts of forgiveness and reconciliation are consistent with the South African concept of ubuntu, as well as with his Christian beliefs. In his view, the Judeo-Christian God is a god of compassion, not of punishment, and one who seeks to rehabilitate humankind and reconcile with it. So, in his work with the TRC, Tutu argues that the very act of forgiveness is an act of faith that can restore a relationship gone awry. He says that "according to Jesus, we should be ready to do this not just once, not just seven times, but seventy times seven, without limit" (1999, 273). In Tutu's view, forgiveness is not just altruism, it is the best form of self-interest, for it liberates the one who forgives from the burden of resentment and anger. Forgiveness gives people resilience and allows them to survive and end up being completely human in spite of the efforts of others to dehumanize them.

On this view, contrition is not absolutely necessary for forgiveness to take place. On the other hand, forgiveness does not imply forgetting what has happened. Quite the contrary, it requires the victim to acknowledge fully what has happened and to take it seriously, but to also choose to let it go in order to free oneself from the burden of the injury that one suffered. Tutu argues that the process of forgiveness is neither easy nor cheap. Forgiveness opens the door, so to speak, for reconciliation to take place. Reconciliation also requires the acknowledgement of what has gone wrong, the admission of estrangement and alienation for both parties. When the perpetrator acknowledges the wrong actions that he or she has performed and asks for forgiveness sincerely and contritely, then the victim could be motivated to forgive and the process of reconciliation could begin.

The South African notion of ubuntu was equally significant in the work of the TRC. Tutu says that one who has ubuntu is generous, hospitable, friendly, caring, and compassionate. Hence, Ubuntu is the essence of personhood, and personhood is defined by person-to-person relationships.

In other words, a person becomes a person through other people (Tutu 1999, 26–31): "I am a human being because I belong, I share, I participate. A person with ubuntu is open and available to others and is able and good, for he or she has a proper self-assurance that comes from knowing that he or she belongs in a greater whole and is diminished when others are humiliated or diminished, when others are tortured or oppressed and treated as if they were less than who they are."

In this sense, harmony, friendliness, and community are great goods. Social harmony is the greatest good. Anger, resentment, lust for revenge, and even success through aggressive competition would violate this good.

This thread of interconnectedness and compassion is picked up by yet another commissioner of the TRC, Pumla Gobodo-Madikizela, who discusses a concept called *inimba* that refers to the connection a mother has with her child through the umbilical cord (2007). She argues that all human beings are connected to each other, and these mutual connections enable us to have empathy and compassion for each other. She also argues that forgiveness has a profound healing power for victims who have been dehumanized by perpetrators. Victims of oppression, such as those in South Africa, not only experience the loss of freedom, but also the undoing of their self-concept. They feel powerless, helpless, and that they have no control over their lives, and thus feel shame and humiliation. Trauma causes rupture of self for victims, and they need, therefore, validation and affirmation in order to heal. They need to be acknowledged and respected. So, when perpetrators ask for forgiveness, they acknowledge that they have dehumanized the victim, and in so doing they have also dehumanized themselves, and are asking for readmission into human society.

Similarly, victims are also given an opportunity to acknowledge their trauma by talking about it, and to regain control of their memory, thus beginning to turn the trauma around. People of color in South Africa and in the United States live with the memory of the pain of oppression. There is a need for dialogue and acknowledgment of the events that took place. The task of forgiveness begins with truth, that is, the acknowledgement of the events that have taken place. The process of forgiveness has to do with letting go of the pain, and beginning to create the possibility of a relationship with the perpetrator. It requires the ability to empathize with the offender, since, according to Gobodo-Madikizela, we all have the potential to do evil acts. The consequences of forgiveness allow for the restoration of the relationship that has been ruptured. Even if victims do not want a relationship with their oppressors, they can still regain a sense of peace for themselves, as can perpetrators.

In an entirely different part of the world, the thread of compassion and interconnectedness is picked up by the Dalai Lama (Dalai Lama and Chan 2004), who utters a similar message of compassion, empathy, tolerance, and forgiveness. In his view, if we can treat all human beings as though they were members of our family, genuine compassion would be felt towards them. Positive emotions such as compassion are based on the belief that others have the same value as ourselves. If everyone were to practice genuine compassion, then freedom for all human beings would be possible. Destruction of another human being amounts to destruction of oneself. According to the Dalai Lama, this belief is based on the Buddhist metaphysical view that all things in the universe are interdependent and interconnected. All living entities are one in the "ocean of life." So, what affects one living being ends up affecting all. This view is strikingly similar to the South African concept of ubuntu described above.

The Dalai Lama's approach toward China—which has been occupying his country and which forced him, as well as many of his fellow citizens, to live in exile—is supported by his view of cosmic interdependence, for he, like Desmond Tutu and Nelson Mandela in South Africa, says that he has forgiven the Chinese. He says that he does not seek independence for Tibet, because Tibet is dependent on China both economically and environmentally, although he does seek Tibetan autonomy and self-governance. On the other hand, he argues that Tibetan traditions and spirituality would be quite beneficial to the Chinese. So, even China and Tibet in his view cannot be totally separate, because they are quite interdependent. He points out that there has been a lot of destruction and death in Tibet, which have caused a lot of pain and unhappiness, but if Tibetans were to respond similarly to the Chinese, there would be even more unhappiness. So the only option is forgiveness—which, however, just as in South Africa, does not mean forgetting what has happened. To the contrary, one remembers all the suffering that has taken place in the past in order not to repeat it in the future.

According to the Dalai Lama (ibid., 109), it is possible to forgive the Chinese by remembering that they too are humans, and therefore they also want to be happy and avoid suffering. Since Tibetan interests are interrelated with Chinese interests, as stated above, then taking care of the Chinese would result in taking care of Tibetans as well. The Dalai Lama makes an important distinction between the actor and the action. In his view, while one condemns the action of the perpetrator, one does not have to condemn the actor, as well. That is the reason he is able to forgive the Chinese, in spite of the suffering that they have inflicted on his people. For the Dalai Lama, the ability to forgive, as stated earlier, arises from the essence of Buddhism, which encompasses both the notion of cosmic inter-dependence and that of compassion toward all living beings.

Looking at a much earlier time in ancient China, we see a similar thread of interconnectedness and compassion woven in the thoughts of two different philosophers, Confucius and Lao-Tzu. For Confucius (551–479 BCE), the self is defined in terms of human relationships (Ames and Rosemont 1988, 29). One becomes a *junzi*, an ideal person, by expanding one's empathy indefinitely. We can imagine, according to Confucius, empathy expanding in concentric circles (Smith 1994, 114). The circles begin with oneself and expand to one's family, one's community, one's nation, and ultimately to the whole world. Moving in empathy from oneself to the family, one transcends selfishness; moving from the family to the community, one transcends nepotism; moving from the community to the nation, one transcends parochialism; and when empathy moves from the nation to the whole world, one transcends chauvinistic nationalism.

The central virtue for Confucius is *ren*, which is the ideal relationship between human beings. It is this virtue that distinguishes human beings from other animals. It is the kind of relationship where a person relates to others with an open heart, with kindness, altruism, and empathy. Confucius expresses this view in his *Analects* in the following manner: "Within the four seas all men are brothers" (Smith 1994, 110), to which I would like to add that all women are sisters. This kind of relationship does not allow for adversity, anger, or hatred toward others. The junzi exemplifies this virtue, for he or she represents humanity at its best. The ideal person has self-respect, but also respects others and does not feel any resentment toward others if they do not know him or her, or if they fail to recognize his or her qualities. Rather, ideal persons are concerned about their own inadequacies. Ideal persons are broad and not partisan; they focus on what is right, not on what is profitable. Ideal persons carry out what they say into action and live in harmony with others. These persons would not be inclined to elevate people because of what they might say, nor would they reject a person's message or ideas because of that person's identity or external characteristics.

Confucius further advocates the doctrine of the mean, *wu-wei*, which teaches that moderation is the preferred way to behave because it ensures harmony and balance. Wu-wei encourages compromise and avoids fanaticism. Excess in any direction brings about undesirable consequences. The doctrine of the mean, as well as the "rectification of names" and the "five constant relationships" constitute the framework of *li*, which indicates how people ought to behave towards each other. The rectification of names spells out what people's obligations toward each other are in the very definition of terms. For example, the word "parent" should encompass not only the fact that a person has had a child, but also the responsibilities that a parent has toward his or her child!

One ought to govern oneself with *de*, which is moral power. As Confucius says, "Governing with excellence can be compared to being the North Star: the North Star dwells in its place, and the multitude of stars pay it tribute" (Ames and Rosemont 1998, 76). When one of Confucius's followers, Tzu-kung, asked him if there was one universal principle that one could always focus on, Confucius replied that it is: "Never do to others what you would not like them to do to you" (Confucius 1986, 114). This principle resonates easily with many Westerners, for it is a slightly different formulation of the Golden Rule (i.e., one should treat others as one would like others to treat oneself), which is often attributed to the Christian Bible, but which also has analogues among the sacred texts of many other religions.

Lao-Tzu (604–? BCE), who is recounted as an older contemporary of Confucius, emphasizes not only harmony and balance with other human beings, but also with the world of nature itself. This is achievable through non-action, or wu-wei. According to Lao-Tzu, nature itself operates passively, quietly in a natural rhythm. The sages who are in harmony with the world of nature are neither aggressive nor violent nor do they seek reward or position. Such people live spontaneously without any rules or plans, they accept both joy and sorrow with equanimity. Such people, then, are truly free. Chuang-Tzu (369–286 BCE), a disciple of Lao-Tzu, points out that conventional thinking creates dichotomies such as good as opposed to evil, pleasure versus pain, or life versus death, whereas the Tao transcends all these dualities because it encompasses all forms of existence. Thus, to be in harmony with the world of nature and thereby with the Tao allows one to transcend all dualities and experience total happiness. The Tao embraces everything and therefore is in a constant process of change. Instead of reacting to change, the sage accepts all change as a natural process and goes along with it.

In the *Tao Te Ching*, Lao-Tzu (1986, 133) uses water imagery and says that the highest good, like water, benefits everything and does not compete. The highest good puts itself in places that no one wants. Similarly, people who achieve the highest good remain low, however they are profound in their thinking and compassionate when interacting with others. Such people keep their promises and are effective at work. People of the highest good do not make any enemies, because they do not compete. Lao-Tzu also points out that when people are born, they are soft and weak, but when they die, they are hard and stiff—like plants that are supple and crisp when they are young, but dry and brittle when they die. He concludes that those who are soft and weak are followers of life, while those who are strong and hard follow death. Therefore, in his view, when the army is strong, it will not be victorious. Conversely, Lao-Tzu (1986, 135) makes the point that it is those who yield that will be preserved. As he says,

The Yielding will be preserved.
The bent will be straightened.
The hollow will be filled.
The old will be renewed.
Having little, he will get more.
Having much, he will be confused.

Therefore the sage holds to the One and becomes the model of the
   world.
He who does not show himself will be illustrious.
He who does not boast will be meritorious.
He who is not conceited will be lasting.
What the ancients say "The yielding will be preserved" is not empty
   words.
The yielding is truly preserved and followed.

Thus, for Lao-Tzu, yielding, and not aggression, is the means to preservation and life.

In an entirely different location, Lucania (today's southern Italy), and at about the same time as Confucius and Lao-Tzu, the Pythagorean philosopher Aesara also picks up the thread of compassion and forgiveness and weaves it through her moral philosophy. In the fragmentary remains of Aesara's work, *On Human Nature* (Waithe 1987, 19–26), we see that she addresses the question of whether people need two different kinds of moral philosophy: virtue ethics in the home, and a theory of justice for society at large. Aesara's answer is a resounding "No," for in her view all moral decisions, whether they relate to the individual, the family, or the larger society, should reflect the appropriate proportions of rationality, compassion, and willpower.

In her discussion of morality and justice, Aesara, like Plato, conceives of the soul as having three parts, but unlike Plato, one of the parts of the soul has to do with emotions such as love and compassion. This emphasis on love and compassion as a necessary condition for moral action constitutes Aesara's important contribution to the history of philosophy. Aesara argues that we can discover the natural and philosophic foundations of all human law through introspection. Her concept of the natural law involves the application of the moral law in three areas: (1) individual and private morality, (2) the moral foundation of the family, and (3) the morality on which social institutions are based.

In a Platonic fashion, Aesara conceives of the soul as consisting of three parts: the mind, spiritedness, and desire. The mind, which is analogous to the intellect, analyzes ideas and arrives at decisions. Spiritedness, which is analogous to the will, provides the motivations for action. Desire is analogous to positive affective emotions, such as love and compassion. Aesara argues that human nature provides a standard of morality, law, and justice for the individual, the family, and the state. All moral decisions need to show the appropriate proportions of rationality, willpower, and compassion. Aesara also argues that morality, law, and justice need to be rational because they need to consider all relevant ideas, arguments, and principles. Morality, law, and justice are involved in decisions having to do with matters of fact, obligations, and duties. Yet, in order for morality within the individual, rules and discipline in the family, or societal laws to be effective, spiritedness is essential in order for these rules, principles, or laws to function well, either as deterrents or as incentives for action. Personal moral principles, family rules, and discipline, as well as societal laws all need to also include love, either as compassion and kindness toward others, or as self-esteem.

In Aesara's view, individuals need to formulate moral standards for themselves in such a way that they can reasonably follow their own dictates. Nevertheless, if one falls short of one's own moral standards, then compassion needs to play a role in being self-forgiving and not unduly obsessing about one's own moral shortcomings. In the family, compassion also plays a role in that each member's needs ought to be considered, and forgiveness ought to be exercised vis-à-vis individual members' shortcomings. Finally, in society, the justice system needs to be compassionate and forgiving, as well, taking into account extenuating circumstances and reasons for noncompliance.

Aesara's moral philosophy is as relevant to us today as it must have been to her own society. Whether we are at home trying to decide how to discipline our children, or at a public debate on whether punishment or rehabilitation is more effective in our system of justice, or in the United Nations Security Council trying to decide whether additional sanctions against Iran would be morally justifiable, we need to apply our rationality, motivations, and compassion appropriately and in a balanced manner to the decisions that we make.

We have seen from the twentieth century in South Africa, Tibet, and China, all the way back to the fifth century BCE in China and ancient

Greece, that a thread of interconnectedness and compassion is woven to support the conceptual framework of peaceful coexistence. To the extent that compassion is the basis of our modus operandum, we can transform conflicts nonviolently through forgiveness, and ultimately with reconciliation. In the work of the TRC, and in the ideas expressed by the Dalai Lama, Confucius, Lao-Tzu, and Aesara, we have seen that compassion is a necessary condition for justice and peace.

Indeed, compassion is the central theme of every tradition, and it should be practiced all day and every day. The golden rule expresses it best: "Do unto others as you would like them to do unto you." In order to explore the meaning and application of compassion, we are summoned to action. We are told to love our neighbor as we love ourselves by many traditions, for we cannot love anyone else if we do not love ourselves. As the Dalai Lama suggests, we need to cultivate compassion in ourselves. Until the pain of others resonates with us, we cannot deal with it intelligently and creatively. The TRC in South Africa gave victims of apartheid the opportunity to share their suffering, and thus allowed them to confront it and deal with it constructively. The question arises whether justice was achieved in South Africa through the work of the TRC. If what we mean by "justice" is retributive justice, then probably not, but if what me mean by "justice" is restorative justice, then yes, justice was achieved, for it allowed the victims who had been dehumanized to reenter the ranks of full-fledged human beings. By forgiving their perpetrators, the victims were able to restore relationships that had gone awry and allow the perpetrators to be restored, as well. This is only possible through compassion, which allows one to look into the heart of the other and acknowledge his or her full humanity.

14

Toward a Moral Psychology of Nonviolence

The Gandhian Paradigm

Nancy E. Snow

Scholars have used many traditions to interpret Mohandas Gandhi's approach to nonviolence, known as *satyagraha*. For example, using the life and work of Gandhi as depicted in Richard Attenborough's film *Gandhi* (1982), Joseph Kupfer (2007) argues that Gandhi displayed central aspects of the feminist ethics of care. Others have interpreted Gandhi as a reformed liberal (Gier 2003), in terms of Buddhism (Gier 2004), and through the lens of psychoanalysis (Erikson 1969). All of these interpretations offer valuable insights into the complexity of Gandhi and his moral philosophy.

There are three distinct, yet interwoven layers in Gandhi's thought: (a) a deep spiritual and metaphysical foundation in Hinduism that is informed by values from other traditions, both Eastern (for example, Buddhism, Jainism) and Western (for example, Tolstoy, Thoreau, Ruskin); (b) a moral psychology of nonviolence; and (c) a political philosophy. In this chapter, I interpret the moral psychology of satyagraha as an outgrowth of deeper roots in Hindu philosophy and religion, especially Vedanta philosophy, which is drawn from the doctrines of Atman and Brahman as articulated in ancient Indian texts, the Upanishads. First, I lay out Gandhi's moral psychology of nonviolence and trace some of its Hindu roots, and then I argue that Gandhi's approach should be taken as paradigmatic for any moral psychology of nonviolence that seeks to link the practice of nonviolence with political activism on behalf of oppressed people. Finally,

I conclude by addressing an objection to the notion that Gandhian nonviolence should be taken as a paradigm for nonviolent activism.

Satyagraha as a Moral Discipline and Way of Life Grounded in Vedanta Philosophy

It is tempting to refer to satyagraha as a "method" of nonviolence, but it is more than just a method. It is, instead, a moral discipline, a way of life, and a form of therapy and recovery from the devastating psychological effects of oppression. To see this, let us consider the central concepts of satyagraha, as well as the virtues and requirements of the *satyagrahi*, or practitioner of satyagraha.

The two central values of satyagraha are *sat*, or truth, and *ahimsā*, or nonviolence. "Satyagraha" means "grasping for truth," or "truth-force," and is sometimes also translated as "soul-force" or "love-force" (Lal 1978, 113). Gandhi understands truth to be the supreme value of human life, and believes that truth is equivalent to God, or, more abstractly, to the spiritual force that guides the universe. Ahimsā, or nonviolence, is the way to attain truth. Though Gandhi values ahimsā almost as much as truth, he is willing to abandon ahimsā if it does not lead to truth (Iyer 2000, 229). One may in certain circumstances resort to violent action, though never with hatred or ill will (see Gier 2004, 53–54; Tähtinen 1976, 122; Verma 1970, 59; Parel 1997, 86). Thus, ahimsā is a vitally important means or pathway to the attainment of truth (Verma 1970, 41).

What, then, is ahimsā? As a translation of ahimsā, the term "nonviolence" is inadequate. This is because the meaning of ahimsā, though overlapping in some ways with the meaning Westerners give to "nonviolence," goes beyond it in important respects (see Lal 1978, 108–13). As with our term "nonviolence," ahimsā requires that one refrain from using physical force against others. It also requires that one refrain from harming others in nonphysical ways, for example, by lying, cheating, spreading rumors, or even by having negative thoughts about others. In addition to these demands that we refrain from harming others, ahimsā requires that we go beyond that to love others—to help and support them in positive, active ways. Grasping this positive sense of ahimsā is essential for understanding the nature of Gandhi's approach to nonviolence. That ahiṃsā requires love for others, including oppressors, imbues its use as a political tool with moral authority. This point will be developed below. For now, let us note that techniques of noncooperation or resistance, for example, strikes, were not to be used to coerce oppressors, but, instead, to convert them (Lal 1978, 115). Satyagraha was an appeal to the hearts and minds of oppressors, an attempt, through communicative action, to bring the oppressor to admit the legitimacy of the claims of the oppressed. Techniques of nonviolent resistance were to be chosen not to embarrass or burden oppressors, but, instead, to make a point.

The idea was for practitioners of satyagraha to take upon themselves the sacrifice of nonviolent resistance while instructing oppressors about the nature of their grievance through their choice of tactics. Yet, should oppressors resist acknowledging the claims of the oppressed, tactics such as strikes and deliberate civil disobedience, such as the Salt March of 1930, could legitimately increase pressure on oppressors. Helping oppressors see and acknowledge the point of the oppressed was essential to the conversion process of winning oppressors over to the side of the satyagrahi. Thus, satyagraha was a love-force. It was the use of the force of love and respect for the oppressor, as well as self-sacrifice, to convert them to the cause (Lal 1978, 115; Parel 1997, 90).

Not just anyone can practice satyagraha. Practicing satyagraha requires a moral discipline that is a purification of the self. This purification of the self is meant to control desires and emotions such as anger, which are forms of corruption that disturb the practitioner's balance, equanimity, and single-mindedness—qualities that are needed if the satyagrahi is to be effective in the pursuit of nonviolent goals. Gandhi's conception of the self and his belief in the need for purification are rooted in early Indian philosophy and religion, especially in the Vedanta doctrines of Atman and Brahman as articulated in the Upanishads and expanded in the Bhagavad Gita. In the Upanishads, ancient Indian philosophical texts, we learn that our true Self, Atman, is Brahman, or God. Atman lies at the deepest core of our being, and is not to be identified with *dehin*, the embodied spatiotemporal self, which is composed of body, senses, mind, and soul (Parel 1997, xlix). Brahman is in everyone, and in all of creation. According to

Vedanta, at the deepest level of reality, we are all one, and divinity is present in all of us. Because of the divinity in all of us, we are required not to harm—through thought, word, or deed—anyone: not ourselves, not other humans, not other living beings. Even oppressors embody divine goodness and consequently, are worthy of love and respect.

The Upanishads teach that the Self that is Brahman lies at the core of our innermost being and is accessible only through the fourth state of consciousness, waking in dreamless sleep. (The other three states are waking, dream-filled sleep, and dreamless sleep [see "The *Brihadaranyaka* Upanishad" and "The *Mandukya* Upanishad"].) To reach this innermost Self, we must move beyond the realm of the senses, *samsara*, to achieve a state of stillness of the soul. Purification, or learning to control or expunge desires and emotions, is part of the discipline needed to achieve the Self. When we reach our innermost being, we realize that the distinctions between inner and outer and public and private are mere appearances. They are part of the realm of samsara that prevents us from achieving unity with our divine being. At a deeper level of reality, all Selves are one in Brahman. As Raghavan Iyer notes, Gandhi explicitly believes in *Advaita*, the Indian doctrine of monism, maintaining "the essential unity of God and man and for that matter of all that lives" (Gandhi, quoted in Iyer 2000, 91; see also Hardiman 2003, 75–76). Thus, Gandhi's is a deeply spiritual, pantheistic worldview. This outlook profoundly shapes his moral psychology and social ethic.

The Upanishads are deeply spiritual and metaphysical, and develop few, if any, ethical themes. They do, however, discuss several stages of life: those of the student, the householder, the retiree, and the "renunciate." Each stage represents a higher level of spiritual development, with the renunciate at the topmost stage. At this level, the mature individual renounces family and social and civic life, and withdraws to the forest to meditate. Surendra Verma (1970, 70) notes that Gandhi does not preach renunciation, as do the Upanishads. Instead, Gandhi holds that perfect salvation, or *moksha*, can only be attained when the whole world is redeemed (ibid., 54–55). Thus, renunciation of the world is not the path to salvation. Right action in the world is needed.

Verma (77–78; 89–94) argues that the tension between the lives of renunciation and of action is reconciled in two Vedantic texts that influence Gandhi, the *Isha* Upanishad, and the Bhagavad Gita (or "Gita," sometimes referred to as "Krishna's Counsel in Time of War"), which is part of the longer epic, the Mahabharata. Since the *Isha* is more suggestive, and the Gita, more explicit, we will focus on the Gita (see also Parel 1997, xlix–l). The storyline is this: After all attempts at peacemaking have failed, Arjuna, the hero of the Gita, is called upon to do battle with his kinsmen. Contemplating the prospect of slaughtering his cousins, Arjuna loses heart. He is counseled by the god Krishna, who is his charioteer. Krishna offers Arjuna much advice that Gandhi finds significant. Among this is an explanation of three states of mind: lucidity, passion, and dark inertia (see "Seventeenth Teaching," Bhagavad Gita). Lucidity is the peaceful, confident, calm state of mind achieved by those who are disciplined. It is a state of self-understanding attained through virtuous living, self-control, patience, and relinquishment of the fruit of action, that is, nonattachment to consequences. The lucid person performs actions for their own sake because they are right, and is not bothered by lack of success in attaining desired ends. He or she has the patience and perseverance to continue striving to do what is right, even in the face of failure. By contrast, the person of passion is roiled by unruly emotions, is angry when her actions fail or are frustrated and is plagued by unrestrained desires. The person of dark inertia renounces her ends and lacks the will to pursue projects.

Verma (1970, 91) reads the Gita as offering a middle way—the way of nonattachment to the fruits of action, or lucidity—between two ideals: *pravritti*, the active life of passion; and *nivritti*, renunciation or dark inertia. Verma (1970, 90) notes that the Gita defines "yoga" as "skill in action." Thus, the teaching of the Gita that Gandhi finds so important is the teaching of the yoga of nonattachment to the fruits of action. We act—our lives are active, but we renounce the fruits. What does it mean to "renounce the fruits" of action? Verma (1970, 91–92) explains: "Renunciation of fruit in no way means indifference to the result. It simply means there should be no selfish purpose behind actions. To be detached from fruits of action is not to be ignorant of them or to disregard or disown them. On the contrary, it is proof of the immovable faith in the certainty of the contemplated result following in due course."

The yoga of nonattachment to the fruits of action cannot be successfully practiced unless one has achieved purity of mind and strength of character. These states are essential if one is to follow one's dharma, or way, and achieve one's own moksha, or salvation, as well as the salvation of the world. To attain these states, Gandhi prescribes a way of life marked by the practice of five traditional Indian virtues, or *yama*, and two nontraditional virtues (Lal 1978, 135–38; see also Gier 2004, 126–35). The five traditional virtues are: *ahimsā* (nonviolence), *satya* (truthfulness), *asteya* (non-stealing), *aparigraha* (nonacceptance), and *brahmacharya* (celibacy). The two that Gandhi adds are *abhaya* (fearlessness) and faith in God. Verma (1970, 68) identifies eleven vows of the satyagrahi and argues (1970, 82) that the five yama listed here are taken by Gandhi from a traditional Vedantic text, Patañjali's Yoga-Sūtras. Patañjali defines "yoga" as "inhibition of the properties of the mind" (Verma 1970, 90). Each of the virtues applies to a range of desires that must be controlled or expunged in order to purify the satyagrahi and free her from the restraints that prevent her from following her dharma. Each of the virtues is necessary for *swaraj*, understood here as self-rule or self-control over mind, senses and passions, as well as for successful engagement in the rigors of nonviolent resistance. A word about each virtue is in order.

We have already briefly explored ahimsā. The virtue of nonviolence is mentioned in the Gita as a divine trait that leads to freedom and helps us escape the "net of delusion"—the temptation to satisfy worldly desires ("Sixteenth Teaching," Bhagavad Gita). At the heart of ahimsā is love and toleration for all beings. Ahimsā requires moral equality for all persons; consequently, Gandhi deeply opposes the doctrine of untouchability. As with all the virtues, cultivating ahimsā is a deeply personal task, requiring discipline in thought, speech, and action. Yet, the development of ahimsā cannot be done on a purely personal or private level. That is, we cannot simply "work on ourselves," seeking to expunge our own demons and leaving it at that. To have the virtue of ahimsā, we need to show love for others in our daily lives and in public practices and policies. We need to oppose policies, such as untouchability, that display hatred or contempt for others (Patel 1997, 172). Our public opposition to such policies is an example of our personal ahimsā at work. But Gandhi goes further. Unless based on personal virtue, public opposition to immoral policies lacks moral worth. Similarly, private virtue that does not issue in public deeds is morally empty. As Iyer (2000, 123) writes, "Gandhi was concerned with socializing the individual conscience rather than internalizing the social conscience." This statement means that Gandhi was interested in facilitating the moral growth of individuals, then effecting social change through individual efforts. What is private must reach outward so that private values become public. This is an implication of the doctrine of Advaita (monism): essentially, all is one; there is, in reality, neither public nor private, neither inner nor outer. The appearance of a public/private distinction is a misleading artifact of the way in which Westerners categorize social realities.

Satya or truthfulness is the second of the yama that Gandhi espouses. Satya, like ahimsā, is a divine trait prescribed by Krishna in the Gita. It combats the vices of ignorance and delusion, which are unnatural to humans, cloud the mind and create confusion ("Sixteenth Teaching" and "Seventeenth Teaching," Bhagavad Gita). To cultivate satya, we must, according to Gandhi, combat the six deadly enemies of lust, anger, greed, infatuation, pride, and falsehood (Lal 1978, 135). Following an ancient Indian maxim, as well as the advice given in the Ramayana, an ancient Indian epic, Gandhi believes the truth should be spoken pleasantly, so as not to create unnecessary social harm (Lal 1978, 136; Narayan 1972, 110). Thus, one should avoid anger or bitterness in speaking the truth, thereby respecting the essential goodness of the one to whom the utterance of an unpleasant truth is directed.

Gandhi understands asteya or non-stealing to require both not taking another's property, as well as not keeping possessions that are not needed. Aparigraha, nonacceptance, is being contented with the necessities of life and not wanting more (Lal 1978, 136). Asteya and aparigraha both combat the vice of greed—wanting more and more—what Aristotle calls *pleonexia* or "graspingness." The desire for material goods is an enemy that diverts us from spiritual and moral growth, and is socially divisive. Gandhi follows several Indian traditions—those of the ancient ascetics and yogins—as well as Jainism in believing that stealing, as well as keeping unnecessary possessions, are forms of *himsa*, or harm (Lal 1978, 136; Tähtinen 1976, 86).

The fifth yama that Gandhi prescribes is brahmacharya, or celibacy. Etymologically, brahmacharya means "living in Brahman" (Lal 1978, 137). Gandhi uses the term in both the narrow sense of the control of sexual desire and abstinence from sexual relations, and in the broader sense of restraining the mind and the senses (Lal 1978, 137; Gandhi 2001, 95–98). Since the senses delude and misguide us, they need to be reined in. Gandhi's understanding of brahmacharya is close to those of the Indian ascetic tradition, Jainism, and Theravada Buddhism. These traditions interpret brahmacharya to mean the renunciation of self-indulgence in every form (Tähtinen 1976, 73–74). Even our desires for food need to be restrained. Gandhi advocates *asvada* or control of the palate (Gier 2004, 129). The literal meaning of asvada is that we should not eat simply for the sake of the taste of the food. The point of eating is, instead, bodily sustenance (ibid., 129). Evidently Gandhi thinks that indulgence in rich food causes sexual desires to arise (Lal 1978, 137). Whatever the merits of this view, it is clear that a diet of simple, nutritious food is consistent with or perhaps a manifestation of aparigraha—not desiring more than one needs.

What is Gandhi's objection to sexual relations? Gandhi thinks that sexual relations should be used only for procreation (Parel 1997, 97). He does not regard sexual pleasure as sinful, but as a distraction and waste of vital energy (Gandhi 2001, 95–98). Desires for material goods, for rich foods, for sex, waste vital energy needed for the rigors of moral purification and nonviolent resistance. Even thoughts must be controlled. Gandhi (97) writes that

> an impure thought is a breach of brahmacharya; so is anger. All power comes from the preservation and sublimation of the vitality that is responsible for creation of life. If the vitality is husbanded instead of dissipated, it is transmuted into creative energy of the highest order. This vitality is continuously and even unconsciously dissipated by evil, or even rambling, disorderly, unwanted thoughts.

Gandhi (2001, 97–98) is under no illusions about the difficulty of self-purification, observing:

This control is unattainable save by the grace of God. There is a verse in the second chapter of the Gita which freely rendered means: "Sense-effects remain in abeyance whilst one is fasting or whilst the particular sense is starved, but the hankering does not cease except when one sees God face to face." This control is not mechanical or temporary. Once attained it is never lost.

Nicholas Gier (2004, 129–130) links brahmacharya to the virtues of asteya and aparigraha—celibacy or restraint of desire is related to non-stealing and non-possession. In the case of each virtue, the practitioner renounces the desire to possess or control.

Brahmacharya forcefully reminds us that Gandhi's is an ascetic discipline. It is reasonable to think that Gandhi is here influenced by Hindu asceticism. Yet, it should be noted that Gandhi's reinterpretation departs from traditional Hindu practices in some respects. Hindu rishis or holy men practiced brahmacharya by withdrawing from society and thus, from sexual temptation. For Gandhi, this would have been the coward's way out. Gandhi believes that temptation and desire should be confronted and conquered head on. As Gier (2004, 130) notes, Gandhi's test of the practice of virtues is openness. The test of one's commitment to celibacy is one's ability to sleep openly with another person and not be tempted to have sexual relations; the test of non-stealing and non-possession is for belongings to be displayed openly, so that those tempted to theft can confront and overcome their desire to possess what is rightfully another's. By confronting and overcoming desire, we conquer it, just as, in the Gita, Krishna urges Arjuna to confront and overcome his kinsmen, who represent the desires with which Arjuna struggles.

As noted earlier, Gandhi adds two virtues of his own to the traditional yamas: abhaya, or fearlessness (also mentioned as a divine trait in the Gita ("Sixteenth Teaching," Bhagavad Gita); and faith in God (Lal 1978, 137–38). Fearlessness is the virtue of having courage in the face of adversity or danger; it includes not fearing starvation, humiliation, imprisonment, beating, poverty, etc. (Lal 1978, 137–138). Gandhi is said to have remarked that cowards can never be moral (Lal 1978, 138). Certainly, cowards do not have the strength squarely to confront their desires and moral failings, and struggle to overcome them.

Finally, what does Gandhi mean by "faith in God"? This means a faith in the essential morality of the universe, a faith that there is a force or forces for good that extend beyond the individual. Our faith in this greater power for good is what sustains us when we flag, when we are weak, tired, sick, lonely, etc. Faith in God saves us from succumbing to despair. Many further elements could be added to this picture or amplified. The account gives a sense of the complexity of Gandhi's moral psychology and of its deep roots in Hinduism.

Why Gandhi's Approach Should be Considered Paradigmatic

Gandhi's thought should be considered paradigmatic as an approach to nonviolence. By "paradigmatic," I mean that the way Gandhi thinks about nonviolence—the method he takes—is a useful model for anyone who believes that nonviolent resistance to oppression is necessary at a specific time and place. I do not mean that the actual content of his thought, for example, the substance of the virtues and requirements of the satyagrahi, should be copied and transferred to different contexts without modification. In his efforts to wrest control of India from the British Raj, three factors make Gandhi's thought socially and politically effective—the extent to which he: (a) understands and values the Indian tradition (Parel 1997, 7, 66–71); (b) understands the psychological situation of the Indian people under British rule; and (c) revitalizes the Indian spiritual tradition in an effort to rebuild the moral psychology of Indian individuals and Indian culture as a whole.

Gandhi understands that the Indian people lost partial touch with their individual and cultural identities under the British, and had adopted some of the "modern" ways of the British. Partial cultural alienation was a fact of daily life. Commenting on his father, who was an irrigation official under the British Raj, Gurcharan Das (2002, 13) notes: "My father seemed to lead two separate lives, neatly divided into two compartments. During the day, at work, he wore Western clothes, spoke English, and followed the rational, individualistic life of an official of the British Raj. In the evening he wore a loose-fitting kurta, spoke Punjabi, ate Indian food, listened to Indian music, and meditated like a good Hindu." Das (13) uses the term "cultural commuter" to describe his father's lifestyle during that period. His reminiscence portrays a schism in the lives of Indians under colonial rule—a fragmentation of cultural identity. Yet, he also writes that religion pervaded ordinary discussions (12), and that the Raj "did not interfere with our ancient traditions and our religion" (15).

Gandhi takes advantage of people's adherence to the ancient traditions and religion of India. He knows that the deepest and most effective motivational forces are those that appeal to higher values—to our best selves. Not only are higher values—love for all, respect for the essential goodness of humanity, compassion, humility, and an ethic of selfless sacrifice—capable of exerting profound motivational force, they also imbue their possessors and their possessors' actions with moral authority. Satyagraha, with its ethic of universal love, its spiritual depth, and its moral discipline of self-purification, is both motivationally efficacious and morally authoritative. Satyagraha is an exercise in revitalization and recreation: in Gandhi's time, the revitalization of the Indian moral and spiritual tradition—its extension from the private to the public realm—and the recreation of integrated Indian personal and cultural identities.

Revitalizing the Indian cultural and spiritual tradition would not have been an effective tool against oppression without Gandhi's understanding of the psychology of the Indian people under the British Raj—his fine attunement to the psychological dynamics of oppressor and oppressed. Oppression causes the deformation and fragmentation of personal and cultural identities. It causes people to feel belittled, inferior, angry, and resentful. Having experienced discrimination himself, Gandhi appreciates these feelings in others and takes them seriously. He understands that people need to heal psychologically before confronting the British and, after expelling the British from India, undertaking self-rule. Consequently, in addition to social action, satyagraha prescribes a form of psychological and moral therapy. Gandhi understands swaraj or self-rule, in a double sense: individuals need to be able to "rule themselves," that is, to exert self-discipline and self-control before undertaking the self-rule of the nation. If the British quit India and personal swaraj is not attained, Gandhi believes that true national independence cannot be achieved. The personal discipline of satyagraha—the moral purification of the self—is thus key to genuine national independence.

Gandhi's approach to the moral psychology of nonviolence should be considered a paradigm or a blueprint for others in the following ways. First, those who believe that nonviolent resistance is called for in a specific setting should be attuned to the psychology of oppressor and oppressed. The Gandhian paradigm urges us to take seriously the damaged self-conceptions and negative feelings of the oppressed—anger, alienation, despair, resentment, inferiority. Through habituated efforts on the part of the oppressed to cultivate self-control and virtue, and to see themselves as integral to an ongoing, morally and culturally vital tradition, such negative thoughts and emotions can gradually be transformed into productive personal revitalization and social activism.

Second, to sensitively apply these methods of satyagraha to non-Indian social and cultural contexts, a series of questions should be addressed. What tradition has been undermined, ignored, or relegated to an inferior status? What values does this tradition prescribe? Among the values of the tradition of the oppressed, are there some which, though interpreted through the prism of traditional cultures, have universal appeal? How might the traditional cultural and moral values of the oppressed be revived and used to motivate individuals whose sense of their personal and collective identities has been damaged or overlain with the values of oppressors? How can the damaged personalities of these people be healed and revitalized?

Furthermore, how can nonviolent resistance be given moral authority? What is the moral discipline that will prepare individuals to face the wrath and scorn of those who oppose them without losing their moral compass? How will practitioners of nonviolence be motivated to undertake the burdens, risks, and costs of nonviolent resistance? The Gandhian paradigm offers answers to all of these questions. More importantly, it recommends asking these questions, but answering them requires scrutinizing the culture, traditions, and psychology of those on whose behalf nonviolence is undertaken with an eye to empowerment.

Nonviolent resistance is, in many contexts, not only a fight for social justice and for better political, social and economic conditions. It is a battle for people's souls. It is a setting in which oppressed individuals seek to reclaim and recreate their own personal and cultural identities. They are best empowered in this venture by paying attention to the method shown by the Gandhian paradigm and drawing on the strength, motivational power, and moral forces of their own values and traditions. Values imported by oppressors, such as the Western distinction between the public and the private that the British brought and enforced in India, might have to fall by the wayside. But that is a small price to pay for the revitalization of people and cultures.

An Objection and a Reply

To conclude, let us consider an objection to the proposal that Gandhian nonviolence should be used as a paradigm for nonviolent activism. The objection is as follows: Gandhi's approach is so successful because it draws on an especially powerful element in the Hindu spiritual tradition, namely the insight that Atman is Brahman—Self is God. The identification of Self with God and the recognition that all Selves are God forces one to the radical ethical conclusion that each Self is sacred, and that no Self should be harmed. In short, it is the very identification of all Selves with the divine that gives the Vedantic tradition of Hindu ethics, and by extension, satyagraha, its spiritual depth and moral authority. Other traditions, such as Christianity, cannot match the moral power implicit in this thought, insofar as these traditions do not identify persons with the divine, but insist on separating God from humanity. Consequently, even if one were to follow the suggestion of this essay, and put Gandhi's approach into practice in other traditions and contexts, such tradition-based nonviolent movements would lack the power and moral force of satyagraha simply because its central driving force—that Self is God—is not part of those traditions.

To respond, let us note first that the foregoing line of thought is deeply incompatible with Gandhi's own way of seeing diverse moral and spiritual

266 • Ethics and Practices of Nonviolence

traditions. Gandhi is an eclectic thinker whose worldview assimilated aspects of Christianity through the works of Ruskin, Thoreau, and Tolstoy, and incorporates elements from other Asian traditions, such as Buddhism and Jainism. Moreover, Gandhi works to draw Muslims into his movement and to unify Hindus and Muslims in India. Gandhi sees the differences between spiritual traditions as inessential. Instead, he sees different religions as alternative paths to the same ultimate reality of Truth.

Let us add to this line of reasoning another observation. Even those religions that do not identify God with humanity, but, instead, insist that God and humanity are separate, allow that humans can and should imitate and follow God. That is, even though we are not divine, we should seek to be God-like or Christ-like in how we live and act. We should follow the word of God. Furthermore, religions such as Christianity and Islam admit of mystical traditions in which spiritual seekers achieve forms of union with God, as in the case of Sufi mystics and Christian mystics such as Meister Eckhart and St. Teresa of Ávila. Less mystical seekers who do not achieve union with God sometimes report, after deep prayer in the face of challenging or agonizing situations, the feeling of spiritual power and renewal.

Consider, for example, the life of Dr. Martin Luther King Jr. King was not an otherworldly mystic, but a passionately engaged activist. As a theist, he adhered to the Christian notion of the separation of the human and the divine. His speeches eloquently attest to the very human obstacles and disappointments that he and others encountered in the nonviolent struggle against racial injustice in the United States, as well as to fear in the face of physical attacks, and deep sadness when comrades were hurt or killed (see Carson and Shepard 2001). Yet, pervading this all-too-human testimony is his enduring faith and a palpable sense that God is with and speaks through King. Reading his speeches and sensing his deep faith, one is convinced that God is never far from Dr. King.

The Jewish tradition, too, combines social justice activism with God's presence. Consider the following reading of a familiar story from the Book of Exodus, which I heard several years ago while attending a local synagogue. Moses is commanded by God to go to Pharaoh and demand the release of the Israelites. According to the rabbi at the service I attended, the common translation of God's words to Moses is, "Go unto Pharaoh." The rabbi proposed an alternative interpretation of the Hebrew text as "Come unto Pharaoh," thereby suggesting that God is not commanding Moses to go to Pharaoh on his own but is inviting Moses to come with God to confront Pharaoh. This reading of the story suggests that we come with God as we work together for the common cause of social justice. It is compatible with the Jewish idea that God depends on us to do His work in the world.

The foregoing reflections suggest the following response to the objection. First, though there is a doctrinal difference between Vedantic Hinduism's identification of Atman and Brahman and other religions for which God and humanity are separate, many of those other religions admit that God and humans can be united through beatific visions and other mystical experiences. Consequently, even at the level of doctrine, the difference between the spiritual tradition of the Vedanta and other religions is not as stark as the objection makes it seem. Second, at the pragmatic level of experience, the doctrinal separation between God and humanity counts for little. What is essential in nonviolent struggle is the practitioner's ability to draw strength from a power that goes beyond the embodied, individual self, as well as the recognition that God resides in oppressor as well as oppressed. Such spiritual sustenance is available in many spiritual traditions. In the final analysis, then, the similarities among these traditions are more important than their differences—especially those that empower and encourage practitioners of nonviolent resistance. Here again, Gandhi's insights into the value of making common spiritual cause in the quest for justice are instructive for our own day and well worth emulating.

Conclusion

*Cultivating Transformative Wisdom and the Power
of Peace to Create Futures of Nonviolence*

Elavie Ndura and Randall Amster

> O Great Spirit of our Ancestors, I raise my pipe to you. To your
> messengers the four winds, and to Mother Earth who provides for
> your children. Give us the wisdom to teach our children to love, to
> respect, and to be kind to each other so that they may grow with
> peace in mind. Let us learn to share all the good things that you
> provide for us on this Earth.

The above Native American prayer is one of the twelve prayers for peace
that were prayed in Assisi, Italy, on the Day of Prayer for World Peace
during the United Nations International Year of Peace, 1986. The twelve
prayers for peace included Hindu, Buddhist, Jain, Muslim, Sikh, Baha'i,
Shinto, Native African, Native American, Zoroastrian, Jewish, and Christian prayers. (They are reprinted in Mallick and Hunter's 2002 edited volume, *An Anthology of Nonviolence: Historical and Contemporary Voices*).
These twelve prayers for peace capture the essence of the present volume,
purposefully titled *Exploring the Power of Nonviolence*—namely, to inspire
and shape the dispositions, worldviews, commitments, and actions necessary to create and sustain cultures of peace and nonviolence in our families, communities, and the world.

Kenneth Boulding (1999) discusses three faces of power in relation to
nonviolence: threat power, economic power, and integrative power. Citing
Mohandas Gandhi's nonviolence movement, Boulding argues that a case

can be made for a fourth face of power: organizational power. Considering the diversity and depth of the contents of the chapters included in this volume, we have great hope that this book will make a significant contribution to the nonviolence movement. Every chapter is inspired by broad knowledge and vast experiences from across disciplines, and by intentional commitments to foster social change—which, as Stephen Zunes, Lester Kurtz, and Sara Beth Asher (1999) argue, is the ultimate goal of the nonviolence movement. Whereas most history courses from educational systems throughout the world often focus on violent conflicts and wars, the contributors to this volume offer knowledge and strategies that shift our thinking from a violence paradigm to a social transformation paradigm as a prerequisite to peaceful and nonviolent coexistence. We hope that this book will inspire readers to more purposefully challenge threat power and work together to create mechanisms that sustain shared economic power, foster deeply rooted integrative power, and cultivate effective organizational power for the common good.

By opening this volume with the timeless question whether there is a natural nexus between love and revolution—which would inspire greater possibilities for positive, lasting social change—Matt Meyer and Elavie Ndura call each of us to higher levels of social responsibility. We are called to ponder the foundation of our principles and the essence of our actions. Why do we teach? What do we teach? Why do we work on a particular line of scholarship? Why do we participate in demonstrations? What motivates our acts of service?

Such questions not only help us clarify our thinking, but also complicate our understanding and interpretation of many of the critical messages shared in this book. For example, Jenice View redirects our attention to the structural and cultural violence that has marked the history of the United States, thus creating a system of racialized oppression. Pat Lauderdale reminds us that respect for human diversity and caring for nature is central to civil law and peace. Stephen Zunes problematizes our understanding of democracy by arguing that true democracy should empower the people to challenge the excesses of national and global capitalism, and to openly defend the rights of women, minorities, and the poor. Supriya Baily urges us to validate the contributions of "unheralded peacemakers" who work daily to help dismantle prejudices and thus ensure a safer future for their communities. Nancy Snow unequivocally contends that nonviolent resistance is a battle for people's souls because it empowers oppressed individuals to recreate their own personal and cultural identities.

These and the other contributors to this book challenge us to examine our often taken-for-granted assumptions more intentionally, to consider building alliances of peace and nonviolence across academic disciplines and diverse communities, and to henceforth broaden both the scope and impact of the movement. Ultimately, the quest for social transformation that is the essence of the nonviolence movement begins with the transformation of self. Randall Amster argues in his chapter that the search for nonviolence connects the personal and political spheres of our lives, and provides a moral compass for evaluating our interactions with ourselves, others, and the environment. It is this moral compass that empowers us to heed that call by Tülin Levitas urging that we cultivate compassion within ourselves. This moral compass empowers us to stand united in the unshakable testimony of Peter Ackerman and Jack Duvall's (2001) conviction that, indeed, nonviolence can be a "force more powerful" in our quest for cultures of peace and our pursuit of the common good.

In the foreword to the *Report on the Decade for a Culture of Peace*, published in May 2010, Ambassador Anwarul K. Chowdhury stresses that "in today's world, the culture of peace should be seen as the essence of the new humanity, a new global civilization based on inner oneness and outer diversity." He adds that the flourishing of a culture of peace will generate the mindset in us that is a prerequisite for the transition "from force to reason, from conflict and violence to dialogue and peace." He concludes by stating that "a culture of peace will provide the foundation for a stable, progressive, and prosperous world for all."

The *Report*, which is documented by over 5,000 pages of information provided by over 1,000 civil society organizations spanning all continents, highlights the progress achieved in the eight program areas that were identified in 1999 at the onset of the International Decade for a Culture of Peace and Nonviolence for the Children of the World: (1) peace through education; (2) sustainable economic and social development; (3) respect for all human rights; (4) equality between women and men; (5) democratic participation; (6) understanding, tolerance, and solidarity; (7) participatory communication and the free flow of information and knowledge; and (8) international peace and security. Through its focus on the history and theory of nonviolence, nonviolent movements, peace pedagogy, and ethics and practices of nonviolence, this broad-ranging volume contributes significant insights to the actualization of the mission and goals of the Decade for a Culture of Peace.

The Report states that striving for "peace through education" is the program area that was ranked as the highest priority by the majority of participating civil society organizations. This finding has several implications for the future of attaining a world of peace and nonviolence. First, as the *Report* concludes, the Decade for a Culture of Peace may be at a close, but the global movement for a culture of peace and nonviolence is just beginning. The wide scope and diversity of voices represented by this volume vividly supports this conclusion. Thus, it behooves proponents, practitioners, scholars, policy makers, and all who dream to live in communities of peace, to multiply our efforts to strengthen and sustain the nonviolence movement, and to more intentionally trust in the power of nonviolence to achieve needed social change.

Second, it is imperative to create educational systems and develop curricula that empower educators and students to become culturally competent citizens of their communities and of the world with the wisdom, skills, and commitments necessary to erect bridges of caring consciousness—because only they can unite humanity into communities of peace and nonviolence. George Lakey and Laura Finley, respectively, develop practical frameworks and competent educational tools for cultivating nonviolence, indicating that we are all teachers charged with the responsibility to promote the realization of a better world. This means that for the nonviolence movement to achieve higher levels of success, it must be far-reaching and inclusive of diverse voices across cultures, disciplines, traditions, and professions.

Finally, the greatest implication takes us back to the beginning of this volume to once again consider the main question raised in guiding our desire for peace and nonviolence: Is there a natural nexus between love and revolution, a meeting point where the two enrich one another and spur on greater possibilities for lasting, positive change? Indeed, that nexus may be what we refer to as "nonviolence" in its broadest sense: a moral philosophy grounded in universal love, and a set of practices with unabashedly revolutionary potential.

Love, education, and inclusiveness will liberate our minds and our hearts and open them to greater possibilities for social change. Thich Nhat Hanh (2002, 127) teaches that "when your mind is liberated, your heart floods with compassion: compassion for yourself, for having undergone countless sufferings because you were not yet able to relieve yourself of false views, hatred, ignorance, and anger; and compassion for others because they do not yet see and so are still imprisoned by false views, hatred, and ignorance and continue to create suffering for themselves and for others." As we labor to cultivate compassion for ourselves and others, the following words from the Buddhist Prayer for Peace adorn our journeys with hope: "May all beings everywhere plagued with sufferings of body and mind quickly be freed from their illnesses. May those frightened cease to be afraid, and may those bound be free. May the powerless find power, and may people think of befriending one another. May those who find themselves in trackless, fearful wildernesses—the children, the aged, the unprotected—be guarded by beneficent celestials" ("Peace Seeds: Prayers for Peace" 2002, 47).

May we continue to learn and teach to love, to respect, and to be kind to one another, so that we may each grow with peace in our minds and compassion in our hearts as we journey together and work side by side to create futures based on the tenets of nonviolence. And may this collection of grounded insights and heartfelt renderings serve in some small way to aid in that eternal shared journey toward peace.

References

Contributors

Index

References

Ackerman, Peter and Michael J. Glennon. 2007. "The Right Side of the Law." *American Interest* (September/October): 41–46.

Ackerman, Peter, and Jack DuVall. 2001. *A Force More Powerful: A Century of Nonviolent Conflict*. New York: Palgrave Macmillan.

Adams, David. 2009. "The Dawning of Peace." In *I Have Seen the Promised Land*, 82. Self-published via CreateSpace.com (Amazon.com). Accessed August 20, 2013. http://www.culture-of-peace.info/books/novella.pdf.

Adolf, Antony. 2009. *Peace: A World History*. Cambridge, MA: Polity.

Adolf, Antony. 2010a. "Globalizations of Cultural Criticism and the Transformative Roles of Critics." *New Global Studies* (August).

Adolf, Antony. 2010b. *Nonkilling History: Shaping Policy with Lessons from the Past*. Honolulu, HI: Center for Global Nonkilling.

Adolf, Antony and Israel Sanmartin. 2009. "How to Historicize What Did Not Happen (But Makes the Past Present, and Future Possible)." In *Toward a Nonkilling Paradigm*, edited by Joam Evans Pimm, 203–18. Honolulu, HI: Center for Global Nonkilling.

Alberle-Grasse, Melissa. 2000. "The Washington Study-Service Year of Eastern Mennonite University: Reflections on 23 Years of Service Learning." *American Behavioral Scientist* 43:848–57.

Alfred, Gerald T. R. 1995. *Heeding the Voices of Our Ancestors: Kahnawake Mohawk Politics and the Rise of Native Nationalism*. Oxford: Oxford University Press.

Alfred, Taiaiake. 1996. *Peace, Power, and Righteousness: An Indigenous Manifesto*. Oxford: Oxford University Press.

Ali, Saleem H., ed. 2007. *Peace Parks: Conservation and Conflict Resolution*. Cambridge, MA: MIT Press.

Allen, Paula G. 1986. *The Sacred Hoop: Recovering the Feminine in American Indian Traditions*. New York: Beacon.

Amabile, Teresa M. 1985. "Motivation and Creativity: Effects of Motivational Orientation on Creative Writers." *Journal of Personality and Social Psychology* 48:393–99.

Amabile, Teresa M. 1996. *Creativity in Context.* Boulder, CO: Westview.

Amabile, Teresa M., Beth Hennessey, and Barbara Grossman. 1986. "Social Influences on Creativity: The Effects of Contracted-For Reward." *Journal of Personality and Social Psychology* 50:14–23.

Amabile, Teresa M., Sigal G. Barsade, Jennifer Mueller, and Barry M. Staw. 2005. "Affect and Creativity at Work." *Administrative Science Quarterly* 50:367–403.

Ames, Roger T. and Henry Rosemont Jr., trans. 1998. *The Analects of Confucius: A Philosophical Translation.* New York: Ballantine.

Amster, Randall. 2009a. "Water, Water Everywhere? Sustaining Scarce Resources in the Desert." *Huffington Post,* March 5. Accessed August 11, 2013. http://www.huffingtonpost.com/randall-amster/water-water-everywhere-su_b_17 1291.html.

Amster, Randall. 2009b. "Pax Gaia: The Ecology of War, Peace, and How to Get from Here to There." In *Building Cultures of Peace: Transdisciplinary Voices of Hope and Action,* edited by Elavie Ndura-Ouédraogo and Randall Amster, 242–57. Newcastle upon Tyne, UK: Cambridge Scholars.

Amster, Randall. 2009c. "It's Time to Escalate the Peace." ZNet, December 14. Accessed August 11, 2013. http://www.zcommunications.org/its-time-to -escalate-the-peace-by-randall-amster.

Amster, Randall. 2010a. "What the Muslim World Can Teach Us about Nonviolence." *Truthout,* February 5. Accessed August 11, 2013. http://www.truth -out.org/archive/item/87961:what-the-muslim-world-can-teach-us-about -nonviolence.

Amster, Randall. 2010b. "Arizona Bans Ethnic Studies and, Along with It, Reason and Justice." *Truthout,* December 28. Accessed August 11, 2013. http://www.truth-out.org/archive/item/93603:arizona-bans-ethnic-studies-and -along-with-it-reason-and-justice.

Anderson, James. 1988. *The Education of Blacks in the South, 1865–1930.* Chapel Hill: University of North Carolina Press.

Andress, David. 2000. *Massacre at the Champ de Mars: Popular Dissent and Political Culture in the French Revolution.* Suffolk, England: Royal Historical Society.

ANI. 2010. "Gandhi's Words Are Shakira's Personal Motto." *Indian Express*, March 19. Accessed August 20, 2013. http://www.indianexpress.com/news /gandhis-words-are-shakiras-personal-motto/592996/.

Apple, Michael. 2000. *Official Knowledge: Democratic Education in a Conservative Age*. New York: Routledge.

Archives départementales de l'Indre, Châteauroux, France. L 110 49.

Archives municipales de Marseille, Marseille, France. 4 D 43 69, 97, 108, and 115.

Archives nationales de France, CC 24. Paris.

Archives parlementaires de 1787 à 1860: recueil complet des débats législatifs et politiques des chambres françaises. Series I, Vol. 28. Paris.

Ariz. Rev. Stat. § 15-112 (2010), enacting H.B. 2281, 49th Leg., 2d Reg. Sess. (Ariz. 2010), "An Act . . . Relating to School Curriculum."

Arrianus, Flavius. 2010. *Discourses of Epictetus*. New York: Nabu.

ASALH (Association for the Study of African American Life and History). n.d. "History of ASALH." Accessed November 11, 2008. http://www.asalh.org /asalhstory.html.

Åslund, Anders and Michael McFaul, eds. 2006. *Revolution in Orange: The Origins of Ukraine's Democratic Breakthrough*. Washington, DC: Carnegie Endowment for International Peace.

Atkin, Jonathan. 2003. *A War of Individuals: Bloomsbury Attitudes to the Great War*. Manchester, UK: Manchester Press.

Aung San Suu Kyi and Alan Clements. 1997. *The Voice of Hope*. New York: Seven Stories.

Bacic, Roberta. 2002. "Dealing with the Past: Chile—Human Rights and Human Wrongs." *Race and Class* 44:1.

Baily, Supriya. 2009. "Can You Eat Peace? Addressing Development Needs and Peace Education in Gujarat, India." In *Building Cultures of Peace: Transdisciplinary Voices of Hope and Action*, edited by Elavie Ndura-Ouédraogo and Randall Amster, 217–41. Newcastle upon Tyne, UK: Cambridge Scholars.

Baker, Keith Michael. 1990. *Inventing the French Revolution: Essays on French Political Culture in the Eighteenth Century*. Cambridge: Cambridge University Press.

Balaban, John. 1991. *Remembering Heaven's Face: A Conscientious Objector's Moving Memoir of the Vietnam War*. New York: Touchstone.

Banks, James A. 2007. *Educating Citizens in a Multicultural Society*. 2nd ed. New York: Teachers College Press.

Barlow, Maude. 2002. *Blue Gold: The Fight to Stop the Corporate Theft of the World's Water.* New York: New Press.

Barrionuevo, Alexei. 2010. "A Sign of Latin America's Fading Polarization." *New York Times*, January 19. Accessed August 11, 2013. http://www.nytimes.com /2010/01/20/world/20chile.html?_r=0.

Bauman, Garrett M. 2005. "But Can You Teach?" *Chronicle of Higher Education*, October 28. Accessed August 11, 2013. http://chronicle.com/article /But-Can-You-Teach-/6605.

Bennett, Scott. 2003. *Radical Pacifism: The War Resisters League and Gandhian Nonviolence in America, 1915–1963.* Syracuse, NY: Syracuse University Press.

Bentham, Jeremy. 1879. *An Introduction to the Principles of Morals and Legislation.* London: Clarendon.

Berrigan, Daniel. 2004. *The Trial of the Catonsville Nine.* New York: Fordham University Press.

Berry, Barnett, Mandy Hoke, and Eric Hirsch. 2004. "NCLB: Highly Qualified Teachers—The Search for Highly Qualified Teachers." *Phi Delta Kappan* 85 (9): 684–89.

Betit, Amy and Mary Elizabeth Lynch. 2004. "Venture Inward." *Leadership and Peacemaking.* Accessed January 31, 2010. http://www.leadersthroughpeace .com/art1026l.shtml.

Bigler, Rebecca, Christia Spears Brown, and Marc Markell. 2001. "When Groups Are Not Created Equal: Effects of Group Status on the Formation of Intergroup Attitudes in Children." *Child Development* 72 (4): 1151–62.

Black History Now! n.d. "About." *Black History Now!* (blog). Accessed August 12, 2013. http://blackhistorynow.blogspot.com/.

Blackmon, David A. 2008. *Slavery by Another Name: The Re-Enslavement of Black Americans from the Civil War to World War II.* New York: Anchor.

Bluehouse, Philmer and James W. Zion. 1993. "Hozhooji Naat'aanii: The Navajo Justice and Harmony Ceremony." *Mediation Quarterly* 10 (4): 328–31.

Bondurant, Joan V. 1971. *Conquest of violence: The Gandhian Philosophy of Conflict.* Berkeley: University of California Press.

Boorman, John. 1995. *Beyond Rangoon.* Feature film. Castle Rock Entertainment.

Bossut, Nicole. 1998. *Chaumette, porte-parole des sans-culottes.* Paris: CTHS.

Boulding, Kenneth E. 1977. "Commons and Community: The Idea of a Public." In *Managing the Commons*, edited by Garrett Hardin and John Baden, 280–94. San Francisco: W. H. Freeman.

Boulding, Kenneth E. 1999. "Nonviolence and Power in the Twentieth Century." In *Nonviolent Social Movements: A Geographical Perspective*, edited by Stephen Zunes, Lester R. Kurtz, and Sara Beth Asher, 9–17. Malden, MA: Blackwell.

Bowen, Murray. 2002. *Family Therapy in Clinical Practice*. Northvale, NJ: Jason Aronson.

Branch, Andre. 2001. "Increasing the Numbers of Teachers of Color in K–12 Public Schools." *The Educational Forum* 65:254–61.

Branch, Taylor. 1988. *Parting the Waters: America in the King Years, 1954–63*. New York: Simon and Schuster.

Branch, Taylor. 1998. *Pillar of Fire: America in the King Years, 1963–65*. New York: Simon and Schuster.

Branch, Taylor. 2006. *At Canaan's Edge: America in the King Years, 1965–68*. New York: Simon and Schuster.

Brayboy, Bryan McKinley Jones. 2008. "The Lives and Work of Beatrice Medicine and Vine Deloria Jr." *Anthropology and Education Quarterly* 38 (3): 231–38.

Bretherton, Di and Jackie Bornstein. 2003. "The Qualities of Peacemakers: What Can We Learn from Nobel Prize Winners about Managing Conflict within Organizations?" In *Handbook of Conflict Management*, edited by William J. Pammer and Jerri Killian, 33–48. New York: Marcel Dekker.

Bretherton, Diane. 1996. "Nonviolent Conflict Resolution in Children." *Peabody Journal of Education* 71 (3): 111–27.

Breyman, Steve. 2001. *Why Movements Matter: The West German Peace Movement and U.S. Arms Control Policy*. Albany, NY: State University of New York Press.

Brown v. Board of Education, 347 U.S. 483 (1954).

Brown, Anthony L. and Keffrelyn D. Brown. 2010. "Strange Fruit Indeed: Interrogating Contemporary Textbook Representations of Racial Violence toward African Americans." *Teachers College Record* 112 (1): 31–67.

Brown, Dee Alexander. 2001. *Bury My Heart at Wounded Knee: An Indian History of the American West*. New York: Macmillan.

Buchez, Philippe-Joseph-Benjamin. 1845. *Histoire parlementaire de la Révolution française*. Paris: Paulin.

Buff, Rachel Ida, ed. 2008. *Immigrant Rights in the Shadows of Citizenship*. New York: New York University Press.

Buffalohead, Roger W. and Paulette Fairbanks Molin. 1996. "'A Nucleus of Civilization': American Indian Families at Hampton Institute in the Late Nineteenth Century." *Journal of American Indian Education* 35 (3): 59–94.

Burke, J. 2001. "Graduate Schools Should Require Internships for Teaching." *Chronicle of Higher Education*, October 5. Accessed August 11, 2013. http://chronicle.com/article/Graduate-Schools-Should/23560.

Burrowes, Robert J. 1996. *The Strategy of Nonviolent Defense: A Gandhian Approach*. Albany, NY: State University of New York Press.

Butselaar, Jan van. 2001. *Church and Peace in Africa: The Role of the Churches in the Peace Process*. Assen, Netherlands: Uitgeverij Van Gorcum.

Cammarota, Julio and Michelle Fine, eds. 2008. *Revolutionizing Education: Youth Participatory Action Research in Motion*. New York: Routledge.

Carson, Clayborne and Kris Shepard, eds. 2001. *A Call to Conscience: The Landmark Speeches of Dr. Martin Luther King, Jr.* New York: IPM/Warner.

Carius, Alexander. 2006. *Environmental Cooperation as an Instrument of Crisis Prevention and Peacebuilding: Conditions for Success and Constraints*. Report commissioned by the German Federal Ministry for Economic Cooperation and Development. Berlin, Germany: Adelphi Consult.

Cassuto, L. 1998. "Pressures to Publish Fuel the Professionalization of Today's Graduate Students." *Chronicle of Higher Education*, November 27. Accessed August 11, 2013. http://chronicle.com/article/Pressures-to-Publish-Fuel-the/5317.

Castro, April. 2010. "Texas OKs School Textbook Changes." MSNBC.com, May 21.

Cavanagh, Tom. 2009. "Creating Schools of Peace and Nonviolence in a Time of War and Violence." *Journal of School Violence* 8:64–80.

Cerutti, Furio and Rodolfo Ragionieri. 1990. *Rethinking European Security*. New York: C. Russak.

Chan Sucheng. 1991. *Asian Americans, an Interpretive History: Chronology of Asian American History*. Accessed November 21, 2008. http://web.mit.edu/21h.153j/www/chrono.html.

Chapman, Audrey and Hugo van der Merwe, eds. 2008. *Truth and Reconciliation in South Africa: Did the TRC Deliver?* Philadelphia: University of Pennsylvania Press.

Chapple, Christopher Key. 1993. *Nonviolence to Animals, Earth, and Self in Asian Traditions*. Albany, NY: State University of New York Press.

Chapple, Christopher Key. 2002. *Jainism and Ecology: Nonviolence in the Web of Life*. Boston: Center for the Study of World Religions, Harvard Divinity School.

Chernus, Ira. 2004. *American Nonviolence: The History of an idea*. Maryknoll, NY: Orbis.

Childs, John Brown. 2003. *Transcommunality: From the Politics of Conversion to the Ethic of Respect*. Philadelphia: Temple University Press.

Chiu Chi-Yue and Hong Ying-Yi. 2005. "Cultural Competence: Dynamic Processes." In *Handbook of Motivation and Competence*, ed. Andrew J. Elliot and Carol S. Dweck, 489–505, New York: Guilford Press.

Chiu Chi-Yue and Angela K. Y. Leung. 2007. "Do Multicultural Experiences Make People More Creative? If So, How?" Accessed January 3, 2008. http://www.in-mind.org/special-issue/do-multicultural-experiencesmake-people-more-creative-if-so.html.

Chowdhury, Anwarul K. 2010. Foreword to *Report on the Decade for a Culture of Peace*. United Nations International Decade for a Culture of Peace and Non-violence for the Children of the World (2001–10). Accessed August 5, 2010. http://decade-culture-of-peace.org.

Christie, Nils. 1971. *Hvis skolen ikke fantes* [If school did not exist]. Oslo, Norway: Universitetsforlaget.

Chu Y-K. 1970. "Oriental Views on Creativity." In *Psi Factors in Creativity*, edited by Allan Angoff and Betty Shapin, 35–50. New York: Parapsychology Foundation.

Cock, Jacques de. 2001. *Les Cordeliers pendant la Révolution française*. Lyon, France: Fantasques.

Collins, Patricia Hill. 1998. "The Tie That Binds: Race, Gender and US Violence." *Ethnic and Racial Studies* 21 (5): 917–38.

Confucius. 1986. The Analects. In *World scriptures: An Introduction to Comparative Religions*, edited by Kenneth Kramer, 110–14. Mahwah, NJ: Paulist.

Cook, David Jackson. 2010. "Every Teacher a Peace Teacher." *YES! Magazine*, June 29. Accessed August 11, 2013. http://www.yesmagazine.org/peace-justice/every-teacher-a-peace-teacher.

Cook, K. 2000. "Grandmother Moon." In *Words That Come Before All Else: Environmental Philosophies of the Haudenosaunee*, edited by Haudenosaunee Environmental Task Force, 140–59. Cornwall Island, ON: Akwesasne Territory, Mohawk Nation, Native North American Traveling College, Haudenosaunee Environmental Task Force.

Cooper, Jonathan J. 2010. "Arizona Ethnic Studies Law Signed by Governor Brewer, Condemned by UN Human Rights Experts." *Huffington Post*, May 12. Accessed May 26, 2010. http://www.huffingtonpost.com/2010/05/12/arizona -ethnic-studies-la_n_572864.html.

Corvette, Barbara A. Budjac. 2007. *Conflict Management: A Practical Guide to Developing Negotiation Strategies*. Upper Saddle River, NJ: Pearson Education.

Craft, Anna. 2003. "The Limits to Creativity in Education: Dilemmas for the Educator." *British Journal of Educational Studies* 51 (2): 113–27.

Craft, Anna. 2005. *Creativity in Schools: Tensions and Dilemmas*. Oxford: Routledge Falmer.

Crawford, Stanley. 1989. *Mayordomo: Chronicle of an Acequia in Northern New Mexico*. New York: Anchor.

Crews, Robin J. and Kathleen M. Weigart. 1999. *Teaching for Justice: Concepts and Models for Service-Learning in Peace Studies*. Washington, DC: American Association for Higher Education.

Crowder, Ralph L. 1977. "Historical Significance of Black History Month." *Western Journal of Black Studies* 1 (4): 302–4.

Dalai Lama. 2002. "The Nobel Peace Prize Lecture." In *An Anthropology of Nonviolence: Historical and Contemporary Voices*, edited by Krishna Mallick and Doris Hunter, 117–24. Westport, CT: Greenwood.

Dalai Lama and Victor Chan. 2004. *The Wisdom of Forgiveness: Intimate Conversations and Journeys*. New York: Riverside.

Das, Gurcharan. 2002. *India Unbound: The Social and Economic Revolution from Independence to the Global Information Age*. New York: Anchor.

Das, Samarendra. 2010. Morning speech to the War Resisters International conference: "Nonviolent Livelihood Struggle and Global Militarism: Links and Strategies," Willoughby-Sutherland Hall, Gujarat Vidyapith, Ahmedabad, India, January 23.

Dasgupta, Sugata. 1984. *Philosophical Assumptions for Training in Nonviolence*. New Dehli: Gujarat Vidyapith.

Deere, Phillip. 1978. *Cheyenne River Swift Bird Project (Development Staff): Operations Guide*. Washington, DC: Law Enforcement Assistance Administration, US Department of Justice.

Delgado, Richard and Jean Stefancic. 2001. *Critical Race Theory: An Introduction*. New York: New York University Press.

Dellinger, David. 1970. *Revolutionary Nonviolence*. Indianapolis: Bobbs-Merril.

Dellinger, David. 1975. *More Power than We Know*. Garden City: Anchor.

Deloria, Vine Jr. 1992. *God Is Red*. 2nd. ed. Golden, CO: North American.

Democracy Now! 2008. "LA School Teacher Fired for Being Too 'Afrocentric'; Arizona Bill Proposes to Prohibit Teachings Critical of Western Civilization." June 18. Accessed August 11, 2013. http://www.democracynow.org /2008/6/18/la_school_teacher_fired_for_being.

DeMulder, Elizabeth K., Elavie Ndura-Ouédraogo, and Stacia M. Stribling. 2009. "From Vision to Action: Fostering Peaceful Coexistence and the Common Good in a Pluralistic Society through Teacher Education." *Peace and Change* 34 (1): 27–48.

Déposition de François-Paul-Nicolas Anthoine, député à l'Assemblée nationale, au tribunal du 6eme arrondissement, sur les troubles, sur la pétition, et sur l'affaire du Champ de Mars. 1791.

Desai, Narayan. 1972. *Towards a Nonviolent Revolution*. Rajghat, India: Sarva Seva Sangh Prakashan.

Desai, Narayan. 2010. Closing speech to the War Resisters International conference, "Nonviolent Livelihood Struggle and Global Militarism: Links and Strategies," Willoughby-Sutherland Hall, Gujarat Vidyapith, Ahmedabad, India, January 25.

Dewey, John. 1902. *The Child and the Curriculum*. Chicago: University of Chicago Press.

Dewey, John. 1966. *Democracy and Education*. New York: Free Press.

Dickens, Charles. 1859. *A Tale of Two Cities*. London: Chapman and Hall.

Dietrich, Wolfgang. 2005. "A Call for Trans-Rational Peaces." Accessed Sept. 19, 2006. http://www.tirol.gv.at/themen/bildung/einrichtungen/grillhof/library/.

Doughman, Pamela M. 2002. "Water Cooperation in the U.S.-Mexico Border Region." In *Environmental Peacemaking*, edited by Ken Conca and Geoffrey D. Dabelko, 190–219. Washington, DC: Woodrow Wilson Center.

Du Bois, William E. B. 1995. *Black Reconstruction in America: 1860–1880*. New York: Free Press. First published 1935.

Duerr, Maia, Arthur Zajonc, and Diane Dana. 2003. "Survey of Transformative and Spiritual Dimensions in Higher Education." *Journal of Transformative Education* 1 (3): 177–211.

Duncan-Andrade, Jeffrey M. R., and Ernest Morrell. 2008. *The Art of Critical Pedagogy*. New York: Peter Lang.

Early, Gerald. 2006. "28 days." *In the Center of It All* (blog). *New York Times*, February 2. http://early.blogs.nytimes.com/2006/02/02/.

Eastman, Clyde, J. Phillip King, and Nicholas A. Meadows. 1997. "Acequias, Small Farms, and the Good Life." *Culture and Agriculture* 19 (1/2): 14–23.

Easwaran, Eknath, trans. 2000. *The Upanishads*. Tomales, CA: Nilgiri.

Easwaran, Eknath. 1999. *Nonviolent Soldier of Islam: Badshah Khan*. Tomales, CA: Nilgiri.

Edmo, Se-ah-dom. 2008. "Building a Sovereignty Curriculum: A Conversation with Denny Hurtado (Skokomish)." *Democracy and Education* 17 (2): 44–47

Eisenberger, Robert and Judy Cameron. 1996. "Detrimental Effects of Reward: Reality or Myth?" *American Psychologist* 51:1153–66.

Eisler, Riane. 1987. *The Chalice and the Blade: Our History, Our Future*. New York: Harper and Row.

Eisler, Riane. 2000. *Tomorrow's Children*. Boulder, CO: Westview.

Erikson, Erik. 1969. *Gandhi's Truth: On the Origins of Militant Nonviolence*. New York: W. W. Norton.

Esteva, Gustavo and Madhu Suri Prakash. 1998. *Grassroots Post-Modernism: Remaking the Soil of Cultures*. Boston, MA: Zed Books.

Evans, Brad. 2009. "Revolution without Violence." *Peace Review* 21:85–94.

Everett, Charles Warren. 1969. *Jeremy Bentham*. London: Weidenfeld and Nicolson.

Feist, Gregory J. 1998. "A Meta-Analysis of the Impact of Personality on Scientific and Artistic Creativity." *Personality and Social Psychological Review* 2:290–309.

Feldman, David H. 1994. *Beyond Universals in Cognitive Development*. Norwood, NJ: Ablex.

Feldman, David H. and Ann C. Benjamin. 2006. "Creativity and Education: An American Retrospective." *Cambridge Journal of Education* 36 (3): 319–36.

Feldman, David H., Mihaly Csikszentmihalyi, and Howard Gardner. 1994. *Changing the World: A Framework for the Study of Creativity*. Westport, CT: Praeger.

Fellman, Gordon. 1998. Rambo and the Dalai Lama: The Compulsion to Win and Its Threat to Human Survival. Albany, NY: State University of New York Press.

Ferrera, Stephanie J. 1996. "Lessons from Nature on Leadership." In *The Emotional Side of Organizations: Applications of Bowen Theory*, edited by Patricia A. Comella, Joyce Bader, Judith S. Ball, Kathleen K. Wiseman, and Ruth Riley Sagar, 200–210. Georgetown, MD: Georgetown Family Center.

Finley, Laura L. 2003. "Militarism Goes to School." *Essays in Education* 4 (Winter).

Fitzpatrick, Peter. 1992. *The Mythology of Modern Law.* London: Routledge.

Fitzsimons, Patrick. 2002. "Neoliberalism and Education: The Autonomous Chooser." *Radical Pedagogy* 4 (2): 1–10.

Florida, Richard L. 2004. *The Rise of the Creative Class and How It Is Transforming Work, Leisure, Community, and Everyday Life.* New York: Basic Books.

Flowers, Nancy and David Shiman. 1997. "Teacher Education and the Human Rights Vision." In *Human Rights Education in the 21st Century*, edited by George J. Andreopoloulos and Richard P. Claude, 161–75. Philadelphia, PA: University of Philadelphia Press.

Fong, Ting C. 2006. "The Effects of Emotional Ambiguity on Creativity." *Academy of Management Journal* 49:1016–30.

Fontana, Alessandro, Francesco Furlan, and Georges Saro, eds. 1997. *Venise et la Révolution française: les 470 dépêches des ambassadeurs de Venise au Doge, 1786–1795.* Paris: Laffont.

Forcey, Linda R. 1991. "Women as Peacemakers: Contested Terrain for Feminist Peace Studies." *Peace and Change* 16 (4): 331–54.

Forcey, Linda R. and Ian Harris. 1999. "Introduction." In *Peacebuilding for Adolescents*, edited by Linda R. Forcey and Ian Harris, 1–14. New York: Peter Lang.

Förster, Jens, Ronald S. Friedman, and Nira Liberman. 2004. "Temporal Construal Effects on Abstract and Concrete Thinking: Consequences for Insight and Creative Cognition." *Journal of Personality and Social Psychology* 87:177–89.

Forsythe, Harold. 2002. "Review of Educating the Disfranchised and Disinherited: Samuel Chapman Armstrong and Hampton Institute, 1839–1893, by Robert Francis Engs." *Journal of Southern History* 68 (4): 984–86.

Foster, Catherine. 1989. *Women for All Seasons: The Story of the Women's International League for Peace and Freedom.* Athens, GA: University of Georgia Press.

Fox News. 2010. "America's Future: Texas Board of Education Adopts New Social Studies, History Guidelines." May 21. http://www.foxnews.com/us/2010/05/21/state-board-education-adopts-new-social-studies-history-guidelines-texas-high/.

Francis, David J. 2006. "Linking Peace, Security and Developmental Regionalism: Regional Economic and Security Integration in Africa." *Journal of Peacebuilding and Development* 2 (3): 7–20.

Franklin, John Hope. 1995. *Reconstruction after the Civil War*. Chicago: University of Chicago Press.

Franklin, John Hope, Harold W. Cruse, Allen R. Ballard, and Reavis L. Mitchell Jr. 1997. "Black History Month: Serious Truth Telling or a Triumph in Tokenism?" *Journal of Blacks in Higher Education* 18:87–92.

Fredrickson, Barbara L. 2001. "The Role of Positive Emotions in Positive Psychology: The Broaden-and-Build Theory of Positive Emotions." *American Psychologist* 56:218–26.

Freire, Paulo. 1970. *Pedagogy of the Oppressed*. New York and London: Continuum.

Freire, Paulo. 1972. *Pedagogy of the Oppressed*. Harmondsworth, UK: Penguin.

Freire, Paulo. 1974. *Pedagogy of the Oppressed*. New York: Seabury.

Freire, Paulo. 1983. "The Banking Concept of Education." In *The Hidden Curriculum and Moral Education*, edited by H. Giroux and D. Purpel. Berkeley, CA: McCutchan.

Freire, Paulo. 2000. *Pedagogy of Freedom: Ethics, Democracy, and Civic Courage*. Lanham, MD: Rowman and Littlefield.

Freire, Paulo and Donaldo Maceo. 1987. *Literacy: Reading the Word and the World*. Oxford: Routledge.

Friedman, Edwin. 1985. *Generation to Generation: Family Process in Church and Synagogue*. New York: Guilford.

Friedman, Edwin. 1987. "How to Succeed in Therapy without Really Trying." *Family Therapy Networker* (May–June): 27–34.

Friedman, Edwin. 1991. Bowen Theory and Therapy. In *Handbook of Family Therapy*, edited by Alan S. Gurman and David P. Kniskern, 134–70. New York: Brunner/Mazel.

Friedman, Edwin. 1996. *Reinventing Leadership*. New York: Guilford.

Fritz, Robert. 1994. *The Path of Least Resistance: Learning to Become the Creative Force in Your Own Life*. New York: Ballantine.

Froebel, Friedrich. 1887. *The Education of Man*. New York: D. Appleton.

Fryberg, Stephanie A. and Hazel Rose Markus. 2007. "Cultural Models of Education in American Indian, Asian American, and European American Contexts." *Social Psychology of Education* 10:213–46.

Fuller, Laurie. 2006. "Teaching Peace in the Feminist Classroom: Starhawks's *The Fifth Sacred Thing*." *Radical Teacher* 75:28–35.

Furet, François. 1981. *Interpreting the French Revolution*. Translated by Elborg Foster. Cambridge, MA: Harvard University Press. First published 1978.

Gallegos, Joseph C. 1998. "Acequia Tales: Stories from a Chicano Centennial Farm." In *Chicano Culture, Ecology, Politics: Subversive Kin*, edited by Devon G. Peña, 235–48. Tucson, AZ: University of Arizona Press.

Galtung, Johan. 1965. "On the Meaning of Nonviolence." *Journal of Peace Research* 2:228–56.

Galtung, Johan. 1969. "Violence, Peace, and Peace Research." *Journal of Peace Research* 6 (3): 167–91.

Galtung, Johan. 1984. *There Are Alternatives*. Nottingham, England: Spokesman.

Galtung, Johan. 1990. "Cultural Violence." *Journal of Peace Research* 27 (3): 291–305.

Galtung, Johan. 1996. *Peace by Peaceful Means: Peace and Conflict, Development and Civilization*. London: Sage.

Galtung, Johan. 2010. *The Fall of the US Empire—And Then What?* Stadtschlaining, Austria: Transcend University Press.

Gandhi, Mohandas K. 1929. *The Story of My Experiments with Truth*. Ahmedabad, India: Navajivan.

Gandhi, Mohandas K. 1938. *Hind Swaraj or Indian Home Rule*. Ahmedabad, India: Navajivan.

Gandhi, Mohandas K. 1983. *Autobiography: The Story of My Experiments with Truth*. New York: Dover.

Gandhi, Mohandas K. 1996. *An Autobiography, or, the Story of My Experiments with Truth*. Ahmedabad, India: Navajivan.

Gandhi, Mohandas K. 1997. *Hind Swaraj and Other Writings*, edited by Anthony J. Parel. Cambridge: Cambridge University Press.

Gandhi, Mohandas K. 2001. *Non-Violent Resistance (Satyagraha)*, edited by Bharatan Kumarappa. Minneola, NY: Dover.

Garcia, Paula and Miguel Santistevan. 2008. "Acequias: A Model for Local Governance of Water." In *Water Consciousness: How We All Have to Change to Protect our Most Critical Resource*, edited by Tara Lohan, 111–19. San Francisco: AlterNet.

Garcia, Paula. 2000. "Community and Culture vs. Commodification: The Survival of Acequias and Traditional Communities in New Mexico." In *Voices from the Earth* 1 (2). Accessed March 11, 2009. http://www.sric.org/voices /2000/v1n2/waterNM.html.

Garcia-Reid, Pauline. 2008. "Understanding the Effects of Structural Violence on the Educational Identities of Hispanic Adolescents: A Call for Justice." *Children and Schools* 30 (4): 235–41.

Gardner, Howard. 1999. *Intelligence Reframed*. New York: Basic.

Garnier, Katja von. 2004. *Iron Jawed Angels*. DVD. New York: HBO Video.

Garrigues, Georges. 1931. *Les districts parisiens pendant la Révolution française*. Paris: Spes.

Gay, Geneva. 2000. *Culturally Responsive Teaching: Theory, Research, and Practice*. New York: Teachers College Press.

George-Kanentiio, D. 2000. *Iroquois Culture and Commentary*. Santa Fe, NM: Clear Light.

Gernet, Jacques. 1999. *A History of Chinese Civilization*. Translated by J. R. Foster and Charles Hartman. Cambridge: Cambridge University Press.

Gibble, H. Lamar. 2006. *Ecumenical Engagement for Peace and Nonviolence: Experiences and Initiatives of the Historic Peace Churches and Fellowship of Reconciliation*. Elgin, IL: Brethren.

Gier, Nicholas F. 2003. "Nonviolence as a Civic Virtue: Gandhi and Reformed Liberalism." *International Journal of Hindu Studies* 7 (1/3): 75–97.

Gier, Nicholas F. 2004. *The Virtue of Nonviolence: From Gautama to Gandhi*. Albany, NY: State University of New York Press.

Gilbert, Roberta M. 1996. "A Natural Systems View of Hierarchy." In *The Emotional Side of Organizations: Applications of Bowen Theory*, edited by Patricia A. Comella, Joyce Bader, Judith S. Ball, Kathleen K. Wiseman, and Ruth Riley Sagar, 130–37. Georgetown, MD: Georgetown Family Center.

Giroux, Henry. 1988. *Teachers as Intellectuals: Toward a Critical Pedagogy of Learning*. Westport, CT: Bergin and Garvey.

Giroux, Henry. 2007. "Youth and the Politics of Disposability: Resisting the Assault on Education and American Youth." *State of Nature* (Winter): 1–20.

Glass, David Ronald. 2001. "On Paulo Freire's Philosophy of Praxis and the Foundations of Liberation Education." *Educational Researcher* 30 (2): 15–25.

Gobodo-Madikizela, Pumla. 2007. "Language Rules: Witnessing about Trauma on South Africa's TRC." *River Teeth: A Journal of Nonfiction Narrative* 8 (2): 25–33.

Goggin, Jacqueline. 1993. *Carter G. Woodson: A Life in Black History*. Baton Rouge, LA: Louisiana State University Press.

Goldsmith, Benjamin and He Baogang. 2008. "Letting Go without a Fight: Decolonization, Democracy and War, 1900–94." *Journal of Peace Research* 45:587–611.

Goleman, Daniel. 2006. *Social Intelligence: The New Science of Human Relationships*. New York: Bantam.

Gonzalez, Gilbert G. 1997. "Culture, Language, and the Americanization of Mexican Children." In *Latinos and Education: A Critical Reader*, edited by Antonia Darder, Rodolfo D. Torres, and Henry Gutierrez, 159–73. New York: Routledge.

Gonzalez, Norma E., Luis C. Moll, and Cathy Amanti, eds. 2005. *Funds of Knowledge: Theorizing Practices in Households, Communities, and Classrooms*. Mahwah, NJ: Lawrence Erlbaum.

Grand récit de ce qui s'est passé hier au CdM et des assassinats qui s'y sont commises, avec le nombre des morts et des blessés. 1791. Paris: Imprimerie de la rue St. Honoré.

Grande, Sandy. 2004. *Red Pedagogy: Native American Social and Political Thought*. Lanham, MD: Rowman and Littlefield.

Greene, Maxine. 1995. *Releasing the Imagination: Essays on Education, the Arts, and Social Change*. San Francisco: Jossey-Bass.

Gresson III, Aaron David. 2008. *Race and Education: Primer*. New York: Peter Lang.

Griffin, Nicholas, ed. 2002. *The Selected Letters of Bertrand Russell: The Public Years, 1914–1970*. London: Routledge.

Grimshaw, Anna, ed. 1992. *C. L. R. James: The C. L. R. James Reader*. Cambridge: Blackwell.

Gross, Jean-Pierre. 1997. *Fair Shares for All: Jacobin Egalitarianism in Practice*. Cambridge: Cambridge University Press.

Groves, Joseph W. 2000. "Revisiting 'self-suffering': From Gandhi and King to Contemporary Nonviolence." In *Nonviolence for the Third Millennium: Its Legacy and Future*, edited by Simon G. Harak, 201–27. Macon, GA: Mercer University Press.

Guevara, Ernesto "Che." 2001. *The African Dream: The Diaries of the Revolutionary War in the Congo*. New York: Grove.

Guevara, Ernesto "Che." 2005. "From Algiers." In *The Che Reader*. Havana: Ocean.

Guilford, J. P. 1950. "Creativity." *American Psychologist* 5:445–54.

Hamilton, Kendra. 2006. "From Then to Now." *Diverse: Issues in Higher Education* 22 (26): 30–32

Hanh, Thich Nhat. 2002. "The Almond Tree in Your Front Yard." In *An Anthology of Nonviolence: Historical and Contemporary Voices*, edited by Krishna Mallick and Doris Hunter, 125–31. Westport, CT: Greenwood.

Hanley, Mary Stone and George W. Noblit. 2008. *Cultural Responsiveness, Racial Identity and Academic Success: A Review of the Literature*. Pittsburgh, PA: Heinz Endowments.

Hanson, Randel D. 2002. "Half Lives of Reagan's Indian Policy: Marketing Nuclear Waste to American Indians." *American Indian Culture and Research Journal* 25 (1): 21–44.

Hardiman, David. 2003. *Gandhi in His Time and Ours: The Global Legacy of His Ideas*. New York: Columbia University Press.

Harnecker, Marta. 2007. *Rebuilding the Left*. London: Zed.

Harris, Ian. 2002. "Challenges for Peace Educators at the Beginning of the 21st Century." *Social Alternatives* 21:28–31.

Harris, Ian and M. Morrison. 2003. *Peace Education*. 2nd ed. Jefferson, NC: McFarland.

Hartranft, Chip, trans. 2003. *The Yoga-Sūtra of Patañjali: A New Translation with Commentary*. Boston, MA: Shambhala.

Hastings, Tom H. 2004. *Nonviolent Response to Terrorism*. Jefferson, NC: McFarland.

Hastings, Tom H. 2006. *Lessons of Nonviolence: Theory and Practice in a World of Conflict*. Jefferson, NC: McFarland.

Haukoos, Gerry D. and Archie B. Beauvais. 1996. "Creating Positive Cultural Images: Thoughts for Teaching about American Indians." *Childhood Education* 73 (2): 77–82.

Hazler, Richard. 1996. *Breaking the Cycle of Violence: Interventions for Bullying and Victimization*. New York: Taylor and Francis.

Hennessey, B., and T. Amabile. 1998. "Reality, Intrinsic Motivation, and Creativity." *American Psychologist* 53:674–75.

Henze, Rosemary C. 2000. "A Required Curriculum for Respect." *Principal Leadership* 1 (4): 14–19.

Herr, Kathryn and Gary L. Anderson. 2003. "Violent Youth or Violent Schools? A Critical Incident Analysis of Symbolic Violence." *International Journal of Leadership in Education* 6 (4): 415–33.

Hicks, Gregory A., and Devon G. Peña. 2003. "Community Acequias in Colorado's Rio Culebra Watershed: A Customary Commons in the Domain of Prior Appropriation." *University of Colorado Law Review* 74 (2): 387–486.

Hill, David. 2004. "Sisters in Arms." In *Putting the Movement Back into Civil Rights Teaching*, edited by Deborah Menkart, Alana D. Murray, and Jenice L. View, 346–51. Washington, DC: Teaching for Change and Poverty & Race Research Action Council.

Histoire du 18 avril. 1791. Paris.

Ho, Kathleen. 2007. "Structural Violence as a Human Rights Violation." *Essex Human Rights Review* 4 (2): 1–17.

Hodge, James and Linda Cooper. 2004. *Disturbing the Peace: The Story of Father Roy Bourgeois and the Movement to Close the School of the Americas.* Maryknoll, NY: Orbis.

Homans, George C. 1950. *The Human Group.* New York: Harcourt, Brace.

hooks, bell. 1994. *Teaching to Transgress: Education as the Practice of Freedom.* New York: Routledge.

Hunt, Swanee and Cristina Posa. 2001. "Women Waging Peace." *Foreign Policy* 124:38–47.

Hunter, Daniel and George Lakey. 2004. *Opening Space for Democracy: Third-Party Nonviolent Intervention Curriculum and Trainer's Manual.* Philadelphia: Training for Change.

Huntington, Samuel P. 2004. "The Hispanic Challenge." *Foreign Policy*, March 1. Accessed November 14, 2008. http://www.foreignpolicy.com/articles/2004/03/01/the_hispanic_challenge.

Huntley, Horace. 2007. "Black Historians and Black History: The Early Years." *The Black Collegian Online.* Accessed November 11, 2008. http://www.black-collegian.com/issues/2ndsem07/black_historians.htm.

Illich, Ivan. 1970. *Deschooling Society.* New York: Harrow.

Indian National Commission for Cooperation with UNESCO. *1970 Truth and Nonviolence: Report of the Unesco Symposium on Truth and Nonviolence in Gandhi's Humanism, Paris, 14–17 October 1969.* New Dehli: Gandhi Peace Foundation on behalf of Indian National Commission for Cooperation with UNESCO.

Inverarity, James, Pat Lauderdale, and Barry C. Feld. 1983. *Law and Society: Sociological Perspectives on Criminal Law.* Boston: Little, Brown.

Isambert, Gustave. 1896. *La Vie à Paris pendant une année de la Révolution (1791–1792).* Paris: Alcan.

Isserman, Maurice. 1992. "You Don't Need a Weatherman But a Postman Can Be Helpful." In *Give Peace a Chance: Exploring the Vietnam Antiwar Movement*, edited by Melvin Small and William D. Hoover, 22–34. Syracuse, NY: Syracuse University Press.

Iyer, Raghavan N. 2000. *The Moral and Political Thought of Mahatma Gandhi.* New Delhi, India: Oxford University Press.

Jackson, Norma and Malcolm Shaw. 2005. *Subject Perspectives on Creativity: A Preliminary Synthesis.* York, UK: Higher Education Academy.

Jacoby, Barbara. 1996. *Service Learning in Higher Education: Concepts and Practices*. San Francisco: Jossey-Bass.

Jameson, A. K. and Gene Sharp. 1963. "Non-Violent Resistance and the Nazis: The Case of Norway." In *The Quiet Battle: Writings on the Theory and Practice of Non-Violent Resistance*, edited by Mulford Q. Sibley. Boston: Beacon.

JLove, Calderon and Marcella Runell Hall, eds. 2010. *Love, Race, and Liberation: Till the White Day Is Done*. New York: self-published.

Johns, Beverley H. 2000. "Give Peace a Chance with Research-Based Advice for Teachers." *The Education Digest* 65 (9): 14–20.

Jones, Ellis, Brett Johnson, and Ross Haenfler. 2001. The Better World Handbook: From Good Intentions to Everyday Actions. Gabriola Island, BC: New Society.

Journal des clubs, April 22–28, 1791.

Journal du soir, July 16, 1791.

Kaati, Gunnar, Lars Olov Bygren, and Sören Edvinsson. 2002. "Cardiovascular and Diabetes Mortality Determined by Nutrition during Parents' and Grandparents' Slow Growth Period." *European Journal of Human Genetics* 10:682–88.

Kaplan, Erin Aubry. 2007. "Tell Black History's Ugly Truth: The Story of African American Struggle Isn't Always Uplifting, But None of It Should Be Denied." *Los Angeles Times*, March 23. Accessed August 11, 2013. http://www.latimes .com/news/opinion/commentary/la-oe-kaplan23mar23,0,6186046.column.

Karatnycky, Adrian. 2005. *How Freedom Is Won: From Civic Resistance to Durable Democracy*. Washington, DC: Freedom House.

Kaunda, Kenneth David. 1980. *Kaunda on Violence*. London: Collins.

Keels, Crystal L. 2006. "Celebration or Placebo?" *Issues in Higher Education* 23 (1): 28–31.

Kelly, Kathy. 2000. "Nonviolence and the Ongoing War against Iraq." In *Nonviolence for the Third Millennium: Its Legacy and Future*, edited by S. J. Harak, G. Simon. Macon, GA: Mercer University Press.

Kelly, Petra. 1984. *Fighting for Hope*. Boston: South End.

Kelly, Petra. 1988. "Women and Ecology." In *Women on War: Essential Voices for the Nuclear Age*, edited by D. Gioseffi. New York: Simon and Schuster.

Kerr, Michael. 1981. "Family Systems Theory and Therapy." In *Handbook of Family Therapy*, edited by Alan S. Gurman and David P. Kniskern, 226–64. New York: Brunner/Mazel.

Kerr, Michael E. and Murray Bowen. 1988. *Family Evaluation: An Approach Based on Bowen Theory*. New York: W. W. Norton.

Kilman, Carrie. 2006. "The ABCs of Latino Heritage Month." *Teaching Tolerance*. Accessed November 21, 2008. http://www.tolerance.org/teach/activities /activity.jsp?ar=709.

King, Martin Luther, Jr. 1964. *Why We Can't Wait*. New York: New American Library.

King, Martin Luther, Jr. 1967. "Beyond Vietnam: A Time to Break Silence," speech given at a meeting of Clergy and Laity Concerned, Riverside Church, New York City, April 4.

King, Martin Luther, Jr. 2002. "Letter from a Birmingham Jail." In *An Anthology of Nonviolence: Historical and Contemporary Voices*, edited by Krishna Mallick and Doris Hunter, 99–114. Westport, CT: Greenwood.

King, Tim. 2010. "Illegal Arrests and Shootings in Israel Reach Epic Levels." *Intifada*, March 22. Accessed August 11, 2013. http://www.intifada-palestine .com/2010/03/illegal-arrests-and-shootings-in-israel-reach-epic-levels/.

Klare, Michael T. 2002. *Resource Wars: The New Landscape of Global Conflict*. New York: Owl.

Klopotek, Brian. 2009. "Of Shadows and Doubts: Race, Indigeneity, and White Supremacy." In *Indivisible: African-Native American Lives in the Americas*, edited by Gabrielle Tayac, 87. Washington, DC: Smithsonian Institution National Museum of the American Indian.

Kohn, Livia. 2002. *Daoism Handbook*. Amsterdam: Brill.

Kolb, David A. 1984. *Experiential Learning: Experience as the Source of Learning and Development*. Englewood Cliffs, NJ: Prentice Hall.

Koliba, Christopher J. 2000. "Moral Language and Networks of Engagement: Service-Learning and Civic Education." *American Behavioral Scientist* 43:825–38.

Kool, V. K. 1993. *Nonviolence: Social and Psychological Issues*. Lanham, MD: University Press of America.

Kramer, Kenneth. 1986. *World Scriptures: An Introduction to Comparative Religions*. Mahwah, NJ: Paulist.

Krech, Shepard, III. 1999. *The Ecological Indian: Myth and History*. New York: W. W. Norton.

Kriesberg, Louis. 2007. *Constructive Conflicts: From Escalation to Resolution*. 3rd ed. Lanham, MD: Rowman and Littlefield.

Krishnan, Suneeta. 2005. "Do Structural Inequalities Contribute to Marital Violence? Ethnographic Evidence from Rural South India." *Violence against Women* 11:759–75.

Kuh, George D. 1995. "The Other Curriculum: Out-of-Class Experiences Associated with Student Learning and Personal Development." *Journal of Higher Education* 66 (2): 123–55.

Kuhn, Thomas S. 1962. *The Structure of Scientific Revolutions*. Chicago: University of Chicago Press.

Kuo You-Yuh. 1996. "Taoistic Psychology of Creativity." *Journal of Creative Behavior* 30 (3): 197–212.

Kupfer, Joseph. 2007. "Gandhi and the Virtue of Care." *Hypatia* 22 (3): 1–21.

Kurlansky, Mark. 2008. *Nonviolence: The History of a Dangerous Idea*. New York: Modern Library.

Lacroix, Sigismond, ed. 1908. *Actes de la Commune de Paris*. Paris: Cerf, Noblet and Quantin.

Ladson-Billings, Gloria J. and William F. Tate. 1994. "Toward a Theory of Critical Race Theory in Education." *Teachers College Record* 97:47–68.

Lakey, George. 2009. Nonviolent Responses to Terrorism, Syllabus. In *Peace, Justice, and Security Studies: A Curriculum Guide*, 7th ed., edited by Timothy A. McElwee, B. Welling Hall, Joseph Liechty, and Julie Garber, 169–77. Boulder, CO: Lynne Rienner.

Lakey, George. 2010. *Facilitating Group Learning: Strategies for Success with Diverse Adult Learners*. San Francisco: Jossey-Bass.

Lal, Basant Kumar. 1978. *Contemporary Indian Philosophy*. Delhi, India: Motilal Banarsidass.

Lam Tom Wing-Hong and Chiu Chi-Yue. 2002. "The Motivational Function of Regulatory Focus in Creativity." *Journal of Creative Behavior* 36:138–50.

Lanthenas, François. 1793. *Motifs de faire du 10 août un jubilé fraternel, une époque solemnelle de réconciliation générale entre tous les républicains, en concernant une déclaration des devoirs de l'homme, des principes and maximes de la morale universelle*. Paris: Imprimerie nationale.

Lao-Tzu. 1986. *Tao Te Ching*. In *World Scriptures: An Introduction to Comparative Religions*, edited by Kenneth Kramer, 132–37. Mahwah, NJ: Paulist.

Laozi. 2004. *Dao de Jing: A Philosophical Translation*. Translated by Roger Ames and David Hall. New York: Ballantine.

LaRocque, Emma. 1997. *Re-Examining Culturally Appropriate Models in Criminal Justice Applications in Aboriginal and Treaty Rights in Canada: Essays on Law, Equity, and Respect for Difference.* Edited by Michael Asch. Vancouver, BC: University of British Columbia Press

Latini, Theresa F. 2009. "Nonviolent Communication: A Humanizing Ecclesial and Educational Practice." *Journal of Education and Christian Belief* 13:19–31.

Lauderdale, Pat. 1997. "Indigenous North American Jurisprudence." *International Journal of Comparative Sociology* 38:131–44

Lauderdale, Pat. 2008. "Indigenous Peoples in the Face of Globalization." *American Behavioral Scientist* 51 (12): 1836–43.

Lauderdale, Pat. 2009. "Collective Indigenous Rights and Global Social Movements in the Face of Global Development: From Resistance to Social Change." *Journal of Developing Societies* 25 (3): 419–30.

Lauderdale, Pat and Barbara Gray Kanatiiosh. 2006. "The Great Circle of Justice: North American Indigenous Justice and Contemporary Restoration Programs." *Contemporary Justice Review* 9 (4): 1–19.

Lauderdale, Pat and Richard Harris. 2008. "Introduction to the Light of Andre Gunder Frank." *Journal of Developing Societies* 24 (1): 2–12.

Lauderdale, Pat and Randall Amster. 2008. "Power and Deviance." In *Violence, Peace and Conflict,* 2nd ed., edited by Lester Kurtz. New York: Academic.

Le Jeune, P. 1633. *The Jesuit Relations and Allied Documents: Travels and Explorations of the Jesuit Missionaries in New France 1610–1791.* Ottawa, ON: National Library of Canada.

Le Patriote Français, June 26, 1791.

Lee, Carol D. 2001. "Is October Brown Chinese? A Cultural Modeling Activity System for Underachieving Students." *American Educational Research Journal* 38 (1): 97–141.

Lee, Enid, Deborah Menkart, and Margo Okazawa-Rey. 1997. "Black History Month: Beyond Heroes and Holidays." In *Beyond Heroes And Holidays: A Practical Guide to K–12 Anti-Racist Multicultural Education and Staff Development,* edited by Enid Lee, Deborah Menkart, and Margo Okazawa-Rey, 380. Washington, DC: Teaching for Change.

Lee, Enid. 2010. "The Law against Ethnic Studies Courses in Arizona Schools." Teaching for Change, May 27. http://www.facebook.com/notes/teaching-for-change/enid-lee-on-the-law-against-ethnic-studies-courses-in-arizona-schools/10150199978240646.

Lefebvre, Georges. (1939) 1957. *The Coming of the French Revolution.* Translated by R. R. Palmer. New York: Vintage.

Letter from Paris Mayor Jean-Sylvain Bailly. "Recherches pour l'histoire de ce temps." MSS 870, Bibliothèque Historique de la Ville de Paris. Paris.

Levy, Jacques and Barbara Moulton. 2007. *Cesar Chavez: Autobiography of La Causa*. Minneapolis: University of Minnesota Press.

Lin Jing. 2006. *Love, Peace, and Wisdom in Education*. Lanham, MD: Rowman and Littlefield.

Liu Yuanlong, Shen Jianping, Wilson J. Warren, and Lynne E. Cowart 2006. "Assessing the Factorial Structure of High School History Teachers' Perceptions on Teaching American History." *Teacher Development* 10 (3): 379–91.

Lopez-Reyes, Ramon. 1998. "Flight/Fight Response and Nonviolence." In *The Frontiers of Nonviolence*, edited by Chaiwat Satha-Anand and Michael True, 34–42. Honolulu, HI: International Peace Research Association.

Lubart, Todd I. 1999. "Creativity Across Cultures." In *Handbook of Creativity*, edited by Robert J. Sternberg, 339–50. Cambridge: Cambridge University Press.

Luthuli, Albert. 1963. *Let My People Go*. New York: McGraw-Hill.

Lutz, Catherine, ed. 2009. *The Bases of Empire: The Global Struggle against U.S. Military Posts*. New York: New York University Press.

Lyons, Oren. 1992. "The American Indian in the Past." In *Exiled in the Land of the Free: Democracy, Indian Nations, and the U.S. Constitution*, edited by Oren Lyons, J. Mohawk, V. Deloria Jr., L. Hauptman, D. Grinde Jr., H. Berman, C. Berkey, and R. Venables, 13–42. Santa Fe, NM: Clear Light.

MacKinnon, Donald. 1978. *In Search of Human Effectiveness*. Buffalo, NY: Bearly.

MacKinnon, Mark. 2007. *The New Cold War: Revolutions, Rigged Elections and Pipeline Politics in the Former Soviet Union*. Toronto, ON: Random House of Canada.

MacMaster, Richard. 1979. *Conscience in Crisis: Mennonites and Other Peace Churches in America, 1739–1789*. Scottsdale, AZ: Herald.

MacQueen, Graeme. 1992. *Unarmed Forces: Nonviolent Action in Central America and the Middle East*. Toronto, ON: Dundurn.

Macrine, Sheila, Peter McLaren, and Dave Hill. 2009. *Revolutionizing Pedagogy: Education for Social Justice within and beyond Global Neo-Liberalism*. New York: Palgrave Macmillan

Mahony, Liam, and Luis Enrique Eguren. 1997. *Unarmed Bodyguards: International Accompaniment for the Protection of Human Rights*. West Hartford, CT: Kumarian.

Mallick, Krishna and Doris Hunter, eds. 2002. *An Anthology of Nonviolence: Historical and Contemporary Voices.* Westport, CT: Greenwood.

Mandela, Nelson. 1994. *Long Walk to Freedom: The Autobiography of Nelson Mandela.* Boston: Little, Brown.

Martin, Brian and Wendy Varney. 2003. *Nonviolence Speaks: Communicating Against Repression.* Cresskill, NJ: Hampton.

Martinez, Carlos, Michael Fox, and Jojo Farrell. 2010. *Venezuela Speaks! Voices from the Grassroots.* Oakland, CA: PM Press.

Martinez, Elizabeth. 1976. *Five Hundred Years of Chicano History in Pictures.* Albuquerque, NM: Southwest Organizing Project.

Martinez, Elizabeth. 1997. "Unite and Overcome!" Teaching Tolerance, a project of the Southern Poverty Law Center. Accessed November 12, 2008. http://www.tolerance.org/teach/magazine/features.jsp?p=0andis=13andar=108andpa=6.

Marullo, Sam. 1993. *Ending the Cold War at Home: From Militarism to a More Peaceful World Order.* New York: Lexington.

Marullo, Sam and B. Edwards. 2000. "Editor's Introduction: Service-Learning Pedagogy as Universities' Responses to Troubled Times." *American Behavioral Scientist* 43:746–55.

Maslow, Abraham. 1970. *Motivation and Personality.* 3rd ed. London: Harper Collins.

Mason, Christine. 2005. "Women, Violence and Nonviolent Resistance in East Timor." *Journal of Peace Research* 42 (6): 737–49.

Mathur, S. 1982. "Cross-Cultural Implications of Creativity." *Indian Psychological Review* 22 (1): 12–19

Mayton, Daniel. 2009. *Nonviolence and Peace Psychology.* New York: Springer.

McLaren, Peter. 1998. *Life in Schools: An Introduction to Critical Pedagogy in the Foundations of Education.* New York: Longman.

Mendoza, Sally P. 1984. "The Psychobiology of Social Relationships. In *Social Cohesion: Essays towards a Sociophysiological Perspective,* edited by Patricia R. Barchas and Sally P. Medoza, 3–30. Westport CT: Greenwood.

Menkart, Deborah, Alana D. Murray, and Jenice L. View. 2004. *Putting the Movement Back into Civil Rights Teaching.* Washington, DC: Teaching for Change and Poverty & Race Research Action Council.

Merideth, Martin. 1997. *Nelson Mandela.* New York: St. Martin's Griffen.

Merryfinch, L. 1981. "Militarization/Civilization." In *Loaded Questions: Women in the Military,* edited by W. Chapkis. Amsterdam: Transnational Institute.

Metta Center for Nonviolence. 2010. "Introduction to Nonviolence." Accessed March 8, 2010. http://www.mettacenter.org/nv/nonviolence/intro.

Meyer, Matt and Elavie Ndura-Ouédraogo, eds. 2009. *Seeds of New Hope: Pan-African Peace Studies for the 21st Century.* Trenton, NJ: Africa World Press.

Meyer, Matt. Forthcoming. "Liberation Myths: Resistance Strategies in Mozambique's Independence Struggle." In *Rediscovering Nonviolent History in Independence Movements: Civil Resistance beneath Eulogized Violence,* edited by Maciej Bartkowski. Hampshire, UK: Palgrave Macmillan.

Miles, Steven. 2005. *The Hippocratic Oath and the Ethics of Medicine.* New York: Oxford University Press.

Miller, Barbara Stoller, trans. 2004. *The Bhagavad-Gita: Krishna's Counsel in Time of War.* New York: Bantam Classic.

Miller, William. 1974. *The Baha'i Faith: Its History and Teachings.* Pasadena, CA: William Carey Library.

Mills, Nicolaus. 1992. *Like a Holy Crusade: Mississippi 1964—The Turning of the Civil Rights Movement in America.* Chicago: Ivan R. Dee.

Mindell, Arnold. 1997. *Sitting in the Fire: Large Group Transformation through Diversity and Conflict.* Portland, OR: Lao Tze.

Molomo, Mpho G. 2009. "Building a Culture of Peace in Africa: Using Traditional Knowledge Systems." *Journal of Peacebuilding and Development* 4 (3): 59.

Monnard, Marie-Victoire. 1989. *Souvenirs d'une femme du peuple, 1777–1802.* Creil, France: Dumerchez.

Morales, Miguel. 2010. "Support Carlos Alberto Torres Reentry!" *La Voz del Paseo Boricua* 7(4).

Morrell, Ernest. 2008. *Critical Literacy and Urban Youth: Pedagogies of Access, Dissent, and Liberation.* New York: Routledge.

Morton, Timothy. 2007. *Ecology without Nature: Rethinking Environmental Aesthetics.* Boston: Harvard University Press.

Municipalité de Paris. 1791. "Par le Maire et les Membres du Conseil-Général." Extrait du Registre des Délibérations du Conseil-Général de la Commune de Paris, du Vendredi 24 Juin 1791. Avis sur l'arrivée prochaine du Roi. Paris.

Murangwa, Faustin Bismark and Issa Higiro. 2008. Personal interview conducted by Matt Meyer in Kigali, Rwanda, June 6.

Murithi, Timothy. 2006. "Practical Peacemaking Wisdom from Africa: Reflections on Ubuntu." *Journal of Pan African Studies* 1 (4): 25–34.

Murthy, Srinivasa, B. 1987. *Mahatma Gandhi and Leo Tolstoy Letters*. Long Beach, CA: Long Beach.

Myers, Winslow. 2009. *Living beyond War: A Citizen's Guide*. Maryknoll, NY: Orbis.

NAACP (National Association for the Advancement of Colored People). 2008. "Carter G. Woodson: Father of Black History." Accessed November 11, 2008. http://www.naacp.org/about/history/cgwoodson/.

Narayan, Jayaprakash. 2002. "Notes on Bihar Movement—1975." In *Transforming the Polity: Centenary Readings from Jayaprakash Narayan*, edited by Ajit Bhattacharjea. Delhi, India: Rupa.

Narayan, R. K. 1972. *The Ramayana: A Shortened Modern Prose Version of the Indian Epic*. New York: Penguin.

National Center of Education Statistics. 2009. Various studies. http://nces.ed.gov /search/?output=xml_no_dtdandsite=ncesandclient=ncesandq=teachers+ %2D+race.

Nauriya, Anil. 2006. *The African Element in Gandhi*. New Dehi, India: Gyan.

Ndangiza, Fatuma. 2008. Interview conducted by Matt Meyer in Kigali, Rwanda, June 10, 2008.

Ndura, Elavie. 2006a. "Transcending the Majority Rights and Minority Protection Dichotomy through Multicultural Reflective Citizenship in the African Great Lakes Region." *Intercultural Education* 17 (2): 195–205.

Ndura, Elavie. 2006b. "The Role of Cultural Competence in the Creation of a Culture of Nonviolence." *Culture of Peace Online Journal* 2 (1): 39–48.

Ndura, Elavie. 2007. "Calling Institutions of Higher Education to Join the Quest for Social Justice and Peace." *Harvard Educational Review* 77 (3): 345–50.

Ndura-Ouédraogo, Elavie. 2009. "Diversity, Oppression, and the Challenging Quest for Sustainable Peace." In *Building Cultures of Peace: Transdisciplinary Voices of Hope and Action*, edited by Elavie Ndura-Ouédraogo and Randall Amster, 184–93. Newcastle upon Tyne, UK: Cambridge Scholars.

Ndura-Ouédraogo, Elavie and Matt Meyer. 2009. "Linking NAME and PJSA to Reach New Heights in the Quest for Social Justice and Peace." President's Roundtable Panel presentation, National Association for Multicultural Education conference, Denver, CO, October 30.

Nepstad, Sharon Erickson. 2008. *Religion and War Resistance in the Plowshares Movement*. New York: Cambridge University Press.

Nielsen, Marianne O. and James W. Zion. 2005. *Navajo Nation Peacemaking: Living Traditional Justice*. Tucson, AZ: University of Arizona Press.

Nieto, Sonia. 2000. "Placing Equity Front and Center: Some Thoughts on Transforming Teacher Education for a New Century." *Journal of Teacher Education* 51 (3): 180–87.

Nieto, Sonia. 2004. *Affirming Diversity: The Sociopolitical Context of Multicultural Education.* Boston: Pearson.

Noddings, Nel. 2005. *The Challenge to Care in Schools: An Alternative Approach to Education.* 2nd ed. New York: Teachers College Press.

Norrell, Brenda. 2009. "Zapatistas: In the Language of Love." *Censored News* (blog), December 3. Accessed August 11, 2013. http://bsnorrell.blogspot.com /2009/12/zapatistas-in-langauge-of-love.html.

Nussbaum, Martha C. 2003. *Upheavals of Thought, the Intelligence of Emotions.* Cambridge: Cambridge University Press.

O'Kane, M. 1991–92. "Peace: The Overwhelming Task." *Veterans for Peace Journal* 19 (3), Winter.

Obama, Barack. 2009. "Nobel Lecture: A Just and Lasting Peace." *Nobelprize.org,* December 10. Accessed August 11, 2013. http://www.nobelprize.org/nobel _prizes/peace/laureates/2009/obama-lecture.html.

Okhuysen, Geraldo A., Adam D. Galinsky, and Tamara A. Uptigrove. 2003. "Saving the Worst for Last: The Effect of Time Horizon on the Efficiency of Negotiating Benefits and Burdens." *Organizational Behavior and Human Decision Processes* 91:269–79.

Oliverio, Annamarie. 2008. "On Being 'Frank' about Terrorism." *Journal of Developing Societies* 24 (1): 13–29

Oliverio, Annamarie and Pat Lauderdale. 2005. *Terrorism: A New Testament.* Whitby, ON: de Sitter.

Opotow, Susan, Janet C. Gerson, and Sarah Woodside. 2005. "From Moral Exclusion to Moral Inclusion: Theory for Teaching Peace." *Theory into Practice* 44 (4): 303–18.

Ortiz-Franco, Luis. 1999. "Chicanos Have Math in Their Blood: Pre-Columbian Mathematics." In *Education is Politics: Critical Teaching across Differences, K–12,* edited by Ira Shor and C. Pari, 215–25. Portsmouth, NH: Heineman.

Ostrom, Elinor. 1990. *Governing the Commons: The Evolution of Institutions for Collective Action.* New York: Cambridge University Press.

Ostrom, Elinor. 1992. *Crafting Institutions for Self-Governing Irrigation Systems.* San Francisco: ICS.

Padel, Felix. 2010. *Sacrificing People: Invasions of a Tribal Landscape.* Hyderabad, India: Orient Black Swan.

Page, Jake. 2004. *In the Hands of the Great Spirit: The 20,000 Year History of the American Indians.* New York: Free Press.

Paige, Glenn D. 2009. *Nonkilling Global Political Science.* Honolulu, HI: Center for Global Nonkilling.

Pallares, Amalia. 2002. *From Peasant Struggles to Indian Resistance: The Ecuadorian Andes in the Late Twentieth Century.* Norman, OK: University of Oklahoma Press.

Palmer, Parker J. 1998. *The Courage to Teach: Exploring the Inner Landscape of a Teacher's Life.* San Francisco: Jossey-Bass.

Parel, Anthony J., ed. 1997. *Hind Swaraj and Other Writings.* By Mohandas K. Gandhi. Cambridge: Cambridge University Press.

Parker, Arthur C. n.d. "The Creation of American Indian Heritage Month: A Brief History." US Bureau of Indian Affairs. Accessed November 12, 2008. http://www.infoplease.com/spot/aihmorigins1.html.

Parker-Gwin, R. 1996. "Connecting Service to Learning: How Students and Communities Matter." *Teaching Sociology* 24:97–101.

Parrish, Rick. 2006. *Violence Inevitable: The Play of Force and Respect in Derrida, Nietzsche, Hobbes, and Berlin.* Lanham, MD: Lexington.

Patti, Janet and James Tobin. 2001. "Leading the Way: Reflections on Creating Peaceable Schools." *Reclaiming Children and Youth* 10 (1): 41.

PBS.org. 2007. "Teachers Take on NCLB." *Learning Matters—The Merrow Report,* August 16. Accessed November 21, 2008. http://www.pbs.org/merrow/tv/transcripts/NCLB_TeachersTake.pdf.

"Peace Seeds: Prayers for Peace." 2002 (prayed in Assisi, Italy, 1986). In *An Anthology of Nonviolence: Historical and Contemporary Voices,* edited by Krishna Mallick and Doris Hunter, 44–47. Westport, CT: Greenwood.

Peña, Devon G. 1998. "A Gold Mine, an Orchard, and an Eleventh Commandment." In *Chicano Culture, Ecology, Politics: Subversive Kin,* edited by Devon G. Peña, 249–77. Tucson, AZ: University of Arizona Press.

Peña, Devon G. 2003. "Identity, Place, and Communities of Resistance." In *Just Sustainabilities: Development in an Unequal World,* edited by Julian Agyeman, Robert D. Bullard, and Bob Evans, 146–67. Cambridge, MA: MIT Press.

Peña, Devon G. 2005. *Mexican Americans and the Environment: Tierra y Vida.* Tucson, AZ: University of Arizona Press.

Pepinsky, Hal. 2006. "Peacemaking in the Classroom." *Contemporary Justice Review* 9 (4): 427–42.

Pillay, Navanethem. 2008. " Address by Ms. Navanethem Pillay UN High Commissioner for Human Rights on the occasion of the opening of the 9th Session of the Human Rights Council." United Nations. Accessed September 11, 2008. http://www.unhchr.ch/huricane/huricane.nsf/view01/8F6C6D5B6EE3E7F6C12574BE004A5FB8?opendocument.

Peace and Justice Studies Association. n.d. "About Us." Accessed August 11, 2013. http://www.peacejusticestudies.org/about.php.

Plessy v. Ferguson, 163 U.S. 537 (1896).

Pommersheim, Frank. 1995. *Braid of Feathers: American Indian Law and Contemporary Tribal Life*. Berkeley: University of California Press.

Postman, Neil. 1996. *The End of Education: Redefining the Value of School*. New York: Vintage.

Potorti, David. 2003. *September 11th Families for Peaceful Tomorrows: Turning Our Grief into Action for Peace*. New York: Akashic.

Presbey, Gail. 2009. "George Padmore and C. L. R. James on Strategic Nonviolence as Expressed in the Manifesto of the Fifth Pan-African Congress in Manchester, England 1945." Unpublished paper delivered at the Caribbean Philosophical Association 2009 annual conference, University of Miami, Coral Gables, FL, August 13.

Purdue, Theda. 2009. "Native Americans, African Americans, and Jim Crow." In *Indivisible: African-Native American Lives in the Americas*, edited by Gabrielle Tayac, 21–34. Washington, DC: Smithsonian Institution National Museum of the American Indian.

Randall, Margaret. 2002. *When I Look into the Mirror and See You: Women, Terror, and Resistance*. Piscataway: Rutgers University Press.

Ravitch, Diane. 2000. "The Educational Background of History Teachers." In *Knowing, Teaching and Learning History: National and International Perspectives*, edited by Peter Stearns, Peter Seixas, and Sam Wineburg, 143–55. New York: New York University Press.

Reardon, Betty. 1995. *Education for Human Dignity: Learning about Rights and Responsibilities*. Philadelphia, PA: University of Pennsylvania Press.

Reardon, Betty. 1997. "Human Rights as Education for Peace." In *Human Rights Education for the Twenty-First Century*, edited by George J. Andreopoulos and Richard Pierre Claude, 21–34. Philadelphia, PA: University of Pennsylvania Press.

Reddy, William. 2001. *The Navigation of Feeling: A Framework for the History of Emotions*. Cambridge: Cambridge University Press.

Regina, Wayne and Steve Pace. 2008. "The Personal Intelligences in Experiential Education: A Theory in Practice." In *Theory and Practice of Experiential Education*, edited by Karen Warren, Denise Mitten, and TA Loeffler, 494–506. Boulder, CO: Association for Experiential Education.

Regina, Wayne. 2000. "Bowen Systems Theory and Mediation." *Mediation Quarterly* 18 (2): 111–28.

Reinhard, Marcel. 1958. *La fuite du roi*. Paris: Centre de documentation universitaire.

Report on the Decade for a Culture of Peace. United Nations International Decade for a Culture of Peace and Non-violence for the Children of the World (2001–10). Accessed August 5, 2010. http://decade-culture-of-peace.org.

Rivera, José A. 1996. "Irrigation Communities of the Upper Rio Grande Bioregion: Sustainable Resource Use in the Global Context." *Natural Resources Journal* 36:731–60.

Rivera, José A. 1998. *Acequia Culture: Water, Land, and Community in the Southwest*. Albuquerque, NM: University of New Mexico Press.

Roberts, Nancy. 1984. *Dorothy Day and the Catholic Worker*. Albany, NY: State University of New York Press.

Robinson, Paul. 2003. *Just War in Comparative Perspective*. Surrey, UK: Ashgate.

Robinson, Phil Alden. 2000. *Freedom Song*. Television film. Atlanta: Turner Network Television (TNT). http://www.youtube.com/playlist?list=PL6D54527F71D08A68.

Rodríguez, Sylvia. 2006. *Acequia: Water Sharing, Sanctity, and Place*. Santa Fe, NM: SAR.

Rorty, Richard. 1982. *Consequences of Pragmatism: Essays, 1972–1980*. Minneapolis, MN: University of Minnesota Press.

Roschelle, Ann R., Jennifer Turpin, and Robert Elias. 2000. "Who Learns from Service Learning?" *American Behavioral Scientist* 43:839–47.

Ross, Robert. 1999. *A Concise History of South Africa*. Cambridge: Cambridge University Press.

Ross, Rupert. 1995. "Aboriginal Community Healing in Action: The Hollow Water Approach." In *Dueling Paradigms? Western Criminal Justice versus Aboriginal Community Healing*, edited by Rupert Ross, 241–68. Saskatoon, SK: Native Law Centre of Canada.

Ross, Rupert. 1996. *Returning to the Teachings: Exploring Aboriginal Justice*. Toronto, ON: Penguin.

Rowan, Leona Onderdonk. 2007. "Making Classrooms Bully-Free Zones: Practical Suggestions for Educators." *Kappa Delta Pi Record* 3 (4): 182–85.

Roy, Arundhati. 2002. *The Algebra of Infinite Justice*. New York: Penguin.

Roy, Arundhati. 2010. Opening Speech to the War Resisters International conference, "Nonviolent Livelihood Struggle and Global Militarism: Links and Strategies." Speech given at Willoughby-Sutherland Hall, Gujarat Vidyapith, Ahmedabad, India, January 22.

Rudé, George. 1959. *The Crowd in the French Revolution*. Oxford, UK: Clarendon Press.

Runco, Mark A., and Ruth Richards, eds. 1997. *Eminent Creativity, Everyday Creativity and Health*. Greenwich, CT: Ablex.

Russell, Bertrand. 1985. "The Philosophy of Pacifism." In *Collected Papers*, edited by R. Rempel et al., 147–48. London: Allen and Unwin.

Ryoo, Jean J. and Peter McLaren. 2010. "Seeking Democracy in American Schools: Countering Epistemic Violence through Revolutionary Critical Pedagogy." In *Democracy and Multicultural Education*, edited by Farideh Salili and Rumjahn Hoosain, 99–127. Charlotte, NC: Information Age.

S.B. 2718, Reg. Sess. (Miss. 2006), "An Act . . . to Make Civil Rights and Human Rights Education a Part of the K–12 Curriculum . . . ," codified at Miss. Code Ann. §§ 37-13-191 to -195 (2007).

Salomon, Gavriel and Baruch Nevo, eds. 2002. *Peace Education: The Concept, Principles, and Practices around the World*. Mahwah, NJ: Lawrence Erlbaum.

Salomon, Gavriel. 2002. "The Nature of Peace Education: Not All Programs Are Created Equal." In *Peace Education: The Concept, Principles, and Practices around the World*, edited by Gavriel Salomon and Baruch Nevo, 3–13. Mahwah, NJ: Lawrence Erlbaum.

San Miguel, Guadalupe, Jr. 1997. "Roused from our Slumbers." In *Latinos and Education: A Critical Reader*, edited by Antonia Darder, Rodolfo D. Torres, and Henry Gutierrez, 135–57. New York: Routledge.

Sanchez, George I. 1997. "History, Culture and Education." In *Latinos and Education: A Critical Reader*, edited by Antonia Darder, Rodolfo D. Torres, and Henry Gutierrez, 117–34. New York: Routledge.

Sax, Linda J., Jennifer R. Keup, Shanon K. Gilmartin, Ethan D. Stolzenberg, and C. Harper. 2002. *Findings from the 2002 Administration of Your First College Year (YFCY): National Aggregates*. Los Angeles: Higher Education Research Institute, University of California, Los Angeles.

S.B. 1070, 49th Leg., 2nd Reg. Sess. (Ariz. 2010), "Support Our

Law Enforcement and Safe Neighborhoods Act," codified at Ariz. Rev. Stat. Ann. §§ 11-1051, 13-1509, 13-3883 (2010).

Schama, Simon. 1989. *Citizens: A Chronicle of the French Revolution*. New York: Knopf.

Schell, Jonathan. 2003. *The Unconquerable World: Power, Nonviolence and the Will of the People*. New York: Holt.

Schmidt, Teresa. 1993. *Anger Management and Violence Prevention: A Group Activities Manual for Middle and High School Students*. Center City, MN: Hazelden.

Scott, James Brown. 1909. *The Hague Peace Conferences of 1899 and 1907: a Series of Lectures Delivered before the Johns Hopkins University in the Year of 1908*. Baltimore: Johns Hopkins Press.

Sebarenzi, Joseph. 2009. *God Sleeps in Rwanda: A Journey of Transformation*. New York: Atria.

Sefa Dei, G. 2005. "The Challenge of Inclusive Schooling in Africa." *Comparative Education* 41 (3): 267–89.

Seligman, Martin E. P. and Mihaly Csikszentmihalyi. 2007. "Positive Psychology: An Introduction." *American Psychologist* 55 (1): 5–14.

Sellars, John. 2006. *Stoicism*. Berkeley: University of California Press.

Sen, Amartya. 2006. *Identity and Violence: The Illusion of Destiny*. New York: Penguin.

Sharma, Kalpana. 2009. "Saved by the Women." *India Together*, Oct. 1. Accessed February 14, 2010. http://www.indiatogether.org/2009/oct/ksh-narnaul.htm.

Sharoni, Simona. 2010. "Sexism in our Movements." Peace and Justice Studies Association member listserv (members_pjsa), June 25. http://lists.riseup.net /www/arc/members_pjsa.

Sharp, Gene. 1959. "The Meanings of Non-Violence: A Typology." *Journal of Conflict Resolution* 3 (1): 41–64.

Sharp, Gene. 1974. *The Politics of Nonviolent Action: Power and Struggle*. Boston: Porter Sargent.

Sharp, Gene. 1976. *The Dynamics of Nonviolent Action*. Boston: Porter Sargent.

Sharp, Gene. 2005. *Waging Nonviolent Struggle: 20th Century Practice and 21st Century Potential*. Boston: Extending Horizon.

Shenandoah, Audrey. 1987. "Everything Has to Be in Balance." In *Indian Roots of American Democracy*, edited by José Barreiro, special edition of *Northeast Indian Quarterly* IV (4): 4–7.

Sherwin-White, A. N. 1979. *Roman Citizenship*. Oxford: Oxford University Press.

Shiva, Vandana. 2002. *Water Wars: Privatization, Pollution, and Profit*. Cambridge, MA: South End.

Shivers, Lynne. 1980. "Inside the Iranian Revolution." In *Tell the American People: Portraits of the Iranian Revolution*, edited by David Albert, 56–78. Philadelphia: New Society.

Shorris, Earl. 1992. *Latinos: A Biography of the People*. New York: W. W. Norton.

Siasoco, Ricco Villanueva. n.d. "Origins of APA Heritage Month: A National Celebration Established in 1977." Accessed November 12, 2008. http://www.infoplease.com/spot/asianintro1.html.

Simonton, Dean Keith. 2000. "Creativity: Cognitive, Personal, Developmental, and Social Aspects." *American Psychologist* 55:151–58.

Simonton, Dean Keith. 2003. "Scientific Creativity as Constrained Stochastic Behavior: The Integration of Product, Person, and Process Perspectives." *Psychological Bulletin* 129:475–94.

Sleeter, Christine E. 1996. *Multicultural Education as Social Activism*. Albany, NY: State University of New York Press.

Sleeter, Christine. 1999. Foreword to *Subtractive Schooling: U.S. Mexican Youth and the Politics of Caring*, by Angela Valenzuela, xv–xviii. Albany, NY: State University of New York Press.

Slingerland, Edward. 2003. *Effortless Action: Wu-Wei as Conceptual Metaphor and Spiritual Ideal in Early China*. New York: Oxford University Press.

Smith, Daryl. 2007. "Community Colleges." *Chronicle of Higher Education* 54 (9): B30.

Smith, Huston. 1994. *The Illustrated World's Religions: A Guide to Our Wisdom Traditions*. San Francisco: Harper.

Smith, Watson and John M. Roberts. 1954. "Zuni Law: A Field of Values." *Peabody Museum of American Archeology and Ethnology* 43:46–121.

Snyder, Margaret. 2003. "Women Determine Development: The Unfinished Revolution." *Signs* 29 (2): 619–32.

Soboul, Albert. 1958. *Les sans-culottes parisiens de l'an II: Mouvement populaire et gouvernement révolutionnaire, 2 juin 1793 – 9 thermidor an II*. Paris: Seuil.

Sperber, Murray. 2000. *Beer and Circus: How Big-Time College Sports Is Crippling Undergraduate Education*. New York: Holt.

Stephan, Maria J. and Erica Chenoweth. 2008. "Why Civil Resistance Works: The Strategic Logic of Nonviolent Conflict." *International Security* 33 (1): 7–44.

Sternberg, Robert and Tamara Gordeeva. 1996. "The Anatomy of Impact: What Makes an Article Influential?" *Psychological Science* 7:69–75.

Sternberg, Robert. 1990. *Wisdom: Its Nature, Origins, and Development*. Cambridge: Cambridge University Press.

Strain, Christopher B. 2005. *Pure Fire: Self-Defense as Activism in the Civil Rights Era*. Atlanta: University of Georgia Press.

Stutz, Terrence. 2010. "Texas State Board of Education Approves New Curriculum Standards." *Dallas Morning News*, May 22. Accessed August 11, 2013. http://www.dallasnews.com/news/education/headlines/20100521-Texas -State-Board-of-Education-approves-9206.ece.

Sutherland, Bill and Matt Meyer. 2000. *Guns and Gandhi in Africa: Pan African Insights on Nonviolence, Armed Struggle, and Liberation*. Trenton, NJ: Africa World Press.

Swain, Ashok. 2002. "Environmental Cooperation in South Asia." In *Environmental peacemaking*, edited by Ken Conca and Geoffrey D. Dabelko, 61–85. Washington, DC: Woodrow Wilson Center.

Tähtinen, Unto. 1976. *Ahimsā: Non-violence in Indian tradition*. London: Rider.

Tajfel, Henry and Michael Billic. 1974. "Familiarity and Categorization in Intergroup Behavior." *Journal of Experimental Social Psychology* 10 (2): 159–70.

Takaki, Ronald. 1993. *A Different Mirror: A History of Multicultural America*. Boston: Little, Brown.

Takaki, Ronald. 1998. *Strangers from a Different Shore: A History of Asian Americans*. Boston: Little, Brown.

Tavanti, Marco. 2003. *Las Abejas: Pacifist Resistance and Syncretic Identities in a Globalizing Chiapas*. New York: Routledge.

Terkel, Susan Neiburg. 1996. *People Power: A Look at Nonviolent Action and Defense*. New York: Lodestar.

Timperley, Helen and Viviane Robinson. 2000. "Workload and the Professional Culture of Teachers." *Educational Management and Administration* 28 (1): 47–62.

Toussaint, Laura. 2008. *The Contemporary US Peace Movement*. New York: Taylor and Francis.

Tutu, Desmond. 1994. *The Rainbow People of God*. New York: Doubleday.

Tutu, Desmond. 1999. *No Future without Forgiveness*. New York: Doubleday.

Twemlow, Stuart W. and Frank C. Sacco. 1996. "Peacekeeping and Peacemaking: The Conceptual Foundations of a Plan to Reduce Violence and

Improve the Quality of Life in a Midsized Community in Jamaica." *Psychiatry* 54:156–74.

Tyler, Daniel. 1990. *The mythical Pueblo rights doctrine: Water administration in Hispanic New Mexico.* El Paso, TX: Texas Western Press.

Tyrrell, Frank, Tim Scully, and Jim Halligan. 1998. "Building Peaceful Schools." *Thrust for Educational Leadership* 28 (2): 30–33.

United Nations Development Program. 2007. *Human Development Report.* November 27.

United Nations Office of the High Commission on Human Rights. 2010. "Arizona: UN Experts Warn against 'A Disturbing Legal Pattern Hostile to Ethnic Minorities and Immigrants.'" May 10. Accessed May 11, 2010. http://www.ohchr .org/SP/NewsEvents/Pages/DisplayNews.aspx?NewsID=10035andLangID=E.

United Nations. 1992. *An Agenda for Peace.* Accessed February 24, 2010. http:// www.un.org/Docs/SG/agpeace.html.

Urbain, Olivier. 2009. "Nonkilling Arts." In *Toward a Nonkilling Paradigm,* edited by J. Evans Pim, 73–94. Honolulu, HI: Center for Global Nonkilling.

Vambe, Maurice T. and Abebe Zegeye. 2008. "Racializing Ethnicity and Ethnicizing Racism: Rethinking the Epistemic Conditions of Genocide in Africa." *Social Identities* 14 (6): 775–93.

Van Slyck, Michael and Marc A. Stern. 1999. "A Developmental Approach to the Use of Conflict Resolution Interventions with Adolescents." In *Peacebuilding for Adolescents,* edited by Linda Rennie Forcey and Ian Murray Harris, 177–93. New York: Peter Lang.

Van Wormer, Katherine. 2008. "Anti-Feminist Backlash and Violence against Women Worldwide." *Social Work and Society* 6 (2): 3.

Verma, Surendra. 1970. *Metaphysical Foundations of Mahatma Gandhi's Thought.* New Delhi, India: Orient Longmans.

View, Jenice L. 2007. "Black History Month Student Survey," an informal survey conducted with Teaching for Change with results from three classrooms in the Washington, DC metropolitan area (unpublished).

View, Jenice L. 2010. "Critical Teaching of History: Toward a Human Rights Agenda for Pre- and In-Service Teacher Education." In *Democracy and Multicultural Education,* edited by Farideh Salili and Rumjahn Hoosain, 149–72. Charlotte, NC: Information Age.

Vora, Jay A. and Erika Vora. 2004. "The Effectiveness of South Africa's Truth and Reconciliation Commission." *Journal of Black Studies* 34:301–22.

Waithe, Mary Ellen. 1987. "Late Pythagoreans: Aesara of Lucania, Phyntis of Sparta and Perictione I." In *A History of Women Philosophers,* edited by Mary Ellen Waithe, 19–26. London: Kluwer Academic.

Waller, Signe. 2002. *Love and Revolution: A Political Memoir.* Lanham, MD: Rowman and Littlefield.

Wallström, Margot. 2010. "Turning Words into Deeds: Making Women Actors of Peace and Security." Speech by EU Commission vice-president at the Conference on Women, Peace and Security: "Empowering Women in Peace and Conflict," January 27. Accessed February 24, 2010. http://www.eu-un.europa.eu/articles/en/article_9447_en.htm.

Wals, Arjen E. J. 1999. "Stop the Violence: Conflict Management in an Inner-City Junior High School through Action Research and Community Problem Solving." In *Peacebuilding for Adolescents,* edited by Linda Rennie Forcey and Ian Murray Harris, 239–62. New York: Peter Lang.

Watson, Burton, trans. 1968. *The Complete Works of Chuang Tzu.* New York: Columbia University Press.

Watson, Burton, trans. 2003. *Han Feizi: Basic Writings.* New York: Columbia University Press.

Weinberg, Bill. 2000. *Homage to Chiapas: The New Indigenous Struggles in Mexico.* London: Verso.

Weinthal, Erika, Avner Vengosh, Amer Marei, Alexis Gutierrez, and Wolfram Kloppmann. 2005. "The Water Crisis in the Gaza Strip: Prospects for Resolution." *Ground Water* 43 (5): 653–60.

Weintraub, Shelly. 2000. "What's This New Crap? What's Wrong with the Old Crap? Changing History Teaching in Oakland, California." In *Knowing, Teaching and Learning History: National and International Perspectives,* edited by Peter Stearns, Peter Seixas, and Sam Wineburg, 178–94. New York: New York University Press.

Werlhof, Claudia von. 1997. "Upheaval from the Depth: The Zapatistas, the Indigenous Civilization, the Question of Matriarchy, and the West." *International Journal of Comparative Sociology* 38 (1–2): 106–30.

West, Cornell. 2008. *Hope on a Tightrope: Words and Wisdom.* Carlsbad, CA: Hay House.

Westwood, Robert I. and Donald E. Low. 2003. "The Multicultural Muse: Culture, Creativity, and Innovation." *International Journal of Cross Cultural Management* 3:235–59.

Wilson, James.1998. *The Earth Shall Weep: A History of Native America.* New York: Grove.

Wineburg, Sam and Chauncey Monte-Sano. 2008. "Famous Americans: The Changing Pantheon of American Heroes." *Journal of American History* 94 (4): 1186–202.

Wolk, Steven. 2009. "Reading for a Better World: Teaching for Social Responsibility with Young Adult Literature." *Journal of Adolescent and Adult Literacy* 52 (8): 664–73.

York, Steve. 2000. *A Force More Powerful.* Documentary film. Washington, DC: York Zimmerman.

York, Steve. 2002. *Bringing Down a Dictator.* Documentary film. Washington, DC: York Zimmerman.

Zegeye, Abebe and Richard Harris. 2002. "Media, Identity and the Public Sphere in Post-Apartheid South Africa: An Introduction." *African and Asian Studies* 1 (4): 239–63.

Zegeye, Abebe. 2002. "A Matter of Colour." *African and Asian Studies* 1 (4): 323–48.

Zinn, Howard. 2001. "Nonviolent Direct Action." In *Howard Zinn on History,* 33–45. St. Paul, MN: Seven Stories Press.

Zinn, Howard. 2002. *The Power of Nonviolence: Writings by Advocates of Peace.* New York: Beacon.

Zinn, Howard. 2003. *A People's History of the United States.* New York: Perennial Classics.

Zunes, Stephen. 2009. "The Power of Nonviolent Action." In *Nonviolent Paths to Social Change, eJournal USA* 14 (3), 4–7. http://www.america.gov/media/pdf/ejs/0309ej.pdf#popup.

Zunes, Stephen. 2009. "Weapons of Mass Democracy." *YES! Magazine,* September 16. Accessed August 11, 2013. http://www.yesmagazine.org/issues/learn-as-you-go/weapons-of-mass-democracy.

Zunes, Stephen, Lester R. Kurtz, and Sara Beth Asher, eds. 1999. *Nonviolent Social Movements: A Geographical Perspective.* Malden, MA: Blackwell.

Contributors

Antony Adolf is a teacher, public speaker, independent scholar, and author of *Peace: A World History* (2009). As a regular contributor to Change.org, he has covered peace and conflict globally, and he founded the peace blog *One World, Many Peaces*. Mr. Adolf is currently managing member of Chicago-based Xenos Media Group.

Micah Alpaugh received his PhD in history from the University of California, Irvine, and is currently assistant professor in the Department of History & Anthropology at the University of Central Missouri. He is the winner of the 2009 Marjorie Farrar Award from the Society for French Historical Studies, and is currently completing a book manuscript entitled *Nonviolence, Violence and Revolution: Political Demonstrations in Paris, 1787–1795*.

Randall Amster, co-editor of this volume and director of the Program on Justice and Peace at Georgetown University, holds a JD from Brooklyn Law School and a PhD in justice studies from Arizona State University, and is the executive director of the Peace and Justice Studies Association. Among his recent books are *Anarchism Today* (2012), *Lost in Space: The Criminalization, Globalization, and Urban Ecology of Homelessness* (2008), and the co-edited volume *Building Cultures of Peace: Transdisciplinary Voices of Hope and Action* (2009).

Supriya Baily, PhD, assistant professor of international education at George Mason University, studies the effects that nonformal education has had on women and the communities in which they live. She also explores the effects of education on international students, as well as policy issues affecting education for young adults in developing countries. She has published book chapters and journal articles on these issues, and has presented at many national and international conferences. Dr. Baily is the co-editor of *Internationalizing Teacher Education in the US* (2012).

Laura L. Finley, PhD, is assistant professor of sociology and criminology at Barry University. She is the author or co-author of eleven books, including *Building a Peaceful Society: Creative Integration of Peace Education* (2011), and *Grading the 44th President: A Report Card on Barack Obama's First Term as a Progressive Leader* (2012). Dr. Finley is also actively involved in a number of peace and justice-related organizations in South Florida, and regularly presents on creative strategies for teaching peace.

Tom H. Hastings, EdD, is full-time faculty for the graduate program in conflict resolution at Portland State University and part-time faculty in the Portland Community College peace and conflict certificate program. He is on the governing council of the International Peace Research Association (IPRA), is past co-chair of the Peace and Justice Studies Association, and is on the boards of both the IPRA Foundation and the Oregon Peace Institute (OPI), as well as the Academic Advisory Board of the International Center on Nonviolent Conflict. He directs PeaceVoice, a program of OPI, and has written several books and many articles about nonviolence and other peace and conflict topics. He is a former Plowshares resister and a founding member of two Catholic Worker communities, and currently lives in Whitefeather Peace House.

George Lakey is a visiting professor in Peace and Conflict Studies and a research fellow at the Lang Center, Swarthmore College, and director of the Global Nonviolent Action Database Project there. He is an activist and author of eight books, has led over 1,500 workshops on five continents, and founded Training for Change. His most recent book focuses on direct education, and is entitled *Facilitating Group Learning: Strategies for Success with Diverse Adult Learners* (2010).

Pat Lauderdale, PhD, is professor and director of the PhD/JD and MS programs, Faculty of Justice and Social Inquiry at Arizona State University. His recent publications include research on the world system from a Frankian perspective, global indigenous struggles, and state and international terrorism. He continues his research on the analyses of globalization, nation-statism, rational capitalism, and concentration of power in the post-colonial world by focusing upon the cracks in the armor of the dominant Western paradigm.

Tülin Levitas was born and raised in Izmir, Turkey. She holds an MA from Boston University in philosophy with an historical emphasis, and an MA from the University of Maryland in philosophy with an analytic emphasis. Her interest in peace and justice studies was sparked when a Fulbright-Hays grant took her to South Africa in 2004 and she became acquainted with the work of the Truth and Reconciliation Commission. She has taught in the philosophy program at Montgomery College for the past twenty years, where she has created two honors courses: "Concepts of Forgiveness," based on the South African Model, and "Concepts of Social Justice."

Matt Meyer is an educator-activist based in New York City, and currently serves as a board member for the Peace and Justice Studies Association as well as a representative for the International Peace Research Association. He is co-editor of the two-volume series, *Seeds of New Hope: African Peace Studies and Action for the 21st Century* (2008, 2010). With Bill Sutherland, Meyer co-authored *Guns and Gandhi in Africa: Pan-African Insights on Nonviolence, Armed Struggle and Liberation* (2000), and with Elizabeth Betita Martinez and Mandy Carter, co-edited *We Have Not Been Moved: Resisting Racism and Militarism in 21st Century America* (2012).

Michael N. Nagler, PhD, is professor emeritus of classics and comparative literature at the University of California, Berkeley, where he co-founded the Peace and Conflict Studies Program. He is the founder of the Metta Center for Nonviolence, and has served on the board of directors of the Peace and Justice Studies Association. Among his many publications in the field of nonviolence, Dr. Nagler is the author of *The Search for a Nonviolent Future: A Promise of Peace for Ourselves, Our Families, and Our World*, winner of the 2002 American Book Award.

Elavie Ndura, EdD, co-editor of this volume, is professor and academic program coordinator of multilingual/multicultural education at George Mason University. Her numerous publications on critical multicultural and peace education and immigrants' acculturation have appeared in *Harvard Educational Review*, *Multicultural Perspectives*, and the *Journal of Peace Education*, among others. She co-authored *147 Tips for Teaching Peace and Reconciliation* (2009), and is the co-editor of *Building Cultures of Peace: Transdisciplinary Voices of Hope and Action* (2009), *Seeds of New Hope: Pan-African Peace Studies for the 21st Century* (2009), and *Seeds Bearing Fruit: Pan-African Peace Action for the 21st Century* (2011).

Wayne F. Regina, PsyD, is a licensed psychologist, marriage and family therapist, and certified mediator. He is the former dean and current peace studies and psychology professor at Prescott College. In addition to teaching, Dr. Regina works at the Yavapai County Superior Court of Arizona where he mediates domestic, civil, and victim-offender cases. His book, *Applying Family Systems Theory to Mediation: A Practitioner's Guide,* was published in November 2011.

Nancy E. Snow, PhD, is professor of philosophy at Marquette University. She has published articles on virtue ethics and moral psychology, and is the author of the book *Virtue as Social Intelligence: An Empirically Grounded Theory* (2009). Her current book project is entitled *Landscapes of Hope: The "What," "Why," and "How" of Hope.*

Jenice L. View, PhD, is assistant professor with the Initiatives in Educational Transformation Program at George Mason University. Her research focuses on the critical teaching and learning of history, critical pedagogy in teacher professional development, how the learning of history impacts youth voice and civic engagement, white teacher consciousness, and the use of the arts and arts integration. In addition, she is a co-editor of the award-winning book, *Putting the Movement Back into Civil Rights Teaching* (2004).

Stephen Zunes is a professor of politics and international studies at the University of San Francisco, where he chairs the Middle Eastern Studies Program. He received his PhD from Cornell University, and serves as a senior policy analyst for the Foreign Policy in Focus project of the Institute for Policy Studies, as well as chair of the academic advisory committee for the International Center on Nonviolent Conflict. He is the author of numerous articles, books, and policy publications, including the edited volume *Nonviolent Social Movements: A Geographical Perspective* (1999).

Index

Acequia, 156–66
activism: in Iran, 112; personal, 171; pervasive nature of, 195; political, 253–54; and scholarship, 135; social, 264–66; as structural nonviolence, 32
Aesara, 241, 250–52
Afghanistan, 209
Africa, 1–10, 76, 90, 206–7, 240, 268
African Americans, 58–75, 118, 124, 128, 177
African National Congress (ANC), 7, 127, 242
agency, 23–25, 138, 198, 215
American Indians. *See* Native Americans
American Revolution, 64
anarchism, 3, 14
apartheid, 7–9, 55, 60, 66–67, 127–28, 209, 240–43, 252
Arizona, 58–59, 71–72, 77, 206–8, 217
Asian Americans, 64–66, 75
assumptions: based on experience, 173; and fears, 127; and gender, 148; about nationality, 206–8, 217; about nonviolence, 270

beloved community, x, xii, 13
Bosnia, 136, 182

boycotts, 7, 63, 96, 100, 112, 128, 211
Burundi, 9, 136, 210

Canada, 59, 137
capitalism: anticapitalism, 4; compromises with, 3; critiques of, 76; free market, 99; global, 90, 100, 166, 269; system, 182
Catholicism, 197, 210
Catholic worker, 31, 312
Chavez, Cesar, 69, 129
Chávez, Hugo, 11, 105
Chile, 10, 100, 106
China, 4, 23, 33–34, 100, 246–51
citizenship, 33–34, 57, 60–62, 172, 242
civil disobedience, 5–7, 25, 100, 137, 255
civil resistance, 4, 8, 100, 134
civil rights, x, 31, 55, 119, 128
classism, 14–15, 44, 67, 213
classrooms, 59, 67–74, 171–78, 187–96, 202–4
coexistence, 86, 208, 213, 252, 269
collaboration, 141, 148–49, 191, 217. *See also* cooperation
colonialism, 8, 62–66, 88–89, 133–37, 263
common good, 15, 158, 214–16
communication, 110, 121–22, 157, 197, 213–14. *See also* dialogue

315

Communism: and China, 4, 26; experiments, 2; in Poland, 134; rifts in, 14; and US policy, 99–105

community: colleges, 200–201; and ethnicity, 63–65; international, 130, 243; local, 75; management of resources, 155–66; organizing, 129; peacemaking, 81–83, 144–47; and reconciliation, 9, 79; research, 196; service, 202; value of, 243–45; violence prevention within, 76, 87–89; women and, 136–43; 148–49. *See also* beloved community

compassion, xi, xvi, 24, 191–94, 236–52, 263, 272. *See also* empathy; forgiveness

conflict: alternatives to, 210, 215; armed, 35; complicity with, 28; and education, 171–76, 182–88; intergenerational, 215; prevention of, 83, 87; and resources, 150–66; studies, 120, 124, 176; transformation, 240–52; violent, 190, 211, 269–70; women and, 136–49

conflict resolution, 9, 34–35, 55, 77, 124, 180, 191–94, 223–52

conscientious objection, 13, 35–37

consciousness, x, 31, 59–77, 213–17, 256

cooperation, x, 80, 86, 140–41, 151–66, 189–94, 235. *See also* collaboration

Corrie, Rachel, 120

creative capital, 198

creativity, xiv, 119, 189, 205

cross-cultural engagement, xiii, 214

cultural identity, 81, 208, 213, 263. *See also* identity

cultural violence, 57, 61, 209–10, 269

curriculum, 29, 57–76, 171–81, 192, 202, 215

Dalai Lama, 27, 217, 246–47, 252

Day, Dorothy, 31

decolonization, 8, 137

democracy: direct, 50; electoral, 2, 5; injustice and, 67, 74, 76; participatory, 32, 160, 165; South African, 240–43; struggles for, 99–116, 269; sustainable, 155, 161, 164; water, 155–58, 160

demonstrations, 41–56, 110–12, 129, 225, 269

dialogue, xiii, 6, 35, 43–44, 55, 129, 235–45, 270. *See also* communication

discrimination, 33, 63, 208–15, 243, 263

diversity, ix, 78–93, 158, 171, 176–77, 212–15, 269

Douglass, Frederick, 65, 68, 70

Du Bois, W. E. B., 65, 70

ecology, 27, 91. *See also* environmentalism

education. *See* classrooms; higher education; K–12 education; multicultural education; nonformal education; peace education; pedagogy

empathy, x–xi, xiv, 121, 143, 194, 202, 216, 245–47

empire, 13–15, 33, 57–60

empowerment, 23, 33, 86, 137–38, 155, 263

environmentalism, 13, 27–28, 68, 107, 137, 150–66, 191, 199, 229

equality, xiv, 42, 63, 84–85, 101, 258, 270

ethnicity, 72, 150, 208, 212, 216, 227

ethnic studies, 58, 72, 76

ethnocentrism, 13, 92

faith, 6, 23, 221, 244, 257–66. *See also* religion; spirituality feminism, 3, 58

food, 60, 75, 88, 110, 150, 160, 234, 260, 263

forgiveness, 82, 240–52

freedom, 8–9, 66, 70, 101–13, 120, 212, 243–46, 258

French Revolution, 41–56

Gandhi, Mohandas, ix–xi, xiv–xv, 1–4, 128–29, 217, 253–67

Gandhian nonviolence, 4–10, 23, 31, 55, 109–14, 132–37, 157–61, 171–72, 211, 242, 253–67

gender, 67, 80, 85, 135–49, 176–77, 209, 216–17, 227

genocide, 9, 59, 64, 76, 79, 93, 210

globalization, 90–91, 153

Global North, 12, 14

Global South, 4, 12

grassroots, 11, 58, 84, 102–15, 135–49, 160–61

Guevara, Che, 1, 10

harmony, 49, 82–89, 163, 217, 245, 248–49

higher education, 85, 91, 189–205

humanity, 69, 119, 145–46, 203, 214–15, 248, 252, 263–67, 270

human rights, 72–77, 110–16, 127, 191–205, 208–9, 217, 270

identity, 63, 67, 131, 147, 207–17. *See also* cultural identity

immigration, 33, 60, 65, 207–8

imperialism, 17, 101

independence: African, 8; Indian, 4, 7, 137; individual, 230, 235; in Latin

America, 63; national, 264; Tibetan, 246; women's, 80

India, ix–x, 4–8, 109, 135–49, 152–55, 255–66

indigenous people, x, 10–14, 59–64, 78–94, 125, 133, 157–61, 179–81

Indonesia, 100, 106, 137

inequality, 11, 208

injustice, xiii, 7, 11, 70–77, 84–90, 119–24, 209, 216–18, 237, 266

innovation, 197–98, 200

interconnectedness, 82, 91, 145–46, 155–57, 165, 199, 241, 245–52

interdependence, 74, 79–80, 90, 156, 213, 246–47

intolerance, 210, 216

Iran, 101–7, 111–15, 152

Iraq, 102, 122, 152, 209

Israel, 12–13, 110, 120, 136, 152–54

Jesus Christ, 23, 37, 94, 206–7, 244, 266

Jim Crow, 60–67, 71, 209

justice: comparison of indigenous and Western systems, 81–90; and compassion, 241, 250–51; criminal, 163, 203; economic, 190; environmental, 161, 166; and love, 15; racial, 76–77; and revolution, 3–4; in South Africa, 10, 128, 243, 252; and truth, 10, 217

K–12 education, 59, 67, 69, 73, 77

Kenya, 29, 127

King, Martin Luther, Jr.: actions of, 27, 125, 157, 266; alliances, 55; influence of, 171, 217; leadership of, xiv, 12, 70. *See also* beloved community; civil rights

Lao-Tzu, 24, 247–52
Latin America, 4, 10, 14, 101, 112
law: civil, 78–80, 84; foundations of,
    250–51; international, 37, 102; of love,
    ix, 23, 37; Native American, 78–94;
    role in French Revolution, 44–54;
    shaping behavior and norms, 34; and
    water, 156–63. *See also* Jim Crow
love, ix–xii, 86, 119, 194, 211, 218,
    250–63, 272. *See also* law: of love;
    power: of love; revolutionary love

Mandela, Nelson, 55, 127, 217, 242–43,
    246
Marxism, 7, 10, 42, 101
media, xi, 60, 75, 104, 117–34, 175, 207,
    225
mediation, 9, 55, 82, 191
Mennonites, 37, 210
Mexican Americans, 59, 62–66
Mexico, 12, 59–63, 74, 114, 154
Middle East, 12, 33, 101, 110–16, 152–53
militarism, 15, 106, 108, 112, 192
movements, x–xi, 2–5, 10–14, 31, 41–56,
    69, 85, 99–116, 124–34, 136, 161, 217,
    223, 242, 265–71. *See also* people
    power
multicultural education, 14, 72, 206–18
multiculturalism, 14, 58, 67–75, 159–61,
    172, 210
Muste, A. J., 31

nationalism, 37–38, 55, 111–14, 129, 242,
    247
Native Americans, 58, 61–68, 74–75,
    78–94, 134, 209, 268
nature, x, 27, 78–93, 155, 184, 194,
    225–29, 241–49, 269

neoconservatives, 42, 106
neoliberalism, 33, 42, 91, 108
noncooperation, 5–9, 25, 96, 99, 112–13,
    255
nonformal education, 138, 140
nongovernmental organizations
    (NGOs), 103, 107–12, 182, 217, 237
nonkilling, 28–30, 196, 200
nonviolent action, 8, 25, 31–35, 100–116,
    147, 171–88
nonviolent revolution, 3, 6, 211–12
North America, 2, 11–12, 57–59, 78–94,
    106

Obama, Barack, 43, 58, 103, 115, 207,
    217
oppression, 31–33, 58–61, 69, 72–75,
    90, 114–16, 129, 147, 158, 193–97,
    210–15, 242–45, 262–63
Otpor!, x, 129–30

pacifism, 3–6, 8–11, 14, 37, 108, 210–11
Pakistan, 152
Palestine, 12–13, 107, 120, 152–54
peace: absence of, 78, 84; activists,
    31–32; churches, 37; culture of,
    135–38, 141, 145–49, 268–71; inner,
    36, 224–25; movements, 11, 110–12,
    133–34; negative, 189–91; positive,
    148–49, 190, 193; prayers for, 268,
    272; studies, xv, 9, 14, 32, 55, 91, 120,
    124, 138, 149, 172, 176, 187, 191,
    217; water and, 153–56; world, 36,
    191, 271
Peace and Justice Studies Association
    (PJSA), xvii, 12–13, 311
Peace Brigades International, 110, 118
peacebuilding, 10, 77, 140, 151, 154

peace education, 29, 77, 171–88, 189–205

peacekeeping, x, xiii

peacemaking: and Bowen theory, 223–39; criminology, 203; and education, 76, 191, 202, 204; environmental, 154; failure of, 257; and Native Americans, 81–84; and nonviolence, 10; and women, 136–37, 141–45

pedagogy, xiii, 58, 69–77, 171–88, 194, 197, 212, 215, 271

people power, xiii, 4–6, 99, 104–5, 114, 134

plowshares, 32, 312

poverty, 14, 139, 149, 197, 240, 261

power: asymmetries, 33; communicative, 122; concentration of, 84; forms of, 3, 189–94; local, 54, 78, 158; of love, 2, 10; moral, 248, 265; nonviolent, 9, 12, 82, 113, 118, 129, 134, 148–49, 151, 171–88, 224, 267–72; political, 63, 67, 101, 104, 108; in presence, 238; speaking truth to, 2, 122–23, 164; spiritual, 266–67; state, 4, 8, 11, 34; and will, 25–51; and women, 135–49. See also empowerment; people power

prejudice, 136, 138, 174, 213, 270

protest, 31, 41–56, 100, 110–14, 134, 157, 223

Quakers (Society of Friends), 37, 210

race, 15, 67, 72, 92, 187, 208, 212, 216, 242–43

racism, 13–14, 64, 177, 212–15

reciprocity, 7, 86, 156, 159, 162

relationships, xi, 6, 15, 84–85, 126, 142, 151, 156–60, 165, 176, 185, 212–15, 226–28, 231–38, 244–52

religion: Baha'i, 27, 268; Buddhism, 23–27, 241, 246–47, 253, 260, 266, 268, 272; Christianity, 23–27, 31, 99, 210, 241, 244, 248, 265–66, 268; Confucianism, 26, 241, 247–52; Daoism, 23–27, 36, 133, 241, 249; Hinduism, 27, 253, 261–67, 268; Islam, 23, 25, 33, 99, 101, 112–14, 138, 159, 266, 268; Jainism, 253, 259–60, 266, 268; Judaism, 23, 25, 120, 210, 244, 266–67, 268; Protestantism, 210. See also faith; spirituality

resistance, x, 2–13, 38, 57–77, 99–113, 120–22, 166, 210–12, 217, 242, 255–67

resources: common-pool, 155, 158; conflict over, 150–66; distribution of, 11, 61; educational, 70, 73, 77, 201–3; sharing of, 82, 143, 151, 153; women's access to, 137, 143

respect, 8–9, 58, 70, 78–92, 157–66, 196, 212–16, 248, 255–56, 268–72

revolution, ix–xii, 1–15, 41–47, 101, 105–6, 113–18, 210–12, 269–72. See also American Revolution; French Revolution

revolutionary love, 1–15, 269–71

Rwanda, 9, 210

satyagraha, 1–8, 23, 129, 211, 242, 253–55, 263–65

science, x, 5–6, 22, 73, 157

self-determination, 72, 90, 161

service learning, 202, 204

sexism, 13–14, 213

Shanti Sena, x, 6, 109

Sharp, Gene, 31, 111, 117, 180–81, 210–12
social capital, 150, 156
social justice, 13, 33, 72, 85, 212–13, 217, 265–67
social responsibility, 216–17, 269
solidarity, 9–13, 36, 72, 110–11, 143, 155, 271
South Africa, 9, 55, 65–66, 240–52
spirituality, 23–27, 36, 79–82, 246
strikes, 54, 100, 111–13, 129, 211, 255
structural violence, 31–34, 71, 75–77, 194, 209
Supreme Court, 28, 57, 60
sustainability, 6, 107–8, 154–65, 270

terrorism, 11, 30–32, 118–21, 129–30, 178, 201, 209
Thoreau, Henry David, 25, 217, 253, 266
Tolstoy, Leo, 25, 27, 253, 266
truth and reconciliation, 9–10, 121, 241, 244
truth commissions, 2, 10
truth-force, 2, 254
Tutu, Desmond, 9, 128, 241–46

Ubuntu, 9, 214, 244–46

United States, 31, 58–77, 101–16, 132, 156, 175, 196, 207, 209–11, 266

Venezuela, 11, 103, 105
Vietnam War, 121, 223, 239
violence, xi, xiv–xv, 2, 6–11, 21–37, 41–44, 53–55, 63–77, 78–80, 109–10, 118–28, 136, 143–47, 150–51, 172–75, 190, 209–17, 233, 270. See also conflict; cultural violence; structural violence

war: Cold, 105, 109; crimes, 9, 11; funding of, 123; in Iraq, 122, 209; just, 128; nuclear, 31; over resources, 150, 153, 166; peace as absence of, 91; US participation in, 57, 175, 209
War Resisters International (WRI), 1, 4, 10
water, 110, 139–40, 145–48, 150–66, 249
well-being, 82, 140, 151, 155, 201
women, 3, 70, 80, 85–86, 101, 135–49, 191, 247, 269–70. See also feminism
World War I, 37–38
World War II, 64, 210, 243

Zapatistas, 12
Zeno, 36